To my father, mother and sister; to Anwen, Mali and Efa.
Thank you for everything.

The vast Gothic cathedral of La Seu

Sun. **Museu:** *Open 10am-1pm, 5pm-7pm daily*, T: 93 310 71 95, www.catedralbcn.org

Camp Nou ❶ 1A

On match days you'll hear *'Visca el Barça!'* (Up with Barça!) ringing out through the city's streets. Tickets to the matches are notoriously difficult to get hold of, but you can catch a glimpse of what FC Barça is all about in the museum tacked on to the famous Camp Nou stadium. The museum and stadium tours, known as the Camp Nou Experience, are among the most popular attractions in Barcelona. There are mementos dating back to the club's beginnings more than a century ago, videos reliving the team's most glorious moments, and, in pride of place, the European Cup that FC Barça won in 2011. **Museu:** *Adm. Open 10am-8pm Mon-Sat Apr-mid Oct; 10am-6.30pm Mon-Sat mid Oct-Mar; 10am-2.30pm Sun*, T: 93 496 36 00, www.fcbarcelona.cat

Carrer Montcada ❷ 5F & Museu Picasso ❷ 4F

Carrer Montcada was the city's smartest address in the Middle Ages and is lined with Gothic palaces. Five of them now house the Museu Picasso (Picasso Museum), one of the city's most popular attractions. As well as some important early works, there is a section devoted to his ceramics, a few canvasses from the Rose and Blue periods, and studies based on Velázquez's *Las Meninas*. *Adm free first Sun of month. Open 10am-8pm Tue-Sun and public hols*, T: 93 256 30 00, www.museupicasso.bcn.cat

Casa Milà (La Pedrera) ❶ 3F

Gaudí's huge, curved apartment building was quickly christened

Picasso & Barcelona

Picasso came to Barcelona with his family in 1895 and had his first break when he exhibited at the bohemian tavern of Els Quatre Gats (❷ 2D). Later he found models for the haunting paintings of his Blue Period in the city's dispossessed and poor. The black-eyed women in his ground-breaking work *Les Demoiselles d'Avignon* were supposedly prostitutes from the Carrer d'Avinyó in the Gothic Quarter. He swore never to return to Spain while Franco was ruler and died in France in 1973.

La Pedrera de Nit

On summer evenings you can sit on Gaudí's fabulous rooftop and enjoy cocktails and live music – the perfect backdrop to the stunning views across the city. *Open throughout Jul-Aug, Fri and Sat 8.30-11pm.*

La Pedrera (The Stone Quarry) by enthralled locals when it was completed in 1910. There isn't a straight line anywhere, including inside the apartments, of which one is open to visitors. All the Modernista furniture and fittings were exquisitely wrought by the finest craftsmen of the era. There's a museum dedicated to Gaudí's work in the vaulted attic, but the highlight is undoubtedly the undulating panoramic rooftop, guarded by swirling chimneys covered in shimmering tiles. This splendidly ornate venue plays host to a series of evening concerts *(see web site for details, and box, above)*. Adm. *Open 9am-6.30pm daily Nov-Feb; 9am-8pm daily Mar-Oct.* Passeig de

Gràcia 92, T: 93 484 59 00, www.lapedreraeducacio.org

El Born & Santa María del Mar ❷ 5F

El Born is Barcelona's hippest neighbourhood, crammed with fashionable bars, clubs and shops. It's the best place to begin an evening's *tapeo* (crawl between tapas bars). Looming above the streets is the church of Santa María del Mar, an example of Catalan Gothic architecture, with a soaring central nave. Regular concerts are held here.

The twisting chimneys of La Pedrera

Church: *Open 9am-1.30pm, 4.30pm-8pm Mon-Sat, 10am-1.30pm, 4.30pm-8pm Sun. Plaça Santa Maria, T: 93 310 23 90.*

Font Màgica ❶ 5B

A kitsch aquatic ballet of colourfully lit water leaping in time to Abba and Tchaikovsky. *Free shows. Open 9pm-11.30pm Thu-Sun May-Sep; 7pm-9pm Fri-Sat Oct-Apr. Montjuïc.*

Fundació Joan Miró ❶ 5C

Housed in a light-filled building designed by Josep Lluís Sert, this is

A flamboyant lightshow at the Font Màgica

the largest collection of Miró's work in the world. The Catalan painter invented his own brand of Surrealism, full of bright, fiery colour. As well as the more familiar paintings and sculptures, you'll also find tapestries, bronzes, engravings and sketches, all presented in vast, whitewashed rooms. The foundation also holds excellent temporary exhibitions, contemporary music concerts and puppet shows for kids.

Adm. Open 10am-7pm Tue-Sat Oct-Jun; 10am-8pm Tue-Sat Jul-Sep; 10am-9.30pm Thur; 10am-2.30pm Sun; closed Mon except public hols. Parc de Montjuïc, T: 93 443 94 70, www.bcn.fjmiro.es

Manzana de la Discòrdia ❶ 4E

The three major Modernista architects – Antoni Gaudí, Domènech i Muntaner and Puig i Cadafalch – were each responsible for designing one of the mansions in this block. Choose your favourite between Muntaner's Casa Lleo i Morera, covered with nymphs and flowers, Cadafalch's Casa Amatller, full of neo-Gothic whimsicality, or Gaudí's glittering Casa Batlló, which is the only one of three that's open to the public (*see box, p.13*). *Open 9am-9pm daily. Pàsseig de Gràcia 43, T: 93 216 03 06, www.casabatllo.cat*

Barcelona for Free

There's plenty to do for free in Barcelona besides visiting the Font Màgica (*see left*). Free concerts are staged in the city parks in summer, most museums are free on one day of each month, and you can catch a free exhibition of the national dance (the *sardana*) outside the cathedral on Sundays at 12 noon and in the nearby Plaça Sant Jaume on Saturdays at 6pm (*Easter-end of Nov*). And of course a dip in the waters of the Mediterranean won't cost you a penny. For information on free concerts and days at museums, check with the tourist office (*see p.46*).

Miró's *Dona i Ocell* in the Parc de Joan Miró

7

Museu d'Art Contemporani de Barcelona (MACBA) ❷ 1A

Richard Meier's huge, glassy Museum of Contemporary Art landed in the Raval area in 1995, spearheading the neighbourhood's redevelopment. It's the perfect showcase for celebrated Catalan painters like Antoni Tàpies, Spain's best-known living artist, and newer artists like Miquel Barceló, Perejaume and Susana Solano. International artists such as Nancy Spero and Jo Spence are also shown here in a series of temporary exhibitions. *Adm. Open 11am-7.30pm Mon, Wed-Fri, 10am-8pm Sat, 10am-3pm Sun late Sep-23 Jun; 11am-8pm Mon, Wed-Fri, 10am-8pm Sat, 10am-3pm Sun 24 Jun-end Sep. Plaça dels Àngels 1, T: 93 412 08 10, www.macba.es*

The exterior of Richard Meier's MACBA building

Museu Blau ❸

The National Science Museum has undergone a facelift giving its million-strong collection of rocks, fossils, plants and animals an interactive element that brings the story of evolution to life. *Adm. Open 10am-7pm Tue-Fri, 10am-8pm Sat-Sun Jan-May; 10am-8pm Tue-Sun (& bank holiday Mon) Jun-Sep, Plaça Leonardo da Vinci 4-5, Parc del Fòrum, T: 93 256 60 02, www.museuciencies.bcn.cat*

Museu Nacional d'Art de Catalunya (MNAC) ❶ 5B

This dour, monolithic palace on Montjuïc contains Catalan art from the last millennium. The highlight is a mesmerising collection of Romanesque frescoes gathered from remote churches in the Catalan Pyrenees. The most famous fresco is a hypnotic depiction of Christ in Majesty from the church of Sant Climent in Taüll. The Gothic collection is equally spectacular, with a series of gilded altarpieces dating back to the Middle Ages. 19th-century exhibits include curvaceous Modernista furniture and objets d'art, along with vast historic paintings. *Adm. Open 10am-7pm Tue-Sat, 10am-2.30pm Sun and hols. Parc de Montjuïc, T: 93 622 03 76, www.mnac.es*

Palau de la Música Catalana ❷ 2E

This is the finest of all the work by the great Modernista architect Lluís

Domènech i Muntaner. The lavish concert hall, completed in 1908 on the site of an old monastery, boasts a spectacularly opulent auditorium which is encased in delicate stained glass. The lovely ceiling droops majestically into a pendant shape and illuminates the entire hall with soft rainbow-coloured natural light (the only concert hall in Europe to be lit naturally). Everything the eye

lands on is encrusted in rich ceramic decoration, from the galloping Valkyries erupting from the wings to the whimsical 3-D muses that prance across the stage and are known to be used by the musicians as coat hooks. Even the exterior is a blaze of coloured pillars. The structure of the auditorium is astonishing, and the acoustics have been much improved. *Adm. Open 10am-3.30pm*

Striking architecture of Museu Blau

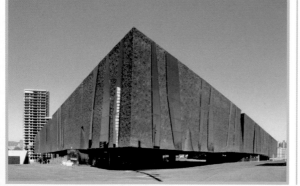

Ruta del Modernisme

'Modernisme' is the artistic movement that, in Barcelona, found its ultimate expression in architecture. During the late 19th and early 20th centuries, Gaudí and his contemporaries created dozens of fluid, fairytale structures with a riot of detail. L'Eixample, the grid-like 'extension' north of Plaça Catalunya, today holds the largest concentration of Modernista architecture in Europe. Buy the guidebook from bookshops or the main tourist office (*see p.46*). *www.rutadelmodernisme.com*

daily and for evening concerts (*see p.25*); visits by guided tour only (may vary according to performances). If ticket office is closed tickets and reservations can be made at the adjacent Muses del Palau gift shop. Carrer de Palau de la Música 4-6, T: 902 442 882, www.palaumusica.org

Palau Güell ❷ 5B

Gaudí's first major commission for his biggest patron, Eusebi Güell, this palace was completed in 1888. It's a strangely forbidding mansion, which is perhaps why Antonioni filmed part of his dark thriller *The Passenger* here in 1977. The rooms are set around a lofty central hall overlooked by a dome with tiny shards of light that represent the heavens. Gaudí spared no expense, using the rarest woods and marble for the richly carved ceilings and fittings. But it is on the playful roof surmounted by mosaic-covered chimneys that he really let his imagination go. A recent restoration project has restored this building to its former glory. *Open 10am-8pm Tue-Sat Apr-Sep; 10am-5.30pm Tue-Sat Oct-Mar, Carrer Nou de Las Ramblas 3-5, T: 93 472 57 75, www.palauguell.cat*

Parc de la Ciutadella ❶ 6G

The city's best-loved and most central park contains a pretty boating lake, an over-the-top fountain (*Cascada*) designed by Josep Fontseré

Fountain in Parc de la Ciutadella

(with the help of Gaudí), shady bench-lined paths and Barcelona's zoo. The Zoo is set to modernize over the next few years to improve and expand its animal areas and habitats - check website for details. **Zoo:** *Open 10am-5pm daily Nov-Mar, 10am-6pm mid Sep-Oct & Apr-mid*

Plaça Reial is across Las Ramblas from Palau Güell

May, 10am-7pm mid May-mid Sep, T: 93 225 67 80, www.zoobarcelona.com

Park Güell ❶ 1G

Perhaps the most emblematic of all Barcelona's sights, the Park Güell is lifted straight from a fairy tale. The

entrance pavilions have ice-cream rooftops and swirling windows, and the glistening tile-covered dragon that guards the main staircase has become the city's unofficial mascot. Beyond the dragon lies the Hall of a Hundred Columns, where each is elaborately decorated with tiny multi-coloured tiles. Gaudí's little

house is now a small museum dedicated to the eccentric architect, with a collection of beautiful furniture that he designed. Best of all is the undulating mosaic-covered bench designed by Josep Jujol, which offers beautiful views out across the whole city. *Carrer d'Olot.* **Park:** *Open 10am–sunset daily,*

T: 93 213 04 88. **Casa Museu Gaudí:** *Adm. Open 10am–8pm daily Apr–Sep; 10am–6pm daily Oct–Mar,* T: 93 219 38 11, *www.casamuseugaudi.org*

Passeig de Gràcia & L'Eixample ❶ 4E, 3F–4F

The Passeig de Gràcia is a sweeping boulevard lined with extravagant wrought-iron lampposts and smart designer boutiques. It's the elegant backbone of L'Eixample, the 19th-century extension to the city that was built when the old city walls were finally tumbled. Here the results of the wealthy competing with one another to create the most fabulous mansions are in evidence everywhere. Modernista masterpieces now rub shoulders with each other, from Gaudí's Casa Calvet on Carrer de Casp to Puig i Cadafalch's maniacally crazy Casa de les Punxes (House of Spikes). This is also where you'll find the famous Modernista houses on the **Manzana de la Discòrdia** (see p.7).

Park Güell – a magical mystery tour

Poble Espanyol ❶ 4B

The 'Spanish Village' was built for the 1929 Universal Exhibition and is enjoyably kitsch, with an Andalucian market square, reconstructed village streets from all over Spain, and the Torres d'Avila, copied from the Castillian town. There are craft shops, restaurants and flamenco shows (*see p.26*). The entrance towers were crafted into a designer bar in the 1980s, which provides a rooftop terrace for summer drinks.
Adm. Open 9am-8pm Mon, 9am-2am Tue-Thu, Sun 9am-midnight Fri, 9am-4am Sat. Avinguda del Marquès de Comillas, T: 93 508 63 00,

The spectacularly fake Poble Espanyol

www.poble-espanyol.com

La Sagrada Família ❶ 3G

The craggy Nativity Façade, completed shortly before Gaudí's death in 1926, is a magical introduction to his masterpiece. Its soaring bulbous spires, seen from all over the city, can be braved by taking a lift halfway up. Slim staircases lead higher still to truly vertiginous views. Work finally began again on the temple in the 1950s, and the building has courted controversy ever since, particularly with the recently completed Passion Façade. There's a museum devoted to the building's progression in the crypt and the story behind its architect.
Adm includes the museum. Open 9am-8pm daily Apr-Sep; 9am-6pm daily Oct-Mar. Carrer de Mallorca 401, T: 93 207 30 31, www.sagradafamilia.org

Las Ramblas ❷ 1C-7A

Barcelona's most famous promenade stretches for almost a mile towards the sea. Lined with kiosks selling

Soaring heights at the Sagrada Família

newspapers, the prettiest part, around the Rambla de Sant Josep (❷ 3B), overflows with flower stalls. Endless entertainment is available here, from Russian dancers to Chinese acrobats, as well as 'human statues'. It is also home to the **Gran Teatre del Liceu** opera house (❷ 4B, *see p.25*), and the **Mercat de la Boqueria** (❷ 3B, *see p.17*).

Houses on the hillside at Tibidabo

Tibidabo ❸

Barcelona's 'mountain of fun' is topped with an old-fashioned funfair, which opened in 1908 and has had a series of new rides added from the 1980s to the present day, such as high-tech rollercoasters and stomach-churning free-fall rides. To get to the top of the mountain take the Tramvia Blau (*see p.49*), a restored antique tram, and then the rickety funicular (*see p.48*). The enormous church at the summit is worth a visit, if only for its wonderful rooftop views across the city, but for an even more spectacular outlook, head on up to Norman Foster's Torre de Collserola (Communications Tower), where a lift whizzes you to a panoramic viewing platform on the tenth floor for views stretching up to 70km on a good day.

Parc d'Atraccions: *Adm. Opening hours and days vary but generally 12noon-7/11pm Wed-Sun Jun-Sep & hols; Sat-Sun & hols only for rest of year; closed Jan-Feb. www.tibidabo.net*
Torre de Collserola: *Adm. Open 12noon-2pm, 3.15pm-7/8pm Wed-Sun Apr-Nov; 12noon-2pm, 3.15pm-6pm. Wed-Sun Mar, Dec Carretera de Vallvidrera al Tibidabo, T: 93 406 93 54, www.torredecollserola.com*

Gaudí & Casa Batlló

Antoni Gaudí (1852-1926), Barcelona's most famous architect, is responsible for some of the city's most emblematic sights. The Casa Batlló opened to visitors to mark its 100th anniversary, and the tour of the interior includes its sinuous rooftop, chimneys and attic. This extraordinary 'house of bones' is covered in bright mosaics, and the wrought-iron balconies are adorned with fine bone-shaped columns and sprouting plants. *Passeig de Gràcia 43, T: 93 216 03 06, www.casabatllo.cat*

barcelona places to shop

Barcelona is shopping heaven and you'll find everything from markets that sell local produce, slick, classy boutiques full of the latest designer fashions to tiny Modernista shops that haven't changed in generations. With the city's unrivalled reputation for style, it's easy to discover original gifts – something special for the home, or an unusual outfit from one of Barcelona's home-grown designers. Even if you are not much of a shopper, one of the best ways to get a feel for the city is to explore the wonderful markets – perhaps the most famous is La Boqueria, located right on Las Ramblas, but art markets, book and coin markets and even honey markets take over the small squares at weekends.

buy it places to shop

Shopping Areas

Avinguda del Portal de l'Àngel ② 2D

This broad, pedestrianised street just off the Plaça Catalunya has a branch of the Spanish department store El Corte Inglés (*see right*), shoe shops and a plethora of fashion stores catering to most tastes. If you've got a sweet tooth, there are a couple of shops devoted to the delicious local nougat (*turrón*), eaten at Christmas.

> ### Closing Time
> Most small shops close for much of the afternoon, and everywhere closes on Sunday. Most shops open at around 9.30am Mon-Fri, and close at around 1pm or 2pm for lunch, reopening at about 4pm or 5pm until around 8pm at night. Department stores and supermarkets don't close at lunchtime. Some small shops close on Saturday afternoon.

Exclusive Loewe in L'Eixample

Carrer d'Avinyó ② 5C

This street may look a bit dingy, but the boutiques are among the hippest in the city. This is the place to pick up something ultra-stylish for your loft apartment or cutting-edge fashion from Barcelona's trendiest designers.

Carrer de la Palla ② 3C

Hidden in the web of streets around here are dozens of antiques shops. Furniture, paintings, books and even antique beaded dresses are on offer – but prices can be surprisingly high.

Carrer de Portaferrissa ② 3C

This is where trendy students come for bargains. There are plenty of good fashion chains, including the cheap but stylish leisurewear label Women's Secret and budget stalwart H&M. The El Mercadillo complex has stalls with new and second-hand clothing.

Carrer de la Riera Baixa ① 5D

The Raval neighbourhood is the best neighbourhood to pick up street fashion, vintage clothes, art books and unusual dance music. The very best street is tiny Carrer de la Riera Baixa, lined with alternative fashion, music and vintage clothes stores. There's an outdoor market on most Saturdays during the summer.

L'Eixample ① 3F-4F

This is the smartest and most exclusive shopping neighbourhood. Designer labels from Chanel to Loewe are crammed along the elegant Passeig de Gràcia, and the Diagonal, around Plaça Francesc Macià, is lined with designer fashion

and accessory stores. Head to Carrer del Consell de Cent for art, with some reputable galleries. Antique-lovers must give Bulevard des Antiquaris (see p.18) a visit.

Passeig del Born ② 5F

This fashionable neighbourhood has all kinds of unusual boutiques in the narrow streets that splinter off it. There's a good range of shops offering everything from household goods to elegant fashions and freshly roasted coffee to gifts.

Department Stores & Malls

El Corte Inglés ② 1D

The most central branch of the enormous Spanish department store with men's and women's fashion, toys, electrical goods, food and home furnishings. There's a supermarket and an excellent delicatessen in the basement, the eighth floor is entirely devoted to oportunitats (bargains), and the

Tax Max
Non-EU residents can claim the tax back (18 per cent on most goods) on purchases of more than €90 bought at participating shops (these display a sign). Ask for a Tax-Free Cheque when you buy your goods and get it signed at the customs desk in the airport as you leave. You can cash it (or get a credit card refund) at the Banco Exterio de España, outside the departure gate in Terminal A.

top-floor café offers amazing views. There's a decent souvenir and gift section too. *Plaça de Catalunya 14, T: 93 306 38 00, www.elcorteingles.es*

El Triangle ② 1C

Large central mall overlooking the Plaça Catalunya, with a FNAC (good for books in English and booking concert tickets), Habitat, Sephora perfumes and Camper (see p.18).

Plaça de Catalunya 1-4, T: 93 318 01 08, www.eltriangle.es

Maremàgnum ① 7E

Located across a bridge over the port, Maremàgnum must be one of the few malls in Europe that offers Mediterranean views. The focus is on fashion, with plenty of outdoor cafés to wind down. *Moll d'Espanya, T: 93 225 81 00, www.maremagnum.es*

Markets

Els Encants Flea Market ① 4H

Early risers might find a bargain at this sprawling flea market near the Plaça de les Glòries Catalanes. Rummage through the junk to find antiques, cheap clothes and wind-up gramophones. *Carrer del Dos de Maig 177-187, T: 93 246 30 30, www.encantsbcn.com*

Mercat de la Boqueria ② 3B

There are about 40 daily produce markets in Barcelona, but this is the best known, with hundreds of stalls under one pretty, Modernista roof. Stalls at the front have inflated

prices for tourists – head to the back for cheaper goods. Unusual local cheeses and hams, vegetables and fruit. *Las Ramblas 91, Open 8am-8.30pm Mon-Sat, T: 93 318 25 84, www.boqueria.info*

Antiques

Bulevard des Antiquaris ① 3E

Upmarket arcade with scores of stalls and a wide range of antiques from porcelain dolls to jewellery, furniture and paintings. *Passeig de Gràcia 55, T: 93 215 44 99, www.bulevarddelsantiquaris.com*

Books & Music

Casa del Llibre ① 3F

An excellent selection of books on most topics, including a good range in English. *Passeig de Gràcia 62, T: 93 272 38 40, www.casadellibro.com*

FNAC ② 1C

A huge store (part of the French chain) right in the city centre, FNAC offers books (including

Fresh vegetables at La Boqueria

some in English), music, a concert ticket service, and an international news-stand and café on the ground floor. *El Triangle, Plaça de Catalunya 4, T: 93 344 18 00, www.fnac.es*

Chains

Camper ② 1C

Trendy, comfortable and affordable shoes. Take advantage – prices here are up to 30 per cent cheaper than in the UK. *El Triangle, Carrer de Pelai*

13-37, T: 93 302 41 24, www.camper.com

Mango ① 4E

Mango caters to young professional women. Great fashion, good-quality fabrics and reasonable prices. Again, there are branches all over the city. *Passeig de Gràcia 65, T: 93 215 75 30, www.mango.es*

Zara ② 1C

Zara has popped up on high streets around the world, but it's still the best place for affordable fashion for the whole family – men, women and

Umbrellas in Bulevard des Antiquaris

Café and bar at FNAC

kids. There are branches all over the city. *Carrer de Pelai 58, T: 93 301 09 78, www.zara.com*

Designer Goods

Galeries Vinçon ❶ 3E
The owner of this influential design emporium has discovered many of Barcelona's most talented young designers. Highly original pieces, including furniture, lighting, rugs and tableware. *Passeig de Gràcia 96, T: 93 215 60 50, www.vincon.com*

Ivo & Co ❷ 4G
Fabulously stylish homeware in retro and rustic styles from this small French chain. *Carrer Rec 20, T: 93 268 33 31, www.ivoandco.com*

WaWas ❷ 4F
Cool, designer souvenirs ranging from retro fridge magnets to kitchen implements designed by Catalan superchef Ferran Adrià. *Carrer Carders 14, T: 93 319 79 02, www.wawasbarcelona.com*

Best Buys
If you want something typically Catalan, buy a pair of ribboned espadrilles to dance the *sardana,* or a floppy Catalan beret called a *barretina.* Local wines, honey or jars of stuffed anchovies make good gifts. Bear in mind that the three big Spanish fashion chains – Zara, Mango and Camper – are up to a third cheaper in Spain than in the UK.

Fashion

Antonio Miró ❶ 4E
Barcelona's very own home grown talent, Antonio Miró produces dashing suits and accessories plus innovative homewares. *Consell de Cent 349, T: 93 487 06 70, www.antoniomiro.es*

Camisería Pons ❶ 2E
Showcasing Spain's talented fashion designers, this century-old clothier now stocks cutting edge fashion to Barcelona's fashion conscious. *Gran*

Pretty summer flip-flops at Camper

de Gràcia 49, T: 93 217 72 92,
www.camiseriapons.com

Loewe ❶ 4E

Luxurious leather handbags,
accessories and luggage
complemented by fashions for men
and women. *Passeig de Gràcia 35,
T: 93 216 04 00, www.loewe.com*

On Land ❷ 4F

This shop, located in the hip
fashion neighbourhood of El Born,
stands out for its own highly
wearable men's and women's
collections that retain a marked
sense of modern style. *Carrer de la
Princesa 25, T: 93 310 02 11,
www.on-land.com*

Purificación García ❶ 4E

An upmarket, affordable, Spanish
fashion chain catering to style-
conscious, urban professionals;
elegant designs and beautiful
fabrics. *Passeig de Gracia 21,
T: 93 487 72 92,
www.purificaciongarcia.es*

Food & Wine

Can Cisa ❷ 4E

This wine shop has been in the
same family for generations.
It's not the cheapest in town,
but the recommendations are
always reliable. Look out for local

Comestibles in Queviures Murrià

Wines at Can Cisa

Denominació d'Origen (DO) such as Priorat, Montsant, Costers del Segre and Penedès. *Carrer de la Princesa 14, T: 93 319 98 81.*

Casa del Bacalao ❷ 2D

A tiny little shop that sells just one thing: dried, salted cod. You should try it while you are here. Staff will vacuum-pack it to take it home. *Carrer Comtal 8, T: 93 301 65 39.*

Formatgeria La Seu ❷ 4D

In the heart of the Barri Gòtic, this Scottish-owned cheese shop specialises in artisanal cheeses from small producers around Spain. It also organises cheese lunches and cheese courses (by appointment only). *Carrer de la Dagueria 16, T: 93 412 65 48, www.formatgerialaseu.com*

Queviures Murrià ❶ 3F

This charming, Modernista grocery contains all kinds of goodies, including local cheeses, excellent hams and a good selection of wines and cavas. *Carrer de*

> ### Sale Time
> Don't miss the sales in Barcelona, where you are likely to find a real bargain. The big New Year sales usually begin on 9 January. You can't miss the huge signs (*rebaixes* in Catalan, *rebajas* in Castilian) blazoned across the windows. Summer sales start in early July and continue until the end of August. Designer boutiques often drop their prices by up to 60 or 70 per cent.

Roger de Llúria 85, T: 93 215 57 89, www.murria.cat

Vila Viniteca ❷ 6E

If you have developed a taste for the local fizz, take a few bottles home with you. This family-run shop has a great selection of wines and cavas. *Carrer dels Agullers 7-9, T: 93 777 70 17, www.vilaviniteca.es*

Traditional Old-Timers

El Ingenio ❷ 4C

This wonderful little shop was founded in 1838 and holds a magical range of puppets, masks and fancy-dress outfits. Kids will love it. *Carrer d'en Rauric 6, T: 93 317 71 38, www.el-ingenio.com*

Flora Albaicín ❷ 2C

A delightfully old-fashioned little shop with a magnificent range of colourful flamenco dresses and accessories. *Carrer de la Canuda 3, T: 93 302 10 35, www.tiendaflamenco.com*

barcelona entertainment

Barcelona loves a good time. Whether you want to sip champagne at the opera, catch a late-night movie in an outdoor swimming pool or dance the night away on the seashore, this is a city that really does have something for everyone. The biggest local passion (besides football) is music; Montserrat Caballé and José Carreras are Catalan, and a night at the sumptuous Gran Teatre del Liceu or the fabulous Palau de la Música Catalana is utterly unforgettable. Contemporary dance and drama thrives here, and the clubs and bars draw some of Europe's biggest DJs and bands. Every sports fan knows FC Barça, perhaps the most popular football club in the world. Getting a ticket to the Camp Nou stadium is difficult, but by no means impossible.

What's On

For information on theatre, classical music and opera, visit the **Palau de la Virreina** (❷ 3B) on Las Ramblas (see p.46). For cinema, restaurants and nightlife, check out the weekly listings guide La Guía del Ocio, on sale at news kiosks, which has a small English section (www.guiadelociobcn. es). The English-language magazine Barcelona Metropolitan (www. barcelona-metropolitan.com) gives details of the hippest clubs and nightspots, and the quarterly bilingual-style magazine b-Guided (www.b-guided.com), which includes a map, is sold at kiosks. Check out www.bcn.cat, Barcelona's excellent multilingual website, which has a good cultural agenda section.

Booking tickets

Most theatre, opera and concert tickets can be bought through one of the two main savings banks: Servi-Caixa and Caixa Catalunya. The Palau de la Virreina (see above) also has a ticket sales counter. For contemporary music concerts, you can get tickets through FNAC (see p.18) or at record shops.

Servi-Caixa
Servi-Caixa machines are usually located near the regular ATMs at banks. You can get information and buy tickets using your credit card for several venues, including the Teatre Nacional and the Gran Teatre del Liceu. There are some English-speaking operators on the phones and you can also book online via

The IMAX at Port Vell

ticketmaster. T: 902 15 00 25, www.ticketmaster.es

TelEntrada
This service is offered by the Caixa Catalunya bank. Buy tickets over the counter at any branch, by phone (some English-speakers) or online. Half-price tickets are sometimes available at the Plaça de Catalunya branch three hours before performances begin, for cash. T: 902 10 12 12, www.telentrada.com

Cinema

Filmoteca de Catalunya ❸ 4A
Funded by the Catalan government, it offers an interesting programme for devoted film buffs and is now housed in new purpose built building. Plaça Salvador Seguí 1-9, T: 93 567 10 70, www.filmoteca.cat

IMAX ❶ 6E
Catch a dinosaur epic or swim with dolphins at the IMAX. The massive domed screen is 21 m (69 ft) high and 29 m (96 ft) wide, with

a 3D system. *Moll d'Espanya, T: 93 225 11 11, www.imaxportvell.com*

Verdi ❶ 2F

This is a charming, slightly battered arthouse cinema in Gràcia, with a mixed programme of both international and Spanish general release and independent films. *Carrer Verdi 32, T: 93 238 79 90, www.cines-verdi.com*

Classical Music & Opera

Gran Teatre del Liceu ❷ 4B

The city's much-loved opera house is extremely popular so if you want to see a performance there, book tickets as early as possible. The small auditorium in the basement holds performances geared to children. *Las Ramblas 51-59, T: 93 485 99 13, www.liceubarcelona.com*

Palau de la Música Catalana ❷ 2E

This opulent Modernista auditorium (*see p.9*) is a feast for the eyes, and the acoustics are catching up after a series of renovations. *Carrer de Palau de la Música 4-6, T: 902 442 882, www.palaumusica.org*

Clubs

Antilla BCN Latin Club ❶ 3D

Open nightly, this massive, cheerfully tacky dance club boasts live bands, free salsa lessons and a *salsateca* at weekends. *Carrer d'Aragó 141, T: 93 451 45 64, www.antillasalsa.com*

Boulevard Culture Club ❷ 5B

Three different rooms play variations of house, R&B and rock, pulling in a young but knowing crowd of

---

Cinema Secrets

Monday night is traditionally the cheapest night to go to the cinema – but it's cheap by UK standards whenever you go. Films marked in listings guides with the symbol 'VO' are subtitled rather than dubbed and will be shown in the original language.

Behind the Scenes

Even if you don't manage to see a performance at Barcelona's most venerable concert halls, the Liceu and the Palau de la Música Catalana are both open for visits during the day (*see left & pp.9, 12*).

Gran Teatre del Liceu at night

students and tourists. It's practically empty before 2am.
Las Ramblas 27, T: 93 301 62 89, www.boulevardcultureclub.es

CDLC off map

Co-owned by ex-Barça footballer Patrick Kluivert, this glam restaurant, lounge-bar and club is right on the beach. The place to see and be seen if you don't mind the snooty attitude of the staff. *Passeig Marítim 32, T: 93 224 04 70, www.cdlcbarcelona.com*

City Hall ① 4E

From 12 midnight, this central club attracts a mixed bag of tourists and locals. Although house and hip-hop is the focus, R&B holds sway on Thursdays. *Rambla de Catalunya 2-4, T: 93 238 07 22, www.grupo-ottozutz.com*

Club Mix ② 4G

A classy combination of cocktails and DJs makes this bar a hit with a slightly more mature crowd. *Carrer de Comerç 21, T: 93 319 46 96, www.mixbcn.com*

Diobar ② 5G

A small but hugely popular basement club, downstairs from Greek restaurant Dionisus and open from Thursday to Saturday with DJs specialising in funk and Latin beats. *Carrer Marquès de l'Argentera 27, T: 93 319 56 19.*

Moog ② 5B

Central location just off the Ramblas, this popular club covers all the bases with techno, electro, drum'n'bass

Flamenco dancer

and trance. Things get started after 1am. *Arc del Teatre 3, T: 93 319 17 89, www.masimas.com*

La Terrazza ① 5B

From Thursday to Saturday between May and October only, this amazing outdoor venue beneath the trees comes alive right behind Le Poble Espanyol (*see p.12*). Hosting some of Europe's biggest DJs, the huge

---

Flamenco Tablaos

Although flamenco isn't a Catalan tradition, Andalucians living in Barcelona keep it alive. There are several touristy spots to see a show (*tablao*), but the best are Los Tarantos (② 5B) (*see right*) and El Tablao de Carmen (① 5B) *Poble Espanyol, Montjuic, T: 93 325 68 95, www.tablaodecarmen.com.* The latter hosts better shows, and if you buy your ticket in advance, entrance to Poble Espanyol is free. However, Los Tarantos has the advantage of being a late-night club.

queues and strict door policy reflect its popularity. *Poble Espanyol, T: 93 272 49 80, www.laterrrazza.com*

Jazz, Latin & Flamenco

Harlem Jazz Club ❷ 5D
Excellent little jazz club with a very creative programme of guest performers. *Carrer Comtessa de Sobradiel 8, T: 93 310 07 55, www.harlemjazzclub.es*

Jamboree ❷ 5B
Perennially popular, the Jamboree is packed out every night. The wide-ranging programme includes jazz, blues, funk and hip-hop, and the Sunday blues night is always excellent. When the live sets are over, the venue becomes a great spot for a groove, featuring funk, soul and R&B. *Plaça Reial 17, T: 93 319 17 89, www.masimas.com*

Los Tarantos ❷ 5B
The *tablao* (flamenco venue) here is geared towards tourists, but features talented dancers and musicians. The live bands, which play anything from jazz and blues to folk or tango, are usually excellent. Later on, the club opens the doors that separate it from the adjoining Jamboree Club *(see left)*. *Plaça Reial 17, T: 93 319 17 89, www.masimas.com*

Rock & Pop

Apolo/Nitsaclub ❶ 6D
This well-known live music and club venue is set in a converted dance hall. It provides an energetic programme of pop and rock, reggae and world music. *Carrer Nou de Las Ramblas 113, T: 93 441 40 01, www.sala-apolo.com*

Bikini ❶ 2C
A huge venue behind the L'Illa shopping mall, offering a wide variety of pop and rock events. *Ave. Diagonal, 547, Les Corts, T: 93 322 08 00, www.bikinibcn.com*

Luz de Gas ❶ 2E
Beautiful old-style theatre converted into a live music venue and club. Live acts range from salsa to blues and jazz. Drink prices and general attitude reflect its uptown location. *Carrer de Muntaner 246, T: 93 209 77 11, www.luzdegas.com*

Razzmatazz ❶ 5H
Five different club spaces in one, which keep the crowds happy with mainstream rock and pop concerts. *Carrer dels Almogàvers 122, Poble Nou, T: 93 320 82 00, www.salarazzmatazz.com*

The stylish Luz de Gas

Sidecar Factory Club ❷ 5C

Located just off the Plaça Reial, this club is a big student favourite and serves up a wide variety of musical treats from indie-pop to local rock bands and Saturday nights; look out for the alternative performance night, which may be anything from poetry reading to dance. *Plaça Reial 7, T: 93 302 15 86, www.sidecarfactoryclub.com*

Street theatre on Las Ramblas

Theatre & Dance

Barcelona is celebrated throughout Spain for its innovative theatre and dance groups. These are avant-garde and experimental in the extreme, drawing on an eclectic range of influences, from circus acts to traditional Catalan music and dance, and they attract an ardent and critical following.

Summer in the City

Barcelona's main performing arts festivals are held during June and July and include the Festival del Grec, named after the open-air amphitheatre on Montjuïc (❶5C). It features world drama, music and dance. http://grec.bcn.cat **Sónar is a festival of multimedia and electronic music.** www.sonar.es

Mercat de les Flors ❶ 5C

This is one of the main venues of the Ciutat del Teatre (Theatre City) in Montjuïc. The former market is one of the main venues for the Festival del Grec (Greek Festival) *(see box, above)* and is renowned for its dynamic contemporary theatre and dance performances. *Carrer de Lleida 59, T: 93 426 18 75, www.mercatflors.org*

Sala Beckett ❶ 1G

Well-known venue for cutting-edge drama and contemporary dance.

What's it all About?

Even if you don't speak a word of Spanish or Catalan, you'll probably understand what's going on in a performance by Barcelona's contemporary theatre and dance groups. Language is just one element – mime, video, projections and even circus acts get thrown into the mix. No wonder the city's art scene is considered to be the most daring in all of Spain.

Carrer l'Alegre de Dalt 55, T: 93 284 53 12, www.salabeckett.com

Teatre Llantiol ❶ 5D

Very atmospheric, pocket-sized, *fin de siècle* theatre in the old town (one of the few that remain) staging fringe cabaret, comedy and music, often in English. Most performances start at 12 midnight and cost €8-15. *Carrer de la Riereta 7, T: 93 329 90 09, www.llantiol.com*

Barcelona's CosmoCaixa

Teatre Nacional de Catalunya (TNC) ❶ 4H

Designed by Ricardo Bofill. Drama and classical music make up the programme. *Plaça de les Arts 1, T: 93 306 57 00, www.tnc.cat*

Kids' Barcelona

L'Aquàrium de Barcelona ❶ 6E

As well as the underwater tunnel, kids will especially enjoy Explora! – get a frog's-eye-view and explore an underwater shipwreck, and Planeta Aqua – see the penguins, feed the stingrays and watch the piranhas and alligators in a tropical river. *Moll d'Espanya, Port Vell, T: 93 221 74 74, www.aquariumbcn.com*

CosmoCaixa (Museu de la Ciència) ❸

Barcelona's glossy Science Museum has been a huge hit, and a visit is highly recommended for kids. The futuristic building, excellent interactive exhibits and the planetarium make learning fun. Younger kids will love ¡Toca-Toca!, which has all different kinds of creatures to pet. *Carrer Teodor Roviralta 47-51, T: 93 212 60 50, www.cosmocaixa.com*

The underwater tunnel of the aquarium

Participation Sports

The city-run *Servei d'Informació* gives info on municipal sports facilities and sporting events. *T: 010.*

Petanca

Some things in Barcelona never change. On summer evenings many families play *petanca* – a kind of

Playing petanca *is serious stuff*

bowls – on quiet squares and catch up with friends between rounds.

Sailing & Watersports

Centre Municipal de Vela ❶ 7H
Sailing courses for all levels. *Moll de Gregal, Port Olímpic, T: 93 225 79 40, www.velabarcelona.com*

Reial Club Marítim de Barcelona ❶ 6E
This private club offers a variety of watersports. *Moll d'Espanya s/n, T: 93 221 48 59, www.maritimbarcelona.org*

Swimming

Club Natació Atlètic-Barceloneta ❶ 7E
By the beach at Barceloneta, this has indoor and outdoor pools, a gym and a café. At weekends, casual visits are only permitted if accompanied by a member. *Adm. Banys de Sant Sebastià, Plaça del Mar, T: 93 221 00 10, www.cnab.org*

Piscina Bernat Picornell ❶ 5B
Indoor and outdoor pools. *Avinguda*

The harbour at Port Vell

de l'Estadi 30-40, T: 93 423 40 41, www.picornell.cat

Tennis

Centre Municipal de Tennis Vall d'Hebron ❸
Clay courts, asphalt courts and pools. *Passeig de la Vall d'Hebron 178-196, T: 93 427 65 00.*

Beg, Steal or Borrow
You'll have to be very determined or well-connected to get a ticket to see FC Barcelona. A week before each match, about 4,000 tickets go on sale; go online to try and snap some up or call ahead to find out what time they will be offered for sale and start queuing at the stadium a couple of hours in advance.
www.fcbarcelona.com

Spectator Sports

Basketball

Basketball is enormously popular in Spain. The FC Barça basketball team has a huge following, as do their rivals, Club Joventut Badalona. The season runs from September to June.

Club Joventut Badalona ❸
*Carrer Ponent 143-161, Badalona (on the outskirts of the city),
T: 93 460 20 40, www.penya.com*

FC Barça ❶ 1A
Tickets from €13. *Palau Blaugrana (next to Camp Nou stadium),
Avinguda d'Aristides Maillol, Les Corts,
T: 93 496 36 00,
www.fcbarcelona.com*

Football

FC Barcelona ❶ 1A
You can buy tickets direct from the stadium ticket office, and an online ticket service is now available. *Camp Nou, Avinguda d'Aristides Maillol, Les Corts, tickets from €19-€265 depending on position and fixture. Ticket hotline:
T: 93 496 36 00, www.fcbarcelona.com*

FC Barcelona scarves for sale

RCD Espanyol ❹
Tickets can be bought online and picked up from the stadium on the day. *Estadi Cornellà-El Prat,
Ave Baix Llobregat 100, Cornellà de Llobregat, T: 93 292 77 00,
www.rcdespanyol.com*

Grand Prix

Formula One Grand Prix ❹
Held in spring at the Circuit de Catalunya. Tickets can be ordered online or bought at the circuit's ticket office. *Carretera de Parets del Vallés a Granollers, Montmeló,
T: 93 571 97 00, www.circuitcat.com*

Tennis

The Barcelona Open takes place during the last week of April. Tickets are available from Servi-Caixa (*see p.24*) and through the club.

Reial Club de Tennis Barcelona-1899 ❸
*Carrer de Bosch i Gimpera 5-13,
Les Corts, T: 93 203 78 52,
www.rctb1899.es*

Looking out over Barcelona at night from the roof of La Pedrera

barcelona places to eat and drink

One of Barcelona's most famous literary creations is the gourmet detective, Pepe Carvalho, whose passion for fine food and wine is shared by everyone in the city. The local cuisine is based on simple combinations of fresh fish from the Mediterranean, game from the Pyrenees and vegetables from the plains. Best of all is the simply delicious Catalan staple, *pa amb tomàquet*, which is bread rubbed with tomatoes, garlic and olive oil. There are thousands of restaurants, from tiny bars dishing out fried sardines washed down with wine straight from the barrel to exclusive establishments serving refined haute cuisine in exquisite Modernista surroundings. And there's a fantastic array of bars and cafés, perfect for people-watching over a glass of cava and some tapas.

taste it places to eat and drink

Price Guide
Prices are for a three-course meal for one without alcohol.
€ = under €15
€€ = €15-30
€€€ = €30-50
€€€€ = above €50

Classic Catalan

Café de l'Acadèmia €€ ❷ 5D
Elegant and romantic with a pretty terrace lit by candles in summer. Fresh Catalan dishes such as *rossejat* (rice cooked in fish broth) are a treat. *Carrer Lledó 1, T: 93 319 82 53.*

Can Culleretes €€-€€€ ❷ 4C
This much-loved restaurant has the honour of being the oldest in the city and it's therefore the perfect place to initiate yourself into classic Catalan cuisine. *Carrer Quintana 5, T: 93 317 30 22, www.culleretes.com*

Casa Calvet €€€€ ❶ 4F
Designed by Gaudí and boasting Modernista stained glass and whiplash wooden fittings. Modern Catalan dishes like smoked foie gras with mango sauce feature along with some great desserts. *Carrer de Casp 48, T: 93 412 40 12, www.casacalvet.es*

Casa Leopoldo €€-€€€ ❸ 3A
This welcoming, family-run restaurant has solid traditional décor and generous portions of hearty Catalan dishes like *albondigas con sepia y gambas* (meatballs with squid and prawns). *Carrer de Sant Rafael 24, T: 93 441 30 14, www.casaleopoldo.com*

Try fresh grilled sardines

Lunch Date
If you want to eat at one of Barcelona's classier places, but can't stretch to the price of dinner, you'll find that most restaurants offer a *menú del día*, a lunchtime menu that offers excellent value. If you are here on a budget, most of the cheaper places also offer inexpensive menus for local workers. It will usually consist of three courses (including dessert) plus wine or water.

Senyor Parellada €€ ❷ 5E

Downstairs from the Banys Orientals hotel (*see p.56*) is this convivial and reasonably priced restaurant, which doesn't flinch from injecting creative twists into the classic dishes of the region. *Carrer de l'Argenteria 37, T: 93 310 50 94, www.senyorparellada.com*

Contemporary

Alkimia €€€€ ❶ 2G

The "Alchemy" suggested from its name is certainly delivered in one of the current favourites with the well-

Inside the Café de l'Acadèmia

Tips on Tipping

Tipping is not common among Catalans. Locals will round the bill up by a euro or two, but waiters hope for a little more from tourists. If you have had good service and you leave 10 per cent, your waiter will definitely go home happy but there is no expectation.

heeled of Barcelona. Chef Jordi Vilà produces Michelin-starred dishes that take Catalan classics and fine tune them down to minimalist food art. Reservations are essential. *Carrer de la Indústria 79, T: 93 207 61 15, www.alkimia.cat*

Pla €€€ ❷ 5D

Candles, vaulted ceilings and brick walls make this spacious restaurant a welcoming spot. Imaginative Mediterranean cuisine with excellent vegetarian options and very friendly service. *Carrer de Bellafila 5, T: 93 412 65 52, www.elpla.cat*

Silenus €€ ❷ 2A

Cool, arty and friendly, this is just around the corner from the MACBA (*see p.8*). The delicious modern Catalan cuisine is imbued with international touches and there are great sofas on which you can while away an afternoon over a coffee. *Carrer dels Àngels 8, T: 93 302 26 80, www.restaurantsilenus.com*

Tickets €€€€ ❶ 5C

Swanky, and ever-popular tapas bar with theatrical and fairground themed décor. The top notch dishes are the creations of the renowned Adrian and Silesians brothers. The restaurant only takes online bookings and its recommended that these are made well in advance due to avoid disappointment. *Avinguda Paral·lel 164, no phone, www.ticketsbar.es*

Tragaluz €€ ❶ 3E

Huge, stylish restaurant with a wonderful glass skylight. Mediterranean dishes are made with ultra-fresh ingredients, and tapas can

---

Opening Hours
Most restaurants are open from around 1pm to 3.30pm and then from 8pm to 11pm. Many are closed on Sunday evenings, and several are closed for the whole of August. It's always worth calling ahead to check opening times before setting off.

Mamá Café serves food from all over the world

be eaten in the downstairs bar. *Passatge de la Concepció 5, T: 93 487 06 21, www.grupotragaluz.com*

DJ Dinners

Bestial €-€€€ ❶ 7G

Part of the Tragaluz restaurant family (*see above*), Bestial serves Italian cuisine, with a cutting-edge design, a terrace overlooking the beach, and DJs on Friday and Saturday nights. *Carrer de Ramon Trias Fargas 2-4, T: 93 224 04 07, www.grupotragaluz.com*

Mamá Café €-€€ ❷ 2B

Live DJs, bright décor and funky design to match the global cuisine cooked up here, and there's plenty to keep vegetarians happy too. *Carrer del Doctor Dou 10, T: 93 301 29 40, www.mamacaferestaurant.com*

Sal Café €€ ❶ 7G

With a perfect beachfront location, this is a trendy restaurant-bar with orange-and-black retro-style décor and a wonderful terrace. The menu is imaginative, the food tasty. *Passeig*

Marítim s/n, T: 93 224 07 07,
www.salcafe.com

Seafood

Agua €€€ ❶ 7G

Overlooking the sea, this is a very
stylish spot to sample creative
seafood and rice dishes. *Passeig
Marítim 30, T: 93 225 12 72,
www.aguadeltragaluz.com*

Can Majó €€€ ❶ 7F

This is a well-known seafood
restaurant with a terrace, where the
local chefs come (praise indeed) for
traditional rice dishes like *suquet* or
sarsuela (a hearty fish stew). *Carrer de
L'Almirall Aixada 23, T: 93 221 54 55,
www.canmajo.es*

El Cangrejo Loco €€€ ❶ 7H

Big, bustling and good value, the

'Crazy Crab' has good paellas and
other seafood dishes. There's also
a terrace right by the shore, but be
prepared to wait for a table.
*Moll de Gregal 29-30, T: 93 221 05
33, www.elcangrejoloco.com*

Set Portes €€€ ❷ 6F

This legendary paella restaurant has
been running for nearly 200 years,
and its popularity shows no signs of

Sea views from El Cangrejo Loco

Child-friendly Restaurants

The Spanish love kids and
you'll see children eating out
with their families in almost
every restaurant and at all
hours of the day and night.
Waiters usually fall over
themselves to accommodate
you and your kids, bringing
toys and special smaller
portions. Note that high
chairs are not usually
common so you should call
ahead to make sure they can
provide you with one.

waning – be prepared to queue. There are various quaintly decorated dining rooms, but only a handful of tables are available for reservations. *Passeig Isabel II 14, T: 93 319 30 33, www.7portes.com*

Tapas

Bar La Plata € ❷ 6D
Don't miss this minuscule bar near the harbour that only serves freshly grilled sardines or whitebait to wash down with wine straight from the barrel. Popular with locals, charming owners too. *Carrer de la Mercè 28, T: 93 315 10 09.*

La Bodegueta € ❶ 3E
This delightful old-fashioned bar is lined with bottles and tucked away in a cellar. Great tapas of ham, cheese and *torrades* (tomato bread with simple toppings). Very good value fixed-price lunch. *Rambla de Catalunya 100, T: 93 215 48 94.*

At the bar in Quimet i Quimet

Watch Out
Tourists – especially tipsy ones – make themselves a prime target for the pickpockets that plague the city's main drags. Watch your bags closely, especially on and around Las Ramblas. Better still, take with you only what you want to spend, and leave extra currency and credit cards safely back at your hotel.

Cal Pep €€€ ❷ 6F
A local legend. Serves excellent tapas, but the real draw is Pep himself who wields a grilling-fork and holds forth on anything and everything at the same time. There are a few small tables in the back room, but no one wants to sit back there for fear of missing out on Pep. *Plaça de les Olles 8, T: 93 310 79 61, www.calpep.com*

Quimet i Quimet € ❶ 5D
A wonderful, old-fashioned little bar, crammed floor to ceiling with a huge

Waiters in La Bodegueta

array of wines and liqueurs. The tapas are among the best in town: get here early, it's standing room only. *Carrer Poeta Cabanyes 25, T: 93 442 31 42.*

Re-Pla €€ ❷ 4F

A gloriously tiled old-style traditional tapas bar, which in fact only opened at the end of 2008. The food isn't cheap, but it is excellent, as is the house wine. *Carrer de Montcada 2, T: 93 268 30 03.*

Taller de Tapas €-€€ ❷ 5E

This large locale takes the stress out of ordering tapas, with written menus and sit-down tables. The selection changes almost daily and although it obviously caters to tourists, the quality is high. *Carrer de l'Argenteria 51, T: 93 268 85 59, www.tallerdetapas.com*

La Vinya del Senyor €€€ ❷ 5E

An elegant wine and tapas bar that has a superb location opposite the beautiful church of Santa Maria del Mar (*see p.6*). The tapas are exquisite and delicious but the portions do come in tiny sizes. *Plaça Santa Maria 5, T: 93 310 33 79.*

Vegetarian

Govinda €-€€ ❷ 2C

A vegetarian Indian restaurant, with a good and tasty set lunch, in a friendly environment. Among the curries and nan bread, you'll find the occasional Spanish dish. *Plaça Vila*

Smoking Rules

In January 2006 Spain's first anti-smoking laws came into effect. In 2011 these restrictions became tougher and now smoking is forbidden in restaurants, bars, clubs, and cafés, as well as public buildings such as train stations and airports. Despite this ban, smoking is still quite commonplace but laws are generally observed.

de Madrid 4, T: 93 318 77 29,
www.amalteaygovinda.com

Juicy Jones € **2** 3B

Upstairs is a cheerful juice counter, and downstairs is the brightly painted, friendly restaurant. Good three-course set menus feature daily, as well as refreshing juices and smoothies, all made right here on the premises. Carrer Cardenal Casañas 7, T: 93 302 43 30.

Organic € **2** 4A

Happy, hippy lunch place with an excellent-value menú del día comprising a salad, main course and a dessert. The communal wooden tables add to the friendly vibe. Carrer Junta de Comerç 11, T: 93 301 09 02, www.antoniaorganickitchen.com

Bars

Bar Marsella €-€€ **2** 4A

Marble-topped tables, creaking paddle fans and the pungent odour of absinthe. This bar was established by a homesick Frenchman almost two centuries ago and hasn't changed a bit since then. Carrer de

Sant Pau 65, T: 93 442 72 63.

Barcelona Rouge **1** 5D

Clandestine watering hole furnished with flea market decor and serving a lengthy list of cocktails to a boho crowd. Carrer Poeta Cabanyes 21, T: 93 442 49 85.

Boadas Cocktail Bar **2** 1C

Exquisite art deco cocktail bar that has barely changed since the 1930s. Excellent, perfectly mixed cocktails and wall-to-wall celebrity tributes with customary doodles. Carrer dels Tallers 1, T: 93 318 95 92.

Gimlet **1** 2D

Small, New York-style cocteleria serving mean martinis to the tune of laid-back jazz. Carrer de Santaló, 46, T: 93 201 53 06, www.gimletbcn.com

Ginger **2** 5D

Split-level design bar that oozes laid-back sophistication, from the retro wood-panelling and yellow leather sofas to the eclectic range of cocktails, wine and tasty and imaginative tapas. Carrer de Lledo 2, T: 93 310 53 09, www.ginger.cat

Marmalade **1** 5D

Located five minutes away from Las Ramblas, the latest incarnation

Refreshing Cosmopolitan

of this former furniture showroom is a jaw-dropping designer cocktail bar, counting a pool table among its many attractions. *Carrer de Riera Alta 4-6, T: 93 442 39 66, www.marmaladebarcelona.com*

Cafés

Café de l'Opéra €-€€ ❷ 4B

This art nouveau café is an institution, providing the perfect vantage point for watching the crowds that flow endlessly up and down Las Ramblas. Prices on the terrace reflect the prime location, but it's a great place to while away an hour or two.
Las Ramblas 74, T: 93 317 75 85, www.cafeoperabcn.com

Café d'Estiu € ❷ 4D

The name means 'Summer Café' and indeed this café is only open from April until September. Set under orange trees in a tranquil courtyard outside the Museu Frederic Marés, this is a wonderfully peaceful spot to take a load off your feet and sample an array of snacks and cakes. *Plaça Sant Iu 5, T: 93 268 25 98. www.cafedestiu.com*

Museu Marítim Café € ❷ 7A

Located near to the Sant Cristòfol gallery, this shady terrace café in the Jardí del Rei provides a relaxed backdrop in which to digest the exhibits within the excellent Museu Marítim. The café serves a good choice of sinful cakes to refuel you for further Barcelona sightseeing. *Av.*

The pretty terrace of the Museu Marítim Café

de les Drassanes s/n, T: 93 342 99 20, www.mmb.cat

La Pallaresa € ❷ 3C

Thick, dark hot chocolate served with fried, doughy *churros* is one delicious way to kick-start your day. The café is regarded as one of the best *xocolaterías* (drinking chocolate shops) in the city. *Carrer de Petritxol 11, T: 93 302 20 36, www.lapallaresa.com*

barcelona practical information

Barcelona welcomes tourists with smooth efficiency, and the provision of very helpful websites in English helps you get the lowdown in advance. This is backed up, once you hit town, by the string of well-equipped tourist information offices. The city is easy to get around too; compact and beautiful, it's perfect for exploring on foot. If you want to take advantage of the public transport system, it is clean, efficient, simple to use and is especially useful for venturing farther afield. For something different, sail high above the bay in a cable car or trundle up a hill in a restored antique tram. For a problem-free trip, make sure you organise accommodation and concert or opera tickets well in advance.

know it practical information

Tourist Information

Barcelona Tourist Office
Plaça de Catalunya 17 ( 1D, main branch), Columbus Monument (**2** 7A), Plaça Sant Jaume (**2** 4D, in the corner of the City Hall), Sants railway station (**1** 3B) and the airport, (Terminals 1 and 2).
T: 93 285 38 34,
www.barcelonaturisme.com

Catalonia Tourist Information 1 3E
Open 10am-7pm Mon-Sat, 10am-2.30pm Sun. Palau Robert, Passeig de Gràcia 107, T: 93 238 80 91,
www.gencat.cat/palaurobert

Cultural Information 2 3B
For information on cultural events contact Centre d'Informació de la Virreina (see p.24). Palau de la Virreina, Las Ramblas 99, T: 93 316 10 00, or City Hall's information service T: 010.

Arriving by Air

Barcelona-El Prat Airport 3
The international airport is 12 km (7½ miles) south of the city. Each airline is allocated to one of the two terminals. Terminal 1 is the newest and most commonly used. For flight information, call:
T: 902 404 704 or visit
www.aena-aeropuertos.es

Bus

The Aerobús departs every 5-10 minutes from outside terminals 1 and 2 for the Plaça Catalunya, via the Plaça d'Espanya (6am-5am daily). Journey times can take between 30 and 40 minutes depending on the traffic (slightly longer on outbound journeys as it takes a different route). A single ticket presently costs €5.30.
www.aerobusbcn.com

Taxi

There are plenty of taxis waiting outside both terminals. A ride into town will cost around €25-30, not including a tip, which is not customary. Journey times depend on traffic. Fares are more expensive after 10pm and at weekends. Luggage and pets carry a supplement. Use the taxi ranks and not the drivers who approach you in the arrivals hall.

Train

RENFE trains leave the airport every 30 minutes from 5.42am to 11.38pm and stop at three stations: Sants **1** 3B, Passeig de Gràcia **1** 4E, and Estació de França **2** 6G; all connect with the Metro **5**. Single tickets cost around €3.15 and return tickets offer a small discount. The journey time is about 25 minutes.
T: 90 232 03 20, www.renfe.es

Sign outside the railway station

Getting Around

For information visit *www.tmb.cat*

Bike Hire

The seafront is the perfect place for a bike ride. there are many options for hiring bikes; try one of the following outlets:

Barcelona Glides ❷ 4D
Glide around Barcelona on Segways. Guided tours only. *T: 93 310 41 08, www.spainglides.com*

Biciclot-Marítim ❶ 7G
Bikes and tandems. *Passeig Marítim, 33-35, Platja de Barceloneta, T: 93 221 97 78, www.biciclot.net*

Bike Rental Barcelona
Delivers folding bikes to your hotel and offers tours. *T: 66 605 76 55, www.bikerentalbarcelona.com*

Un Cotxe Menys ❷ 5F
Bikes and bike tours. *Carrer Esparteria 3, T: 93 268 21 05, www.bicicletabarcelona.com*

Bus

The main hub for buses is the Plaça de Catalunya (❷ 1D). Use the machine behind the driver to stamp your pass or ticket. Buses generally run from 4.30am to 10pm, when the *nitbus* (nightbus) service takes over until 4am. Note that regular transport passes are *not* valid for nightbuses.

Car Hire

Driving in Barcelona is a bad idea; the streets are narrow and crowded, while drivers are impatient and erratic. Parking is a nightmare. If you choose to drive, be sure to park your car in an underground supervised car park with a guard – cars bearing foreign number plates are tend to be prime targets for thieves.

Car hire is expensive. Get the best deals online before you arrive or find out if your airline offers discounts. The following have offices in Barcelona:

Avis
T: 90 218 08 54, www.avis.es

Europcar
T: 90 210 50 55, www.europcar.com

National/Atesa
T: 93 521 90 95, www.atesa.es

Cooltra ❶ 7F
Hires scooters and bikes from 50 to 125 CC. *Passeig Joan de Borbó 80-84, T: 93 221 40 70, www.cooltra.com*

Metro ❺

There are 11 Metro lines in Barcelona, identified by number and colour. The

Sign for the funicular

The funicular building

direction of the train is indicated by the destination at the end of the line. It's clean, efficient and easy. *Open 5am–12midnight Mon–Thu & Sun, 5am–2am Fri, 24 hrs Sat.*

Taxi

Yellow-and-black city taxis are easy to spot. Flag them down on the street when the green roof light is on or head for the taxi rank on Plaça de Catalunya (❶ 5E). Prices are reasonable, but few drivers speak English. There are surcharges for luggage in the boot.

Taxi Numbers

Fono-Taxi: *T: 93 300 11 00.*
Ràdio Taxi: *T: 93 303 30 33.*

Trams provide quick and easy transport

Tickets & Fares

The following tickets are the most useful for visitors and are valid for most forms of public transport within the city, including metro, bus, tram, the Paral·lel funicular, local RENFE trains (*cercanías* in Castilian, *rodalies* in Catalan) and on the FGC (Ferrocarrils de la Generalitat de Catalunya) train lines. They are available at most Metro stations. A single costs €2.

T-Dia
This ticket covers one person for

unlimited travel for one day and costs €6.95. Other tickets are valid for two, three, four or five days.

T-10
Ten single rides for €9.25. This ticket can be shared.

Tram, Funicular & Cable Car

The best way to get up Montjuïc is by funicular from Paral·lel Metro station. For Tibidabo, (*see p.13*) take

ATM machine outside a bank

the Tramvia Blau (Blue Tram) up to Plaça del Funicular, where it meets the funicular. If you don't mind heights, take the cable car from Montjuïc to Barceloneta. Three tram lines (*www.trambcn.com*) link the Ciutadella-Vila Olímpica and Glòries metro stations to Sant Adrià and Gorg to the north. Three other tram lines run along the Diagonal from the Plaça Francesc Macià to the southwestern suburbs.

Banks & Money

There are large banks around the Plaça de Catalunya and *canvis* (bureaux de change) along Las Ramblas and at train stations.

ATMs

ATMs (*cajeros*) are easy to operate and found at most banks. All have multilingual options.

Changing Money

Banks charge hefty commissions for changing money and traveller's cheques; shop around for the best

Euro notes and coins

rates. The bureaux de change are often open 24 hours but they charge crippling rates. The most convenient option is to use your debit or credit card to withdraw money from ATMs, but check your bank fees first.

Currency

The euro is divided into 100 cents, and one euro is worth roughly 82 UK pence or 1.30 US dollars.

Opening Times

Banks are usually open from Monday to Friday, 8.30am-2pm, and many

are open on Saturday mornings in winter. *Canvis* (bureaux de change) are open later.

Climate

Barcelona has a temperate Mediterranean climate with hot summers, cool winters and plenty of sunshine all year round. July average temperatures are 25-30°C, December 8-13°C. The best time to visit is late spring or early autumn when the weather is comfortably warm and the streets are not too crowded.

Disabled Access

Barcelona is getting better at catering for disabled visitors but it still has a long way to go. The sightseeing Bus Turístic (*see p.53*) and Aerobúses (*see p.46*) are equipped for wheelchairs, as are about a third of the public buses. More and more metro stations have lifts. For detailed information on disabled access to museums, restaurants, monuments, theatres

and other establishments, contact the city's bureau for the disabled, the Institut Municipal de Persones amb Disminució. *Avinguda Diagonal 233, planta 1, T: 93 413 27 75 (mornings only), www.bcn.cat/accessible www.accessiblebarcelona.com*

Electricity & Voltage

The voltage in Barcelona is 220v and plugs have two prongs. Adaptors are found at department stores.

Embassies & Consulates

Australia
T: 93 490 90 13, www.spain.embassy.gov.au

Canada
T: 93 270 36 14, www.canadainternational.gc.ca

New Zealand
T: 93 209 03 99, www.nzembassy.com

UK
T: 91 334 2194, www.ukinspain.com

USA
T: 93 280 22 27, www.embusa.es

Emergencies

Ambulance/Ambulància
T: 061.

Fire service/Bombers/Bomberos
T: 080.

General Emergency
T: 112.

Municipal Police/Policia Municipal
T: 088

Insurance

EU residents are entitled to free health care in state hospitals thanks to reciprocal agreements between EU countries, although private insurance is recommended. British citizens need an Emergency Health Insurance Card (EHIC). Apply by phone (*T: 0845 605 0707*), online (*www.ehic.org.uk*) or at your post

Pickpockets are rife along Las Ramblas; look after your valuables

office. Check your insurance policy's small print to ensure that it covers the cost of repatriation in an emergency.

Internet Cafés

These can be found all over Barcelona with a concentration in popular tourist areas such as the Ramblas and Barri Gòtic area. Expect to pay around €2 an hour.

Wireless (Wi-Fi)

Pronounced "wee-fee" in Barcelona, Wi-Fi is widespread through the city in cafes, bars, and hotels. Barcelona city council operates a free public space Wi-Fi service too:
www.bcn.cat/barcelonawifi

Left Luggage

Lockers can be found at the airport, Sants, Estació de França, Passeig de Gràcia stations and Estació del Nord bus station.

Lost Property

If property is lost on the Metro or buses, call TMB customer services on *T: 902 07 50 27*. If it has been longer than seven days since losing the item contact the city council lost property department on *T: 010 (within Barcelona). www.bcn.cat*

Personal Safety

Watch out for pickpockets, especially around Las Ramblas. Violent mugging is not common in Barcelona, but pickpocketing and bag-snatching is. Take care with your belongings in outdoor cafés, crowded streets and on the beaches. As stores require photo ID when making a credit-card purchase, use your driver's licence and leave your passport at the hotel along with other valuables.

Pharmacies

Farmàcia Cervera ❶ 2D

*Carrer Muntuner 254,
T: 93 200 09 96.*

Farmàcia Clapés ❷ 4B

Las Ramblas 98, T: 93 301 28 43.

Post Offices

Post offices may look very grand but the mail service is often unreliable. The price of a postcard stamp for all European countries is €0.70 and €0.85 for all other countries. Postboxes are yellow and you can also buy stamps at *estancs* (tobacconists). Main post office: *open 8.30am-9.30pm Mon-Fri, 8.30am-2pm Sat.* Plaça d'Antoni López (❷ 6E), T: 93 486 83 02, *www.correos.es*

Public Holidays

On public holidays most bars and restaurants will close and the transport service is restricted.
1 Jan *Cap d'Any* (New Year's Day)
6 Jan *Dia dels Reis* (Three Kings)
March/April *Divendres Sant* (Good Friday)
March/April *Pasqua Florida* (Easter Monday)

1 May *Festa del Treball* (Labour Day)
May/June *Dilluns de Pasqua*
(Whit Monday)
24 June *Sant Joan* (St John's Day)
15 Aug *L'Assumpció* (Assumption)
11 Sep *Diada Nacional de Catalunya*
(Catalan National Day)
24 Sep *La Mercè*
(Our Lady of Mercy)
12 Oct *Día de la Hispanitat*
(Columbus Day)
1 Nov *Tots Sants* (All Saints' Day)
6 Dec *Día de la Constitució*
(Constitution Day)
8 Dec *La Imaculada*
(Immaculate Conception)
25 Dec *Nadal* (Christmas Day)
26 Dec *Sant Esteve*
(St Stephen's Day)

Sightseeing

Opening Times

Apart from department stores, malls and shops in the city centre, opening hours are 9.30am-10am until 1.30pm-2pm and then 4pm-5pm until 8pm-8.30pm. Some shops are closed Saturday afternoons and all day Sundays.

Ticket Concessions

Concessions are available on public transport and at most museums and monuments for students, pensioners and children. Students will usually be required to show a valid student card or an ISIC card *(see right)*.

Articket BCN

This covers entrance into Barcelona's seven top art museums: Centre de Cultura Contemporània de Barcelona (CCCB, *see p.59*); La Pedrera *(see p.5)*; Fundació Antoni Tàpies *(see p.59)*; Fundació Joan Miró *(see p.6)*; Museu d'Art Contemporani de Barcelona (MACBA, *see p.8*); Museu Nacional d'Art de Catalunya (MNAC, *see p.8*)

and the Museu Picasso *(see p.5)*. It costs €30 from all the above locations. *www.articketbcn.org*

Barcelona Card

This offers unlimited journeys on the Metro, buses and discounts at many shops, restaurants and museums. It is valid for two to five days and costs between €29 and €47 for adults and €25 and €37 for children (4-12 years). Discounted if purchased online:
www.barcelonaturisme.com

Youth Passes

The ISIC card, available in the UK from STA travel (*www.statravel.com*) and other youth travel organisations, gives discounts on museums, public transport, some sports facilities and cinemas.

Telephones

You will find blue public telephones everywhere in the city, and there are instructions in English pasted up next to them in the booths. Those that take coins are less

A public telephone

frequent, so it's best to buy a phone card (*see right*). *Locutorios* are cheap telephone centres, found in abundance on and around Las Ramblas. These offer good-value international phone calls from booths and many have Internet.

International Codes

To make an international call from Barcelona, dial **00** then add the country code and the rest of the telephone number (minus the first zero if there is one). UK **44**; USA **1**; Australia **61**; Canada **1**; Irish Republic **353**; New Zealand **64**.

Phone Cards

Phone cards are available at *estancs* (tobacconists) and news-stands.

To Call Spain from Abroad

The country code is **34**. The code for Barcelona is **93**, which is incorporated into the telephone number and must be dialled in full, even when calling from within the city.

Tours

Barcelona walking tours

Tours of the Barri Gòtic (**2** 2D) in English are at 9.30am daily. Tours in English of Picasso's Barcelona, which include admission to the Museu Picasso are at 3pm Tuesday, Thursday and Saturday. *T: 93 285 38 32, www.barcelonaturisme.com*

Bus Turístic **2** 1D

This hop-on hop-off service has three routes that take in a variety of the city's famous sights. Buses are adapted for wheelchairs and give commentaries in English. Tickets include discount vouchers to some sights and cost €24 for a one-day

pass, €31 for a two-day pass for all routes. Buy online, on the bus or at tourist offices. *Plaça de Catalunya, www.barcelonabusturistic.cat*

Las Golondrinas **1** 6E

Potter around the harbour in an old-fashioned *golondrina* (swallow boat). Departures from the Moll de la Fusta operate all year depending on weather. *T: 93 442 31 06, www.lasgolondrinas.com*

My Favourite Things

Tailored walking tours of various types, run by English speakers. *T: 637 265 405, www.myft.net*

Stop for the Bus Turístic

Praktik Rambla €€-€€€ ❶ 4E

A charming and intimate little hotel that provides comfortable rooms in a Modernista townhouse which has conserved many of the original details. *Rambla de Catalunya 27, T: 93 343 66 90, www.hotelpraktikrambla.com*

Home-from-Home Hotels

Bonic B&B €€ ❷ 7B

Ideally located near Plaça Reial, this is a B&B with none of the chintz or baked beans for breakfast. Bathrooms are communal but spotless and the décor is cosy. *Carrer de Josep Anselm Clavé 9, T: 626 053 434, www.bonic-barcelona.com*

Granvia €€€ ❶ 4F

Faded grandeur that is accompanied by a warm welcome from the friendly staff. *Gran Vía de les Corts Catalanes 642, T: 93 318 19 00, www.nnhotels.es*

Hostal Girona € ❶ 4F

This is like staying in someone's home; book well ahead for this charming *pensión* that combines faded furnishings with Modernista architecture and friendly service. Superb value. *Carrer Girona 24, 1º, 1º, T: 93 265 02 59, www.hostalgirona.com*

Pensió 2000 € ❷ 2E

A cosy *pensión* with buttercup-yellow walls, large rooms (seven in total) and friendly owners. *Carrer de Sant Pere Més Alt 6, 1º, T: 93 310 74 66, www.pensio2000.com*

Budget Hotels

Banys Orientals €€ ❷ 5E

At around €100 for a double room, this hotel isn't particularly cheap, but it's still probably the best bargain in this rather expensive city. Rooms are small but beautifully styled, and the cool shops and bars

of the fashionable El Born neighbourhood are right on its doorstep. *Carrer Argentería 37, T: 93 268 84 60, www.hotelbanysorientals.com*

Hostal Central € ❶ 4G

This popular hostel is situated in a Modernista apartment in L'Eixample. *Carrer Diputació 346, T: 93 245 19 81, www.hostalcentralbarcelona.com*

Hostal Gat Xino € ❶ 5D

Situated in the heart of the trendy Raval district, this is a sleek hotel boasting a glossy black-and-white décor and offering bright, modern rooms and a very comfortable suite. *Carrer de l'Hospital 155-1º, T: 93 324 88 33, www.gataccommodation.com*

Hostal Goya €-€€ ❶ 4F

This boutique-style pension offers stylish rooms without breaking the bank. Options include individual

rooms plus two apartments to choose from (some with balconies). *Pau Claris 74, T: 93 302 25 65, http://en.hostalgoya.com*

La Terrassa € ❷ 4A

This is a popular cheapie in the Raval. The excellent vegetarian eatery Organic shares the same location (see p.42). *Carrer de la Junta de Comerç 11, T: 93 302 51 74. www.laterrassa-barcelona.com*

Annual Festivals

Many celebrations take place in Barcelona each year. Here follow a selection.

5 January
Festa dels Reis: Festival of the Three Kings.
On the 5th January, the Three Kings parade around the city throwing sweets to children.

February/March
Carnestoltes: Carnival. Street parades and children's activities.

3 March
Festa Sant Medir: Festival of St Emeterius. Crowds process through the streets of the Gràcia area distributing sweets to everyone.

23 April
Sant Jordi: St George's Day. The 'Book and Rose' day celebrating Catalunya's patron saint.

Easter Week
Setmana Santa: Holy Week. Special Masses and solemn processions.

Late April/early May
Feria de Abril: Andalucian April Fair. A colourful event with flamenco performances and street parties.

March-May
Festival de la Guitarra: Guitar Festival. Concerts are held around the city and there is street theatre. *www.theproject.es*

May
Festival de Flamenco i Música Antigua: The Flamenco Festival and the Medieval Music Festival. Offer concerts, both traditional and modern, in various venues around the city.

www.auditori.org
www.flamencociutatvella.com

May/June
Corpus Christi:
This religious festival is celebrated with the custom of the *ou com balla* – hollow eggs dancing on a fountain – around town.

May/June
Formula One Grand Prix.
This takes place in the Circuit de Catalunya, which is out near Granollers (❹, see p.31).

June
Sónar:
Festival of Electronic Music and Multimedia. International DJs, exhibitions and enormous crowds. (see box, p.28) www.sonar.es

23 & 24 June
Festa de Sant Joan: Midsummer's Night, celebrated with fireworks on Montjuïc and Tibidabo, and bonfires on the beach.

June-July
Festival del Grec: A prestigious festival of the performing arts (see box, p.28).

Adm. Open 10am-2pm Tue-Sat, 10am-5pm Sun Nov-Apr; 10am-5pm Tue-Fri, 10am-7pm Sat, 10am-8pm Sun May-Oct. Baixada del Monestir 9, T: 93 256 34 34, www.museuhistoria.bcn.cat

Pavelló Mies Van der Rohe ❶ 5B

♛ ♿

Mies van der Rohe's German pavilion built for the 1929 International Exhibition. Adm. Open 10am-8pm daily. Avinguda Marquès de Comillas, T: 93 423 40 16, www.miesbcn.com

Parks

Parc de la Ciutadella ❶ 6G

See p.10.

Parc de Collserola ❸

A metropolitan park 500 m (1,700 ft) above sea level, with panoramic views of the city towards the sea. There are walking trails and an information centre, as well as guided tours of the countryside. Info Centre: Carretera de Vallvidrera a Sant Cugat km 4, T: 93 280 35 52, www.parccollserola.net

Parc de la Creueta del Coll ❸

A popular modern park with a lake and artificial beach, plus modern sculptures. Open 10am-dusk daily. Metro: Penitents.

Parc de l'Espanya Industrial ❶ 3B

Landscaping includes striking red-and-yellow striped lighthouses at the top of white steps and a boating lake. Sardana dancing takes place here in summer. Metro: Sants.

Parc Estació del Nord ❶ 5G

Grassy five-hectare park with funky contemporary sculptures. Metro: Arc de Triomf.

Park Güell ❶ 1G

See p.10.

Parc del Laberint d'Horta ❸

Huge magical park with restored 18th-century landscaped gardens, pine forests, leafy walks, a lake, waterfalls and an 18th-century maze with Eros at the centre. Open 10am-dusk daily. Metro: Montbau.

Recommended Reading

Local publisher Triangle publish DVD virtual tours on the following subjects:
Casa Batlló
Gaudí, Exploring Form
Temple of the Sagrada Família
For further information, visit www.trianglepostals.com

Barcelona

Learn the secrets of this flamboyant city through the eyes of author Joan Barril and various photographers. Six languages, 424 pages, full colour.

Casa Batlló

Clear colour photography, including shots of many previously unseen details in this architectural oddity. The text by Juan José Lahuerta charts Gaudí's role in the building of the house. Written in seven languages, 208 pages, full colour.

Gaudí

A photographic anthology of Gaudí's work by Pere Vivas and Ricard Pla, with an accompanying

Casa Batlló by
Juan José Lahuerta

essay written by Juan Eduardo Cirlot.
*Written in four languages,
424 pages, full colour.*

The best way to get to know
Barcelona's Modernista architectonic
heritage (*see p.9*) is on foot. The book
Modernisme Route, published by the
Ajuntament (City Hall) and available at
tourist offices, provides a walking map,
colour photos and a history of the
movement, including where to find
the major and minor works of Gaudí.

Gaudí by Juan
Eduardo Cirlot

Other titles on Gaudí include:

*Gaudí, An Introduction to his
Architecture,* Juan Eduardo Cirlot

Gaudí x Gaudí, Joan Bergós et al

La Pedrera, Josep M Carandell

Park Güell, Josep M Carandell

The Gaudí Key, Esteban Martin &
Andreu Carranza (Harper, 2008)

The New Spaniards, John Hooper
(Penguin, 2006)

Catch a glimpse of the real Barcelona
with the following selection of fact
and fiction:

Barça: A People's Passion, Jimmy

La Sagrada Família by Josep M Carandell

Burns (Bloomsbury, 2000)

Barcelona the Great Enchantress,
Robert Hughes
(National Geographic, 2007)

Barcelona, **Robert Hughes**
(Vintage, 1993)

Catalan Cuisine, **Colman Andrews,**
(Grub Street London, 1997)

Gaudí, **Gijs van Hensbergen**
(Harper Perennial, 2003)

Homage to Barcelona, **Colm Toibin**
(Picador, 2010)

Homage to Catalonia, **George
Orwell** (Penguin, 2003)

Offside, **Manuel Vázquez
Montalbán** (Serpent's Tail, 2001)

The Cathedral of the Sea, **Ildefonso
Falcones** (Black Swan, 2009)

The Shadow of the Wind, **Carlos Ruiz
Zafón** (Phoenix, 2012)

The Temple of the Sagrada Família,
Josep M Carandell (Triangle Postal,
2004)

Websites

www.bcn.cat
www.lecool.com

speak it

Barcelona is officially a bilingual city, where locals speak both Catalan and Castilian (Spanish). However, street signs, museum opening times and menus are often exclusively in Catalan. The Catalans are proud of their language and they appreciate efforts by foreigners to speak a few words in it.

hello – **hola**
goodbye – **adéu**
please – **si us plau**
thank you very much – **moltes gràcies**
do you speak English? – **parla anglés?**

Numbers

1 – **un(a)**, 2 – **dos/dues**, 3 – **tres**,
4 – **quatre**, 5 – **cinc**, 6 – **sis**, 7 – **set**,
8 – **vuit**, 9 – **nou**, 10 – **deu**,
11 – **onze**, 12 – **dotze**, 13 – **tretze**,
14 – **catorze**, 15 – **quinze**,
16 – **setze**, 17 – **disset**, 18 – **divuit**,
19 – **dinou**, 20 – **vint**, 100 – **cent**.

Time

What time is it? – **Quina hora és?**
At what time...? – **A quina hora...?**
At 3 o'clock – **A les tres**
...a quarter past 3 – **a un quart de quatre**
...half past 3 – **a dos quarts de quatre**
...a quarter to 4 – **a tres quarts de quatre**

Days of the week

Monday – **dilluns**
Tuesday – **dimarts**
Wednesday – **dimecres**
Thursday – **dijous**
Friday – **divendres**
Saturday – **dissabte**
Sunday – **diumenge**

Eating out

breakfast – **esmorzar**
lunch – **dinar**
dinner – **sopar**
menu – **carta**
fixed price menu – **menú del dia**
bill/check – **el compte**

enjoy your meal – **bon profit!**
toilet/toilets – **lavabos/els serveis**
coffee – **cafè**
wine list – **carta dels vins**
mineral water – **aigua mineral**
bread – **pa**
white wine – **vi blanc**
red wine – **vi negre**

Getting around

museum – **museu**
market – **mercat**
pharmacy – **farmàcia**
post office – **correus**

men – **homes**
women – **dones**

airport – **aeroport**
arrivals – **arribades**
departures – **sortides**

station – **estació de tren**
How can I get to...? – **Per anar a...?**
I'd like a return – **Voldria un bitllet**
return ticket to – **de anada i tornada a...**

Written by Mary-Ann Gallagher, Suzanne Wales.
Updated by Sally Davies, Sophie-Elizabeth Thompson.
Revision Management by Cambridge Publishing Management Ltd.

Pictures © Compass Maps Ltd and Susannah Sayler except Alamy/Terry Harris (p.15), Alamy/Espixx (p.45); Triangle Postals – Pere Vivas/Ricard Pla (pp.3, 5, 6, 23, 24, 32-33); iStockphoto Sam Burt (pp.10R, 11); Shutterstock Pres Panayotov (p.4), csp (p.7), nito (p.9), Veniamin Kraskow (p.12R), Forgiss (p.30L), Antony Rosenberg (p.30R), Liv Friis-Larsen (p.36), 3523studio (p.42), Steven Paul Pepper (p.26); John Heseltine (p.49).

Cover Images: Picture Finders/PCL and Chris Warren/PCL

Whilst every effort has been made to trace the photography copyright holders, we apologise in advance for any omissions. We would be pleased to insert appropriate credits in any future editions.

This PopOut product, its associated machinery and format use, whether singular or integrated within other products, is subject to worldwide patents granted & pending, including EP1417665, CN ZL02819864.6 & CN ZL200620006638.7. All rights reserved including design, copyright, trademark and associated intellectual property rights. PopOut is a registered trademark and is produced under license by Compass Maps Ltd.

8047

Whilst every care has been taken to check the accuracy of the information in this guide, the publishers cannot accept responsibility for errors or omissions or the consequences thereof. No part of this guide may be reproduced without the permission of the publishers. Published by Compass Maps Ltd.
info@popoutmaps.com
www.popoutproducts.co.uk
© 2012 Compass Maps Ltd.

Barceloneta & the Port Olímpic ❶ 7F-7H

Barcelona's beaches and seafront were given a multimillion dollar facelift for the 1992 Olympics. The glistening Port Olímpic is packed with bars, restaurants and shops, all overlooked by swish new urban developments and Frank Gehry's shimmering copper fish. The city's seven beaches stretch for miles and you can do everything from hiring a tandem and cycling along the boardwalk to taking a siesta down on the sand. On summer evenings, DJs play at Mar Bella beach where you can also take sailing and windsurfing lessons. The traditional old fishermen's neighbourhood of Barceloneta is still the best place to find great seafood tapas.

Barri Gòtic ❷ 2D

The Barri Gòtic (Gothic Quarter) is one of the best preserved medieval quarters in Europe. At the huge Gothic cathedral of **La Seu** (❷ 4D), a lift transports you up to experience the dizzying views among the gargoyles. The medieval Plaça del Rei (❷ 4E) is the site of the Palau Reial (Royal Palace) (❷ 4E), which can be visited as part of the Museu d'Història de Barcelona (Barcelona History Museum) (❷ 4E), along with the Roman ruins that are hidden beneath the square. **Catedral:** *Open 8am-7.30pm Mon-Fri, 8am-8pm Sat-*

Frank Gehry's dazzling structure

Més que un Club

You'll see the blue and burgundy strip of FC Barça all over Barcelona – it really is 'more than a club'. Under Franco the team became the embodiment of Catalan national identity, especially when pitted against his pet team, Real Madrid, in fixed matches. The construction of the huge Camp Nou stadium (❶ 1A) in the 1950s was made possible by the dedication of the fans, who were willing to pay their annual subscriptions up to five years in advance. Leading architect, Norman Foster is set to do further remodelling of the stadium over the next few years.

see it places to see

barcelona places to see

Barcelona is a magical city curled around the Mediterranean under a fairytale skyline of soaring spires and Modernista mansions. At its heart is the crooked, shadowy Gothic Quarter, encircled by the elegant grid of L'Eixample, where Gaudí's creamy, organic architecture seems to float above the rooftops. Forget sangría and bullfighting – this is Catalunya, a part of Spain with its own language, customs and long, long history. Most of all, Barcelona is one of Europe's most stylish cities and is right at the vanguard of cutting-edge design. Bold, brash and bent on a good time, it has a spectacular array of restaurants – from the finest haute cuisine to humble seaside taverns – excellent shopping, and a vibrant nightlife that buzzes right through until dawn.

CONTENTS

Map refe
❷ Ciuta .ro Map

D0275356

Belonging

PROLOGUE:
TAITH | JOURNEY

This is where it begins, on match days.

Closing a hotel room door, down into the team room. Up into a hotel lobby full of supporters in red shirts, of cheers and applause and shouts of good luck. Out past the stone columns either side and more people in red. Scarves and pints of beer and Welsh flags being waved. Up the steps of the team bus, walking past Andy the driver in his shirt and tie and the coaches in their Sunday best, walking past teammates in red tracksuit tops, finding your seat.

There's a tightness in your stomach you come to recognize. A strange comfort from the anticipation of pressure to come. After days waiting for it, weeks of pushing yourself so hard you should be broken, it's real. No more meetings, no more plans. It's today. That's what the supporters tell you – the police motorcycle outriders in front of the coach, with their flashing lights; the look on your teammates' faces; the feeling in your own head and heart.

It all builds, with every mile you get closer. First past the golf course on the right, players holding their shots to stand up and wave. The quiet little lanes, bare trees in the early part of a Six Nations, buds and blossom by the end. Thick hedges and little glimpses of the sky above. You look for clouds, for rain. You think about the pitch, in the middle of our capital city. How it will feel under your boots, how the ball will behave.

Across the roundabout, down the slip road onto the M4 and

into the traffic. A nation flowing into the city, all carried along by the same love and hope and devotion, all flags flying proudly from car windows and rosettes and ribbons and old songs being sung. Phones pressed against the windows when they hear the cavalcade coming, when they see the colours on the coach. Fists clenched and shouts you can't hear, grins and horns being sounded.

10 miles, nine.

The adrenaline starting to flow within. You've got to get the timing right. Let the nerves arrive but don't let them take over. You don't want too much time at the stadium – too long to think, to hang around. You don't want too little – rushing your routine, skipping the stuff experience has taught you matters. Glancing around at the boys, headphones on for most, listening to what gets them to the right place. Listening to silence, sometimes. You all do what works for you.

Cars pull over when they see you coming. Down the dual carriageway off the motorway, grey metal barrier down the middle, low trees on the left. Drivers thinking it's the police, at the start. Faces all worry and ready-made excuses, all phones and tooting when they see the coach and its colours and realize.

Past the supermarket superstores, the out-of-town retail parks. Past playing fields, kids with rugby balls running at each other, dropping shoulders. Tall white posts and mud in uneven patches, on the 22s, inside the touchlines.

There's no pre-match apprehension for me. This is where I want to be. This day, this destination. This group of men around me. The fear would be of missing out, of not being here. At the heart of it all, in the heat. Able to influence it, to share in it like these thousands around all will be too.

It's about belonging, playing for Wales. Wanting to be part of it, working your way through the age grades and the club matches and regional sides. Earning the right to be there, driven on by the desire to prove that you're worthy. Feeling the bond to the past, to the traditions, to the great players not long gone.

Feeling the ties to the nation, to the supporters you can see, to the millions in front rooms and pubs across the villages and towns and countryside, the hillsides and the valleys, coast to coast. You all want to belong, and you all do.

Five miles, four.

You can see the stadium in the distance from the end of the dual carriageway. The city laid out in front of you.

Coming in through the eastern suburbs, past the big Asda, the football stadium on your right. The white steel beams of its roof, the heaving bus stops, the drive-thru McDonalds and the Sand Martin pub, streetlights and grey pavements. An ordinary city on a magical day.

You look down at your phone and find the music that works in that moment. Maybe 'My Sacrifice' by Creed. The vocals, the opening line about saying hello to an old friend. A song that always seems to come back, my subconscious hunting it out.

Onwards into the city. The Jubilee recreation ground on your right, rugby posts again. Under the two railway bridges, the sign for Ninian Park train station. Black-and-white Cardiff taxis, new flats and old semis. The red-brick estates, the scaffolding round shopping parades. Corner shops selling cans and crisps.

Building inside you, building all around. Feeling wide awake. Controlled, composed. Senses heightening.

Swinging west onto the Cowbridge Road, towards the hospital. A mile to go.

Pubs are overflowing into the street. Cathedral Road up to your left, to Pontcanna, to Sophia Gardens. Plenty of places to drink up there. People striding through Bute Park, mates behind, mates ahead.

The roads are closed off before the bridge over the River Taff. The Westgate pub to your right, the Holiday Inn as you cross the river, with its Guinness lorry parked on the forecourt passing out dark pints. Always the same man in the same spot in the same suit covered in daffodils, waiting to watch you go by.

The crowd thickening now. Covering the roads, pouring

onwards towards the stadium. 50 minutes to kick-off, and tickets being negotiated at vastly inflated prices.

You swing right, the grand old front of the Angel Hotel on the left. Where the teams used to stay, where the male voice choir will be on the big sweeping staircase inside, belting out all the usual favourites.

They bring the metal bollards down on Westgate Street. It's slow now, the crowds heavy in front of you, opening up and then surging back all around. You're high up in the coach and you see everything – the police horses in front, ready to part the sea, the kids on parents' shoulders, the groups of young lads, swaying already from the sauce, the girls with red dragons painted on their faces or with yellow daffodil hats over their faces. You see the whites of eyes turned up towards you.

Driving on for 200 metres, looking forward and back and just seeing . . . people. Some of them don't want to move, or forget to. They're lost in the drinking and singing and staring at the coach. You spot faces you recognize. Your heart is beating fast now, your throat dry.

It's Gate Four that we head for. Turning right off the street, under the raised security barrier, down the ramp into the heart of the stadium. Under a big sign, white on red:

CROESO – WELCOME

Suddenly, under there, it's dark and quiet. Sombre, the intensity palpable. Grey concrete and pillars painted in yellow hazard stripes. A low roof, shiny aluminium ventilation shafts overhead.

There are television cameras when the bus stops and the door hisses open. Another choral battalion ready to march, providing another link in the chain connecting past and present. Men with neat hair and moustaches in V-neck sweaters. Headphones come off for that.

Double doors ahead of you, pulled back. On the wall to the left, a big red sign:

STADIWM PRINCIPALITY

On the right, the emblem of the Welsh Rugby Union: three white feathers and a gold crown, picked out on black.

You walk in. The walls painted white now, the skirting boards and handrails bright red. A huge silver dragon on the wall, claw up, wings back. Two flights of steps rising up in front of you towards another set of doors. A patch of daylight visible through them. The pitch.

You go into the dressing room first, turning left for the home team. The honours boards on the corridor walls, every man ever to play for Wales. Brown polished wood, names in gold. First your cap number, then given name in lower case, then surname in upper case and the year of your debut.

1045 Ian Richard EVANS 2006.
1046 Alun Wyn JONES 2006.
1047 James HOOK 2006.

Great photos of triumphs past. Tired, muddy faces grinning back at you, trophies being held aloft. Maybe your face, if you're one of the lucky ones.

The dressing room. Pushing the door open, a big photo of the team in a huddle on the wall to your left and a slogan beneath it: HOW DO YOU WANT TO BE REMEMBERED?

Round the corner, through the warm-up area, past the tables of drinks and food, the massage tables set out and ready. The main room round to your left again.

You're in the starting XV, so you turn right. A squared horseshoe of brown wood, each place laid out with a red cushion on the seat and a cupboard above, your name and cap number above your peg. Each of you in position order, the front row the first pegs, then the locks, the back row, the half-backs, centres and back three.

You've brought your boots, your spare boots and your

gumshield. The rest is waiting there: wet top and wet trousers in case of rain, t-shirt, spare t-shirt. Towel. Anthem jacket. Shirt, shorts, socks.

You can feel the noise down here. Muffled and distant, but impossible to ignore. Like the rumble of heavy traffic. Like a nightclub when you're in the alley outside.

Eye contact across the room. A little look, a shared feeling.

Tip sheets on our seats with simple messages, something tight from the coaches: *LINE SPEED. DISCIPLINE.*

Drinks there, everything from water to isotonic to caffeine. The smell of someone's nerves coming in from the toilet area. The sound of retching, spitting. Vomiting.

Jackets on for the huddle. Some with smelling salts. Pulling each other in tight. Staring into each other's faces.

'We're ready?'

There's a shout, with two minutes to go. Telling you the count-down. You close in tighter.

Another shout.

'30 seconds!'

The clatter of studs on concrete, the dressing-room doors open again. A shock of noise as the subs shout you out, 75,000 more waiting beyond.

Turning right into the corridor, turning left into the tunnel, putting your hand on the shoulder of the mascot waiting for you. A smile and a shake of the hand.

Black walls to the tunnel, sloping away to a narrow V of grass and stands and bedlam. Walking, absorbing the energy.

Noise. More noise. A crescendo, a deafening wave of it, break-ing over you.

The away team already out on the pitch. People leaning over the sides of the tunnel, slapping hands on the paint. The heat of the pitchside flamethrowers hot on your forehead, your cheeks. You feel the spray of propellant and its taste, droplets on your face and on your hands.

You can't see the seats, not now. No red and green of the first tier, deep red of the second, dark green of the third. Just shirts, flags and faces, and the choir out on the pitch in front of you. Supporters around you, above you.

You think about everything, when the anthem sounds. Your family, the ones who will tell you how you've played, the ones who can't any more. The villages and towns, the pubs and front rooms.

You're only as good as your next game. Aware there may not be a next one, so make this one count. Thinking: these days are forever, but it's different every time. Different opponents, a different team around you. A day threaded with the familiar but which will never come again.

The anthem peaks, the crowd roars. You unzip your jacket. Throw it to the bench.

You breathe deep. Look around.

This is where it begins.

1

CARTREF | HOME

That's where the journey ends, on that pitch in that city, if you want to play for Wales. If you obsess over it, fight for it, make yourself sick in training. If you keep going when it hurts, stand up again when you don't think you can, work hard through injury and selection. Making your own luck. If you can get past the heartbreaks and regrets, not get swept away in the big days, keep the trust of those around you. If all the things you dream about as a kid come true.

And it starts for me maybe 50 miles west, along the M4, past the steelworks at Port Talbot and then turning south around Swansea Bay, all the way along the coastal road and promenade to the village that sounds made for a shy kid towering over all his mates.

Mumbles. That's me as a boy. As a kid growing up, as a man coming home.

It's all sea views and rocky headlands, Mumbles. It's the rugby club at Underhill Park, the old clubhouse on the sea front. It's the old tumbledown ruins of Oystermouth Castle up on the hill, the lifeboat station and the pier sticking out into the sea, the blue-and-white front of Joe's Ice Cream Parlour on Mumbles Road. The cemetery tucked up the winding path from Newton Road.

The tide comes and goes out in the bay. Sometimes it's all grey, glassy water, sometimes all shiny sand and stretches of mud. In winter the wind comes in and chops it all up into white horses and sweeping currents. You look north to the taller buildings in Swansea and further round again to the smoke rising from chimneys and cooling towers. On clear days you can see all the way across the wind turbines on the hills further north still, up the valleys towards Maesteg and Glyncorrwg and Treherbert.

Go the other way, further west around the headland by the lighthouse, and it's into the Gower Peninsula: big wide beaches, holiday chalets, open heathland and white-painted houses. It's wilder on this side. Big westerlies, all calm on the eastern side when trees are going sideways round here. The coastal path takes you round to Rotherslade beach, then opening out into Langland Bay, a big sweep of yellow sand between the two headlands, Victorian beach huts with green metal struts.

The steep road up from Rotherslade. That was the place. Halfway up on the right-hand side, a two-storey house with big windows looking out from the ground floor, dark brown tiles on the roof, a sloping lawn in front.

It's easier to remember stuff when I go back. The smell of my dad's cigarettes, the kitchen out back. My mum's favourite chair in the front room, the rain splattering against the windows in winter or autumn or during a spring storm.

If you opened the windows of my bedroom, right up under the angles of the roof, you could hear the waves on the beach and rocks outside. Trees opposite, wooden garage doors painted white, houses on the top of the next little hilly ridge along.

There's gaps in my memory, when I try to remember. I've always looked forward. As a player you have to. You spend too long on the last match and you're never ready for the next one. There's things that stand out as a kid and there's weeks and months that won't ever come back.

I'm not complaining. If I never played rugby maybe I would still be exactly the same. Waiting for my dad to come back from his office in town, always the last one there, dealing with all the little legal dramas that make up the life of a local solicitor: wills, contracts, houses, rows.

He loved it, my dad. Always a cigarette on the go, sometimes lighting one, taking a puff, putting it down, forgetting all about it and sparking up another. Piles of paperwork in his office, a sense of duty to the people of Swansea.

The office stank of the smoke. You could have licked the nicotine off the yellow walls. No matter that he'd played for Swansea seconds on the Saturday. The obsession with rugby had been switched for an obsession with work. Monday to Friday was the office, early in the morning to late at night. When you're a kid you just accept it: I'm not going to see Dad today, I'll look after myself. It's only looking back that you realize, I really missed him. I wanted more of him.

So there's me, this kid who's always taller than the ones around me, often heavier too. There's my big sister Lowri, seven years older, way ahead. There's my mum, a working teacher, dedicated to what she was doing.

I was in Aunty Ivy's creche in Gowerton by eight each morning. Picked up by Mum on her way home. I have to rely on her for that detail. And when primary school started at Oystermouth, half a mile's walk up the hill and then back down again, the memories come back again. Me, the new kid, much bigger than a four-year-old should be, sitting on a bench in the playground and taking massive chunks out of my break-time apple. Black trousers, a blue jumper with the emblem of the castle on it, munching everything except the stalk, just in case any of the other kids were in any doubt about my appetite.

There's still kids around from that day. People stay in Mumbles, or they don't get away. You drive around and you see an old mate grown up, or someone comes round to help you with some building work at your house and you hear the surname and think, ah, yeah, I remember your brother.

I'm still the shy kid. But I was always in the school plays, always the one who got the show-off roles. A Galloping Major one year, with the old comedy sponge in my top pocket, soaked in water beforehand so I could dab at my feverish brow and twist it for effect. Another year in a pink satin shirt and black wig, like a young Tom Jones, if Tom Jones had been twice as tall as everyone else on stage.

That probably sounds strange for a boy who was happiest saying nothing, just watching the world around him, listening to the noise from everyone else. I've never played a role since. I'm always me, whether you like it or not. But the pretending then was fun. It's always the quiet ones who surprise you, right?

I didn't mind a sulk. I still don't. When you're a kid and you're quiet, people are okay with it. As you get older and you're still quiet, they tend to assume you're being rude. That's harder.

The stubbornness? That's always been there. My mum spent hours trying to get me to read. I refused, partly because *Stig of the Dump* wasn't working for me. When the family went out on Friday nights for our weekly curry, I'd get my sister to read out the menu for me so I didn't have to. Easy.

Until she refused. Suddenly my curry was on the line, my mum threatening to choose me what she wanted. And so I discovered the motivation to read within a month, although Mum didn't realize until she saw me giggling uncontrollably with the menu in front of my face.

'Alun, what on earth's the matter?'

'Can't tell you.'

'Lowri, what's the matter with your brother?'

'Ah Mum, it's just him.'

How do you tell your mum that you've just spotted chicken breasts on the menu at the point where you've just been told about women's breasts? It's not an easy conversation. It's not an easy thought process. Chickens have breasts too? How do you eat them?

It was easier with my Lego. You follow the instructions and it always turns out okay. Look at the picture, make sure yours is the same, guaranteed satisfaction. If it goes wrong, it's your fault.

I had all my sets lined up on the bottom shelf in my bedroom. My bed on the left as you walked in, next to the radiator – big win in winter. A collection of Micro Machines on the next shelf up, a couple of Transformers given their own space. Posters of Ieuan Evans and Scott Quinnell on the walls, the two of them standing on some rocky outcrop in their Cotton Oxford jerseys.

The Scalextric went in the bay window in the dining room, the cars flying off in the corners, the desolation following when they smashed into the wall and would never work again. *Airwolf* and *The A-Team* on TV.

And always a cigarette in every ashtray. My mum never smoked. She hardly ever drank – maybe a cheeky Cointreau or Tia Maria or Grand Marnier at Christmas, but never a natural. Whereas Dad . . . Dad just had a way of gathering people to him. Or forcing them away.

People loved him or hated him. I found that out as I grew. How loud he was, how intense he could be. How he'd launch straight in when he saw something going wrong. If he was writing a legal letter on your behalf, there would be gleeful anticipation of that letter landing on the recipient's doormat. You knew it would be a rocket. If you had one coming your way – if you were another solicitor in town, or the employer who'd done over a worker, or someone trying to pull a fast one – you feared it and you loathed where it came from. And that stuff would go everywhere, because Swansea is a small place. News would travel fast. 'You hear what Tim Jones has done now?'

There could be quarrels with friends. It was all logic to Dad: the legal process is A leads to B and on to C. There are no shortcuts. There's a way of behaving and there's no blurring of the lines. There was the old mate who casually asked him to speed something along. They didn't speak for three or four months, not after the reply Dad gave.

Black and white, right or wrong. He had an elderly client who he felt was being undercut as he sold his business. That one ended in phones being thrown across the room. There would be shouting matches and storming out. And all those people he helped, all those he pulled out of holes or steered them away, would be loyal to him forever more. They thought he walked on water. The rest? He didn't care.

You ask Mum, it was never going to be Swansea. She grew up in Cardigan, west Wales. She hated Swansea. She was never going to marry a Jones, not as a woman called Ann in an era when the tennis-playing Ann Jones was a Wimbledon champion. She was never going to be involved with anyone who smoked or wore glasses.

And then she got the lot, because he just swept her along, like he did with so many people. The two of them fresh-faced students at Aberystwyth University, and he caught her with his handkerchiefs. Right up until his death, he would always have a clean one in his breast pocket. That's what she says. And she should know; she washed them for 30 years.

When they were students, if anything happened, he would always produce a pristine pocket handkerchief. A friend of hers fell and cut her leg open. Dad was there with the handkerchief, binding the leg, offering to carry her home. The friend never liked him and wasn't going to change her mind; my mum was hugely impressed by his gallantry, his old-fashioned manners. And in such strange ways do stories begin.

Drinks, fags, conversation. That's my dad, as I grew up. You help someone out, they help you out. A partner at his firm had a flat in the south of Spain, so that was holidays sorted for a few years, until the work took back over, because that's where his real satisfaction came from. Always an investment too, looking out for us, looking at the long term, making plans and putting a safety net in place.

You're a solicitor, and you spend your days trying to fix mistakes. The people who have left it late to get a will, the ones who didn't bother. The work contract with the small print that no one bothered to read until they were sacked, the argument over a piece of land that one man thinks he owns until another one shows him something he never remembers signing.

That's Dad, trying to make sure we don't stumble into any of those holes. Buying three holiday chalets up the road as an investment, Lowri on the phone taking the bookings, me climbing up on the roof to fix the tiles until the time I fell through a rotten piece of ceiling that wasn't supposed to be there.

Always work, from both Mum and Dad. It was in them. It was what you did. Mum's own mother had been a teacher at a point where most women in the country were doing it all unpaid at home. Mum had been the one earning more when she and Dad got married, because it takes a solicitor a long time to get qualified. But always more from Dad – longer hours, more time away from home, less time with the family.

We all wished he was around more. Work first, family second. But that made sense to him, and with Dad, you never argued. You just followed.

Work, and family, and rugby. Dad had captained Aberystwyth. Then he comes to Swansea, as a number 8, and he goes straight to the rugby club's ground at St Helen's, just as his own father had as a centre before him, and there's Mervyn Davies swerving everywhere with his Mexican moustache and Wales caps and all those adventures with the British Lions.

So there would be no first-team action with the Whites for Dad, but plenty of chances with the Athletic, the second-string side – not that they saw themselves as second best. Which suited him, because most things came before the Athletic for all of them. You trained once a week, you had a lot of fun playing, you tried your best to have more fun afterwards. All that history at St Helen's – where the Whites had beaten Australia, and the Springboks, and the All Blacks; where Garry Sobers had hit his six sixes off Glamorgan's Malcolm Nash. Seagulls circling overhead, the beach just across the road, whitewashed houses stacked up in neat rows behind the stands.

They called themselves the F Troop, him and his mates. There was a US sitcom on ITV about a group of soldiers out in the Wild West, and that's how they saw themselves – doing it for fun, doing it for the laughs. One pair of boots for the year, bought in Bill Edwards's sports shop on King Edward's Road in Brynmill, dug out from among all the cricket bats and pads. Cleaned by his dad, then by Mum. Hankies and boots, the recipe for true love.

Maybe the only surprise is that it took me a while to follow him. I was playing football for Mumbles Rangers, eight years old, stuck in goal as always because of my size, sticking out for the same reason. There's a team photo of us, and as you look along the line it's child, child, child, small man from Wales under-16s. Shirts baggy on everyone else, skin-tight on me. A puppy-fat roll on my tum, a bowl haircut to complete the look.

The way my mum remembers it is a kid coming down the wing, all pace and balance. Then me charging out towards him with an attitude and body position that made carnage inevitable. And finally Mum apologizing to the other parents even before I hit him.

The coach was blunt in his assessment: *Mrs Jones, it might perhaps be time to put Alun's skills towards rugby.* And soon as I turned up at Mumbles RFC, I felt comfortable. My size was suddenly an asset. Send another kid flying backwards and suddenly everyone was cheering rather than wincing. Mum had the time to take me training because Lowri was old enough by then to look after herself. She never had to ask because I always wanted to go.

But we tried it all, on the way. Mum thought of herself as a facilitator. Rugby was there in the family, and it was there in my physique. But I got the chance to experiment, to double check, to see what else might float my boat.

Including floating boats.

It's easy to get into sailing when Mumbles is home. Water to the east, to the south, to the west. Two sailing clubs along the bay and the old pier. The wind.

You could do it through my primary school, you could move on to the club. A tiny little Oppie and then Toppers and Lasers, doing races at weekends, loving the competition, the fun of it all.

I wasn't the most suitably sized child for a small boat. Yet get out in the great sweep of Swansea Bay, and I could almost disappear. Sometimes I wished I could. There was the occasion Dad invited some of his friends over to watch a race. Ice cream from Verdi's, sit out on the prom and watch me slice by, sails cracking.

Which would have been great, had I not forgotten to put the bung back in the bottom of the hull. I got about 150 yards off shore, felt water sloshing around my feet and found myself flung overboard.

I climbed back in. I'm not stupid. But I could hear the commentary coming from the spectators on the prom, ice creams suddenly forgotten.

'Tim, what's happened to your son?'

'Alun! What on earth you doing?'

'Tim, I don't want to worry you, but is he a strong swimmer?'

There was the time I flipped my Laser on its side, catapulted out again and dislocated my shoulder as I hit the water. Same humiliation, different commentary when I got back to shore.

'Bloody hell, Ann, someone will have to put that shoulder back in.'

'I'm not sure . . .'

'Uncle Bill will do it, won't you?'

'But can he?'

'Hello, Ann? I'm Mike Jefferies, I'm the commodore for the day. Will you give me permission for Uncle Bill to kick your son's shoulder back in?'

'Well, I suppose so. If you're sure . . .'

I considered myself lucky. The bung went back in, as did the shoulder. Neither came out again for a number of years. And the sailing carried on for a long time, and the independence of being out on the water by myself, just me and the wind and the tide, chimed with something inside me.

I liked the silence. I liked the challenge, and the danger. Being reliant on myself, and my effort, as long as Uncle Bill's size 12s weren't required. I kept it going for years, until the faff with the rigging and the maintenance started taking longer than the actual adventures on the high seas. And Mum kept letting me try things – flying big kites down on the beach, great six-foot-long things that could pull you along or test out your shoulder's recovery; a buggy so you could race along the flat sands at low tide. There was the inline skates period, the PlayStation with driving games and snowboarding games, the diablo time – juggling what looks like a giant egg-timer on a long piece of string. I was better with the diablo than the skates. There's a reason why you don't see many adults of six foot six playing roller-hockey.

There was music. I started on guitar and graduated to the simpler pleasures of a drum kit parked up in my bedroom, leaving indentations in the dark blue carpet. Lowri played sax and flute, Dad the trombone. My grandfather could play anything he wanted on the piano, all by ear. There would be skiing, later on. Dad staying back to work, me, Mum and Lowri going happily to Austria. Big Foot short skis for me. Insert your own joke about my physical appearance here.

Nothing was as simple as the rugby. A pair of boots, from the same shop as my dad's, a desire to run about. That's it. Trying everything else helped me. It meant I was never bored; it meant I knew rugby was the one. I wasn't going to get to 13 or 14 and wish I was doing something else instead.

There was Swansea to watch at weekends. Hot toddies passed from adults to kids for a quick sip. New heroes to follow Rob Jones and Richard Moriarty, Dai Young, Bleddyn Bowen and Scott Gibbs. Players who showed you the path: you play here, get in the team, and you can play for Wales, all those miles down the M4 in Cardiff. It's possible. It's real.

And then there was somewhere else, in between. Somewhere like nowhere else. Like nowhere you've been before.

Bonymaen.

2

CYMERIAD | CHARACTER

There's stuff we have to talk about. Stuff you won't know. That I don't normally share, that I don't show, unless you're on the inside.

This is the thing. Some people think I'm arrogant. They come to that conclusion because I won't say much, first time I meet you. I won't be full of chat. I might not be that friendly, at the start.

Some people might think I'm ignorant, when I don't say much. They might think I'm putting the quietness on, or trying to be enigmatic.

I don't think I'm any of those things. I'm just quiet. I'm not an extrovert; I'm not naturally gregarious. You don't like me? Fine. You make up your own mind. I'd rather be perceived the wrong way than have to pretend to be something I'm not.

I'll get asked for my autograph. I'm happy about that. I'm lucky it happens. But I can't give myself to you in that moment, because I don't know you. I'll bide my time, when I meet you for the first time.

I let people show their own intentions. They want to keep talking? That's happy days. I'll find out pretty quick whether they're friend or foe.

I understand how this might make me look. It's not that normal. I'm a sportsman, I captain my country. And I'd rather take the time and be genuine than rush in and have to do a sudden about-turn when I find out what someone's really like. Less embarrassing for me, less embarrassing for them.

Here's another secret, sort of linked, sort of the same thing. I do still have moments when I'm in that coach heading along the M4 on a Six Nations Saturday and I think, I can't believe I'm playing for Wales. Almost 150 caps in, and I'm still pinching myself. I've never got used to it. The mystique has never worn off.

It can become routine to some players, and I can understand that. You get a new car, you love it. It's fast, it's cool, it's closer to what you wanted than the one you had before. Six months later and it's just your car. That's the way the world works. Rugby's a job, too. You work hard every day at it, you get paid, you hope to keep it going as long as possible.

Me? I'm never bored of it. I've never had enough. Maybe this is having a history teacher for your mother, because every time I take the field I think, you're writing a few more words of your own history here, your own story.

You might think that's a load of old nonsense. It's pretend, not profound. And it's true no one's recording my tiny part in it all. Where the game was, the score, who scored, how many supporters were in, the weather – that's all there. How good or bad I was? That slips away with the final whistle, for most people. But it's my life, and it's what matters to me. Every game counts as much as the one before. Every cap I've had I'm thinking only of that one, not how I played last week, last year.

And I'm always conscious of my nerves. I'm a senior player. I have to know my roles. You can make a mistake in the execution of a play, and that's one thing. That's not good, but worse is not understanding the play, not being in the right position to make that mistake.

I still make mistakes. The trepidation about making a mistake is always there. But you have to try things as a professional. You're paid to be a problem-solver. You're given the tools by the coaches, and you go out there, and whatever your opposition does, it's not always going to be what you see in the analysis.

Play it safe and you make fewer mistakes but you also become easier to read and easier to beat. Sometimes it works and sometimes it doesn't work, and that's the game. I never wanted to be a robotic player. I don't ever want to feel comfortable. I don't ever want to think, 'If I mess up, I'll be all right again. They'll still pick me. It won't change what I've done to this point.' Screw that. If you're thinking that, you don't care. And if you don't care, more than anyone else in the world, why are you here?

I'm probably not as hard on myself as I once was. Maybe close, but not all the way. What would still scare me the most is if I didn't give a fuck any more. If it was only a job. If it was only another game. Fear? That's a good thing. It keeps you on your toes. The most dangerous player in the team is the one who's not in control of their emotions. Too cavalier.

The arrogance thing, the mystique thing that's never gone? Here's a moment from the big World Rugby dinner that takes place at the end of a World Cup. On the next table, and then coming over to say hello, was Francois Pienaar: World Cup winner, statesman, champion against apartheid. I was taken aback. I couldn't understand how he recognized me. I just found it weird. I thought, he's just being polite.

I still find it weird seeing Neil Jenkins around the Wales camp. He's been there forever, coaching the kickers, coaching the restarts. He was there when I was an under-19, him cutting his teeth as a coach, getting us up in the morning after we'd sunk a load of Guinness, putting us on the bus and looking after us. Back then I kept staring at him. It's actual Neil Jenkins! 15 years on I still find myself doing the same thing. I'm on the same bus as Neil Jenkins!

The memory thing. For most of my life I've been so focused on the moment that I'm not aware of it in context. It's the tackle I'm making, the ruck I'm running to, the clear-out that's coming. It's never soaking in. And when that game is over, my focus shifts instantly to the next one. My instinct says, right – get on with it, wipe that last one and go again.

The biggest secret of all? It's all worth it. You have to want to be there, and you have to be prepared to give everything to it, but the rewards are like nothing else. When rugby is really good, it's incredibly special. The satisfaction, the exhaustion. The bonds, the collective efforts. The way your body feels, bashed up but with a purpose, a reason to be. The knowledge that you've been pushed past where you thought your limits were, and survived, and then gone on further again.

You play for Wales and you understand what it means. Where it came from, what you're representing. I was there at Wembley in 1999 for the Scott Gibbs try and the Jenks conversion. Me and my dad somewhere near the 10-metre line, halfway up the stands, absolutely covered in beer by the bloke behind us when Scott stepped his last man and stuck his arm up in celebration and dived over the line.

You know what it means for the kids you were at school with, for the coaches at your local rugby club. You know what it means for the hours you put in that no one else will ever see – the time you were on the beach in summer with your mates, aged 14 or so, and it was time for training and the best player you knew, the one everyone knew was going to make it, said *nah, I'm staying here*, and you still went training even when they didn't. You think about the times a few years later when you could have gone out to the pubs on the front, done the Mumbles Mile, gone after those girls you'd been too shy to talk to, and you went training again instead. When you thought, these two hours could be the difference between getting in that team and not. The time, years on, when you pissed off other players in training before an international by going so hard you were like a bear with a headache. The whispers you heard: 'Oh look at him, he's going off again, he's never happy.'

All those little moments that come together, the little decisions you make. The running at Underhill and University Fields, the stuff I've bought and stuck in the garage just in case it makes the tiniest difference to how I train and what I can do.

The further on in my career I've gone, I've come to think of myself as my own small business. I'm essentially a sub-contractor for whoever I'm playing for. You have to invest in yourself, emotionally, financially. Whatever you spend on something that the other lads laughed at gives you more time on the field. Cumulatively, maybe it comes to less than a couple of match fees. How can that not be worth it?

You can't be a carpenter, or a builder, or a plumber, if you don't have the tools to do your job. We're the same. I've talked about this to some of the younger guys, and they can't always see it at first. 'I don't know, I can't do that, I don't need this.' Well. If you do need it now, you've got it, and you'll use it. If you don't need it, you've got it for when you do. I used to go in to Wales training, and Adam Jones would look at me and say, 'What on earth have you bought today?' I'd be gone 10 minutes and he'd be having a go on it. 'Oh, a load of old shit, is it?'

I bought an ice-bath during the first long lockdown in 2020, on the basis that it might help my recovery. Then I bought a Jacuzzi, because there were no massages available for us during that time, so I had to cobble it together myself. Suddenly I could train twice a day and do the same again the next day.

Make your own decisions, take control of your own destiny. In the past I'd go through sessions just to complete them. You want me to do 10 runs? I'll do them regardless of how my body feels. Doesn't matter if I do 10 shit ones, at least I've done what they wanted.

Now? Now I take more responsibility. I'll think about my training load, about change of direction, about quality. Maybe two sets of six done really well is better. My decision, my body, my career. Even if I'd never used the ice-bath again, at least I couldn't blame anyone else if I couldn't train, if I got injured. The more decisions you get taken away from you, the less you're capable of making big decisions yourself.

Maybe it goes back to that fear thing. At 6 a.m. the day after we moved into our new house, I went out and did 10 sets of 50-metre sprints. As I was doing it, the lactic building up in my legs, the sick feeling in my throat, I did think about it. Why am I doing this?

And I knew it was fear – fear that now I'd got a nice big house, I'd be too comfortable.

I had to do that dawn session because it proved something to me. It meant I wasn't going to be complacent. I wasn't going to stop training as hard as I possibly could. I could go back to the house, with its fresh paint and new kitchen and views out over towards the sea, and know I could carry on. I'm still me. It's still inside me. That's what I proved to myself that morning.

I say I don't look back, and I don't look forward. Another secret: you need to look far enough ahead not to let anyone get in. This might sound terrible, but every time I train with Ospreys or Wales, I know other people are after my job. They should be – that's elite sport. They're not supposed to be benign colleagues; this is not sitting in an office, or working for a charity. It's you or them who gets in the team, who keeps playing, keeps walking out at the Principality.

You have to use that to drive you on, just as you can use the knowledge that one day this will all be over. I never wanted the tap on the shoulder. 'Alun, about the game at the weekend . . .' I'd want the conversation to come before. Tell me now that you don't think I'm good enough, and let me make the decision. I don't want to hear the criticism building in the media, read the pieces saying I'm hanging on for my own sake.

I think about why I've managed to play as I have for as long as I have. And all those glamorous attributes that you might want as a rugby player don't matter, not compared to a work ethic. Keep going. Keep working. Go harder and longer than anyone else.

I don't care how good or bad I am on execution, I will always fucking try. If it looked as if I wasn't trying, then I would have retired a long time ago. If I knew I wasn't trying, I couldn't live with myself. Thinking about that kid on the beach, even now. Thinking, if you keep going, you could play for whoever you want. Thinking, you're way better than me. Thinking, I cannot understand what you're doing.

Working hard is the training ground, but it's so much more too. It's an obsession when you're at home. All those little moments when you could have a burger for tea, or a beer with it, or not do your stretching. The times when you could do all your prescribed stuff with your team and then leave it all there at the ground to be someone else at home. The times you go to mates' birthday parties and stay selective around the cake and crisps, not standing around when you need to be tucked up early, recovering. When you're invited to a glitzy event up in London on your day off that would pay well too, but you turn it down because going means driving back late and then being only at 80 per cent in training the next day, and then feeling the lack of recovery on the Friday, and going into Saturday's match knowing that you could have given more.

I've been too hard on myself at times. I can see that now, understand it in a way I couldn't before.

There have been times when I could have taken opportunities and I didn't because I was scared that I would be compromising, that I would be giving someone else an opportunity to get past me. There were times with Wales when Warren Gatland would give me days off, and I'd go back into training anyway.

'Alun, what the fuck are you doing here?'

'Well, you gave me a day off, but I don't want it.'

He would sigh and let me crack on. He'd see me flagging all day, the tiredness piling up on top of tiredness. A week later he would call me aside again.

'Should have had the day off, shouldn't you?'

And I still wouldn't be able to see it. 'No, no, I'm fine, this is good . . .'

That was Gats. When he came in, he made it simple: this is about honest, simple, hard work. You know the phrase, *once you die, you're dead*? That was me in those training sessions. Once you blow up, you're gone, and it happened all the time to me, often quicker than the others.

I don't know whether that's because I was trying harder or

because I was less fit. But as long as it wasn't fake, I didn't care. I had no qualms with being blasted for putting it all out there. I've always been comfortable with doing that. Look at me, I'm in bits. Look at me, and know I've been honest – to you, to myself. And always better that way than the guy who saves himself for the last rep. You're suddenly faster than everyone else now? Where's that come from? Where was that on the nine reps that came before?

There's one of those guys in every training group, every rugby team. That's fine. It's how the world works. I just never want to be that guy. When I play rugby there are guys far quicker than me who make a break and I will always try and chase them down. I know I'm going to screw myself up for the next minute but it's what it's about. That's where the satisfaction comes from. The honesty with myself.

You've given me the world's best environment to train and play in. The best food, coaching, strength and conditioning, recovery. Hotels and perfect pitches. You're telling me all I've got to do is work hard? I can do that. I will always do that.

3

CAREDIGRWYDD | KINDNESS

You don't go to Bonymaen by accident. You don't stay there unless you can handle it.

It's Swansea, sort of, like a thorny crown on top of the city. A rugby club like lots of other rugby clubs in Wales, but also all on its own. A place for a big shy kid to grow up. To be independent. To feel accepted.

You go past the Liberty Stadium, now. Turn left up the B5444, and it's like ascending into a different world. First the dark trees, thick on either side, like you're starting a classic cycling climb, like you're heading into the mountains. Then, as the road rears up in front of you and you change down a gear to get up it, the houses crowding in – small, squashed together, dark terraces with stone cladding and 30 shades of grey paint-work. Cars parked under single streetlights, telegraph poles and wet tarmac. Tyre shops out front, little yards out back. Bus stops and old phone boxes and the cream and dark green front of the Jersey Arms pub.

You turn right before the pub and keep climbing. If the window's open, you can feel the drop in temperature. If the wind's blowing you can hear it on the side of the car. Clouds overhead and the city left far below.

It's right at the top of the hill that you find it. No houses any more, no cars. Like it's the last place on the road, like an outpost that everyone else forgot about but those who are born and live up there. You look one way and you see grey metal railings and a school beyond. You look the other way, and it's a couple of traffic cones and a bumpy car park and then the dark red hand-painted sign above a single turnstile:

BONYMAEN RUGBY FOOTBALL CLUB

It's a little plateau of green grass and a big sky. The pitch in front of you, the concrete terrace of steps back behind you to the two-storey clubhouse, the changing rooms further along. A fence down one touchline, green plastic padding strapped around the posts, white fencing behind the rugby posts at either end.

A scoreboard to your right, backed against the thin line of trees. Bonymaen. Visitors.

Waiting for the scores, waiting for the game.

It looks smaller to me now, yet all the memories still come back when I drive up there again. I was 11 when I first came, some sort of happy accident. Mumbles Rugby Club didn't have the numbers for a team in my age group, so that little period came to an end. No more kids running everywhere, piling into parents holding pads. If I wanted to play for Swansea, like my dad, like my grandfather, there were other options in the area, but a lad I knew called Jamie Williams told me about Bonymaen. *I'm going up, fancy it?*

This school right at the top. Cefn Hengoed. That was the other connection. My mum was teaching there, ending up there almost by accident after another role she went for in Neath fell through. An adventure for me already, another element suddenly there with it too. And I went up there with Jamie Williams, and they welcomed me with open arms.

Maybe it helped that I was a decent size. There were other lads I recognized from school matches. I hope I could play a bit, too. Maybe it helped that I didn't complain about the cold. Even that day in late summer it was coats weather. You'd be down in Mumbles by the beach and it would be tropical. You'd drive up that long, twisting road and the wind would be bashing the long grass about and the temperature would suddenly be early November.

We would train on the second pitch, over the far side of the main one with its slender metal floodlights for training in winter. Never much grass on our one, at least not around the hotspots, the 22s, some of the edges. Horses from the next field along used to get through the fence and wander on. One time one of the lads jumped on board, no saddle, and disappeared over the hill. No control, no hope of getting back for kick-off. The weather came down the valleys to the north and wanted to blow you all the way across the water to Port Talbot.

I never cared. It was another green rectangle where you could charge about and lose yourself and find yourself too. One changing room for all the teams, stacks of shiny metal beer barrels and all the rich strong smells that came out of them. Kids wedging sticks into the tops of the kegs to try to get the beer spraying out and covering each other.

You go back now, and you can still see scrambler tracks in the grass all around. You haven't lived until you've seen a kid with his top off and no helmet come flying up one of those hills and go revving through the air. You could hear the wind whistling through the metal electricity pylons, hear the shouts of the senior players on the main pitch. Tops and bags and water bottles left on the wooden trestle tables on the sidelines, the slap of arms on thighs as tackles went in and the echoing thump of a ball being kicked up into the skies.

I never took that welcome for granted. You'd hear stories about Bonymaen, in other parts of Swansea. What the estates were like all around, what else those kids on scramblers were up to. But there were never any barriers for me. We played rugby; we played together. We won a lot of games, and I was always happy winning.

There's a scene in the film *Twin Town* that'll make sense if you've seen it. *Twin Town*'s the touchstone movie about Swansea. It might be the only movie about Swansea. Came out in 1997, billed as the Welsh answer to *Trainspotting*, but because it's set in Swansea and Mumbles, less about shoplifting, Iggy Pop and heroin than rugby, static caravans, karaoke, massage parlours, male voice choirs, curry houses and a boat being launched from Mumbles pier.

Early in the piece, an intoxicated Rhys Ifans and his brother, having stolen a sports car, drive it to a rugby club and pull doughnuts all over the pitch, scattering the juniors practising on it. The club's owner, Bryn Cartwright, comes out of the prefab clubhouse to vent his fury at the twins, unaware of how much worse things will shortly become for him. Well, that pitch is Bonymaen. The prefab clubhouse is Bonymaen. The road the twins race up is the road that leads to Bonymaen. Bryn Cartwright? A fictional character, and thus never actually involved with the rugby club, yet still a name that carries weight in Swansea on account of *Twin Town*'s iconic status in the area and his behaviour in a curry house a few scenes later.

The real Bonymaen did okay out of the filming. Enough was made for a gentle refit of facilities. But because the Bonymaen that exists in some people's minds is exactly the sort of place where that sort of questionable behaviour would happen, the real Bonymaen has also developed its own mentality: us against the world, a determination to make it a tough place for opposition teams to go, at least until the kegs were opened post-match.

It toughened me up, although that wasn't why I first went. You go up to Bonymaen and play as a kid, and you come back down and go to other places and it all seems relatively soft and easy. You're not thinking about reputations at that age. That comes later. You just know when somewhere makes you feel at home, feel yourself. And that's what Bonymaen did for me.

Mum made a difference. She knew a lot of the boys, knew a lot of the families. She had respect at that school, and it carried over to the club across the road. She'd defend them all, too. Ask her now, in retirement, and she'll talk about how genuine the locals are. If someone says there's rough families up there, she'll say that there's rough families everywhere – they've just got a bit more money behind them, or plastic. If someone calls the kids rude she'll say they're not rude, they're just not accustomed to the same manners as you. She loved the school and the kids and she loved the area. She talks about the time she'd had quite major surgery, and how all the kids were impeccably behaved when she came back to work too early and still in some pain, how without ever spelling it out they gave her the breathing space and recovery time to get better. I've been up there and seen big bears of men stopped in the road, carrying ducklings around a drain that was threatening to suck them into oblivion. That's Bonymaen.

She never felt any resentment aimed at any of us, and that includes Dad. At Bonymaen we were never made to feel like outsiders. There were times at Mumbles Rugby Club when some of that occasional undercurrent you get in a small village would become visible.

Like all dads, my dad was supportive of the club. A simple gesture, putting a bottle of Scotch in the club raffle. He also bought a load of raffle tickets, and with a certain inevitability won his own bottle. That was when one little group started a slow handclap, and when Dad unscrewed the lid, held it aloft like a challenge and said, 'Right, who will have a drink with me?'

At Bonymaen no one bothered at all about who my dad was or what he'd done in his job. They didn't care where he was from or where we lived. He was just another parent on the side of the field, one more rugby disciple who cared about the club. You came to watch games and you cheered when your son did well, but just as much when someone else in the team made a big hit or turnover or ran in a try.

That was all over my head back then. For me it was simple: I played rugby, and I felt at home. And I probably took it for granted, that kindness, everything they did for me, because you do at that age. This is what rugby clubs have always done in Wales. Wherever you are – a mining village, a town once rich on industry, a county town of farmers, a suburb of a big city – there's the rugby club, and it's never just about rugby. It's a youth club, it's a pub. It's an after-school club, it's an accidental weekend creche and hard-play centre. It's food and it's a social life and it's a place to watch far bigger games than yours. It's an identity and a history, a rivalry and a place to belong. That's what rugby is in Wales.

Maybe that's changing now. Kids want more. They look further afield for inspiration. There's everything else competing for their attention. There's gaming and phones and a whole life lived on-line. You get older and there's gyms. Working out on your own, headphones on, everything you're doing all about you.

Us? We lived on that scrubby pitch beyond the fence. We played as a team. Different sizes, different backgrounds, different levels of skill, all aiming for the same thing. That's what I thought about all week. That's where I wanted to go every evening. That's where the weekend went by.

We had a reputation at Bonymaen, but for the way we played the game. Decent bit of size up front, a lot of intelligent rugby players for our age. There's a phrase we have now when someone new comes into a squad and they're decent. We'd say, he knows his trade. Like they're an electrician, like they're an architect.

And in our junior teams at Bonymaen you had kids who just knew rugby. They'd watched it, played it, grown up with it all around them. That's why I describe them as intelligent players. They were clever in how they played the game. Some natural combinations from school teams, a lot of games of touch rugby in training to develop our lines and support play and passing skills.

This was the drill. Roll into the frosty car park in Mum's Daihatsu Sportrak on a Tuesday or Thursday night, pick up a ball, some pads and tackle-bags and away you go. A few cones, nothing more, just like all those other junior sections at all those other rugby clubs across the country. It was about enjoyment and work-ing hard. Winning and losing? They were there, and they mattered too, but not really. It was more to do with occupying kids and developing kids. Go up there, train, have fun, feel good about yourself, come back down incrementally better than when you arrived.

Thursdays were my favourite session. Not because there was a great set difference between plays, as if we were doing starter plays and exits on one day and high-intensity defence drills the next. Thursdays were more like, what have we forgotten from Tuesday? Let's get it done, and now we can play. Thursday was closer to Saturday, and Saturday was the game, and that was where you really wanted to be.

I was always going to be a forward. Size, shape and lack of pace dictated that. But it was never *you, forwards, go stand over there and stay away from the ball*. Everyone had to be able to handle the ball. Everyone had to play.

There are images and scattered moments I'll never forget. Cold evenings with your breath coming white out of your mouth like smoke from a dragon. The floodlights burning bright and then blackness until the streetlights far below in the city, so you felt like you were floating in space, like you were on another planet far away. Horses in that adjoining field, tossing their heads and stamping their feet. Coaches like Kevin Brooks with rugby socks halfway down pronounced calves or rolled up over their tracksuit bottoms. Short shorts and big arms, shouts and swearing, but jokes and laughter too. The red and black of the club badge and the shirt, the old cracked balls we'd get that far down the pecking order, and the giddy excitement if we ever got a slightly newer set.

Depending on your take on beauty, there could be a lot worse places to train. If you were wet and cold, there was always the inducement of a chocolate bar in the back of the car afterwards or a stop-off for a cheeky chicken kebab. And I always wanted to go up there, whatever the weather, all year round. There was never any dragging me. It was pure enjoyment, in the heat of summer, in the snow come winter, in the gales and sideways rain in between.

As I've got older, as I've had kids of my own, I've had pangs about what it meant for Mum. How it must have felt to have driven up there and back again for work, picked me up from home and driven all the way to Bonymaen again. I know she was savvy with her time. Me playing rugby meant her sitting in the car getting her marking done. But there were the matches, and the trips away, and if it was cold playing, it was twice as fresh watching on the touchlines. Contrasting approaches from my parents: Dad vocal in supporting his son but also fully about the collective rather than just his son, Mum whispering about just making sure we came off safe.

There was the kit, too, for a kid growing faster than anyone else. The time everyone thought they had to have the gloves made by Optimum, at least until you realized they weren't actually magic, that you could still spill the ball while wearing them. Up would come the shouts from the other boys: 'Ah, dropped one now, see!' The time, once a year, when you would have a new pair of boots, and time about an hour later when everyone else had made sure they were christened good and proper and covered in mud.

It wasn't always easy finding stuff that would fit. I'd be ushered towards the men's section of shops and the price hikes that would follow. The opening of a Canterbury store in Swansea was big news, and could be exploited if you knew what you were doing. Mum had a certain pride, taking me to her place of work.

'You've got to be looking smart now if you're going up there, Alun.'

'But Mum, I'm going to get stinking!'

'No, you're up there as Mrs Jones the history teacher's son. So we've got to have you looking at least as if you haven't been cobbled together, or I found you on the street . . .'

So I had the old-school Canterbury harlequin shorts, one leg red, one leg black, reverse them for the opposite effect. Old-school Canterbury jerseys with the proper collars and the baggy sleeves. Helly Hansen skins with the chevrons down the sleeve that didn't last long once the hot iron went on them and they melted away.

I always looked after my boots. My dad was adamant about it.

Same as my grandfather. They'd show me how to stuff them with newspaper to dry them off and keep them in shape, brushing the mud off the leather, rubbing in Vaseline to keep them supple. 'Alun, we'll have to buy you men's sizes now – they're more expensive, so if we're having those boots then you've got to look after them . . .'

The pride, the unforgettable moment, when you get your first boil-and-bite gumshield. Putting the hard plastic in the mug of boiling water, putting a stopwatch on it so you leave it in there for exactly 30 seconds and no more. Going too soon out of excitement and burning your lips; going too late out of caution and finding it all softened out of shape. Ending up doing it all three times and scalding yourself twice.

All that's Bonymaen to me. And there are times when I look back on those days, and what they did for me, and wish I had a time machine. To go back and just have another 10 minutes. To feel it all again, to experience it afresh.

Dad loved to record everything. Boxes of reports and cuttings, legal folders stuffed with anything. He was always on at me – *keep a diary, keep a diary*. I always said the same thing to him: *I haven't got time.*

Now? Now I've forgotten more than I can remember. Now I wish I'd written that diary.

4

ANNIBYNIAETH | INDEPENDENCE

These boxes of Dad's. They're still there in the old house, years after he died. Everything I've ever done on a rugby pitch catalogued, absolutely everything kept.

Newspaper cuttings from the local paper. Entire sports sections with only the smallest paragraph concerning his son. Programmes from games I can't even remember taking place. Forms that had been filled in, end of year school reports. Letters – big, small and meaningless.

He was a strong man. Good head of curly hair on him as a young man in the white shirt of Swansea, proper 1970s beard. As he got older that turned grey, and then white. Thinner on top but still bushy under the nose.

And he loved to collect stuff. Memorabilia that could be a smart investment for the future. He had great bags of coins, random remains from different eras and countries, never to be used but stashed away for some unlikely day in the future. Old clothes, old books. Nothing would ever be thrown away. Everything might have a use, some day.

I look at those big brown cardboard boxes now. Each of them indexed to a year or part of a season. It's a curious aspect of Dad's character that doesn't seem to reflect how he was in other ways, or maybe balances that up. All three of us – Mum, Lowri and me – all remember him as being absent, on lots of days, for long periods. Mum reckons that pushed the three of us together. Either way you had to get used to it. He did what he wanted to do. He worked to earn and invest money to keep us safe, and also because he loved to.

Mum had her tactics. If I asked for something for my rugby, some piece of training equipment, she'd work out the cost and then half it before presenting it to Dad. That would be the start of the debate. At one point, when I was 14 and keen to strengthen up my core, I asked for a Swiss ball. The reply came back that I didn't need one. Didn't matter that it was only £15 or so. Then it was ladders, the rope and plastic sort you stretch out on the ground to work on your foot speed and agility. They didn't make sense to him either, particularly when I used them for the first time and churned up the lawn.

But he cared. You take the lid off those brown boxes and you can't ignore it. Why else would you do all that? It's a silent dedication. It's a deep devotion.

And so many elements of what I saw and felt must have rubbed off on me. That obsession with work. Saying what you think, rather than worrying about the consequences. Hating the idea of giving up, when you still have something left. Maybe a certain stubbornness, too.

And an independence, always. Pushing my family away, from an age when most boys are still keeping them close. Understanding that I'd have to stand up for myself. That there were responsibilities I'd have to take on.

You had to speak up to be heard. The time I was due to go training with Bonymaen and felt wrong – listless, sick. I told Mum, and she took me anyway. I told her that night I felt worse, and again in the morning when I knew something serious was up. She told me I had to go to school. I was due to have a couple of teeth out, and I wasn't dodging that. In you go, Alun Wyn.

By lunchtime I was in intensive care with septicaemia. There was a cut on my leg, and something had got in from the pitch – maybe some dog muck, maybe something else. The only time I'd ever said I didn't want to go training.

You had to grow up fast. Mum's sister suffered badly with

multiple sclerosis. We would take Friday afternoons off school and work to drive all the way round to Frome in Somerset to help look after her.

I was a big lad. I could lift my aunt in a way that Mum couldn't at times. I'm not saying this makes me special. Anyone would have done it, course they would. It just changes you a little, nudges you out of your self-obsessed teenage world. When you understand what people are doing for you, when you see the chances you've been given.

A grandfather who played for Swansea, a grandmother on the other side of the family who worked her own magic too. My mum's mother had been brought up in rural poverty in a tiny village in north Wales. Dirt floors and no electricity or running water. A little local school where they weren't much bothered about girls, where you started late and left early to help out with your own family. But then, because she was a bright girl, getting a scholarship with her sister to a school in Dolgellau – walking there together across the mountains, given pennies to stay over until the Friday, getting a lift back on a farmer's cart with another friend.

She used it. Used the scholarship to get educated, to become a teacher herself. So when I got to 16 years old and had the chance to move schools on a partial scholarship myself, she came in with the money to complete the funding. 'Alun, the rugby's going well. But it's never going to get you anywhere for a number of years, see?'

So my world expanded a little more again. From Rotherslade in Mumbles, to Bonymaen on the hill, to Llandovery College, an hour north into rolling green Carmarthenshire. A school founded on the ideals of Welshness, a place built around physical exercise, around the national sport of Wales.

Llandovery is old and it is pure rugby. Representatives there at the table in Neath when the Welsh Rugby Union was formed in 1881; two pupils in the first international game Wales ever played; another pupil, Charles Lewis, the first player to captain

Wales in the Home Nations Championship, the man who led them out against England at St Helen's in Swansea in December 1882. It's all connections, with Welsh rugby, all roots and tendrils reaching back into time, binding the present to the past, the ancient to the new.

I struggled with it at first, being away from home. A mixture of new people, new rules, a long way from home. I remember meeting Mum in the little shop just outside the main entrance and having relatively respectably-sized meltdowns. But I stuck it out, because you had to. Getting upset about it didn't change anything. The more I thought about it the worse it would get, and I still had to say goodbye and go back inside to face the music.

In some ways I got lucky. The usual dorm rooms were small bunks with a bed, but I was never fitting in those. When I lay down I had my feet halfway up the wall. So I was allowed to bring my own bed, and that meant I had a bigger room, just me and one other lad. And I also thought about my grandmother. I knew that she expected me to take every opportunity, just like she had. If there was a choir, I'd join it. If there was a play on, Galloping Major role available or not, I'd throw myself into it. That was how I was going to pay her back. I couldn't waste it. I could feel the pull of duty. It wasn't just about me.

And it settled, as all these things do. You go to Llandovery as a rugby scholar, and as long as you do your work and you're respectful, you'll be respected in return. That's what happens at a school where Carwyn James, maybe the greatest Welsh coach of all time, has been a teacher, where players from Cliff Jones to George North have all been developed. There would be the kids who had been all the way through senior school and often prep school too, and then us lot coming in for the sixth form – not as wealthy, but maybe a little more worldly. There could be friction there, but there was also a sense of how it was challenging us as players – coming up against better sides, better players. Travelling further than I ever could have done had I stayed at home.

You'd travel outside Wales. Onto the school coach, west across the Severn Bridge to play Millfield or Colston's, trundling all the way north to Sedbergh. Into south-west London in summer for the Rosslyn Park Sevens. There would be future internationals in the opposition ranks, lads like Olly Morgan and Tom Varndell. There would always be decent levels of stick from the opposition. Private English schools, or at least the older teachers and parents, seemed to think that every team arriving from Wales had to be full of Valleys lads. 'Got the coal-miners in today, have we?' Even when they were the same balance as we were – some kids fee-paying, more than a few on sporting scholarships. All the way through, you had a sense of adding to the history. Walking in the footsteps of Carwyn, understanding what that meant to the school, to you, to your family.

You developed as a player, and opportunities opened up. Swansea RFC had been there in my family for generations, and now it was my turn. Driving back down from Llandovery every Tuesday and Thursday evening to train, going back to St Helen's at weekends to play or watch matches if I wasn't involved in the intermediate national set-ups. On the same pitch as big beautiful lumps like Garin Jenkins, flyers like Mark Taylor, big lumpy flyers like Scott Gibbs.

As regional rugby began in Wales, as the Ospreys and Scarlets became real entities and began to take flight, the great clubs like Swansea and Neath slipped into semi-professionalism, opening doors for young and older players, and in the period when it was all changing, you could find yourself thrown in with more experienced players with proper miles on the clock and dinks in the bodywork and all the stories and tales to go with it.

I knew what the Whites meant. I understood what an honour it was to play for them, and realized too that it could be a stepping stone to the next level up again. If you wanted to learn, you could. If you could listen, soak it all up.

The older players made sure you knew your place. If you played well, there might be a nod or a tap on the back. That was the acceptance you craved. If you ever thought about stepping out of line, you'd think about some of those stories you'd heard and reconsider pretty quickly.

One of my first captains there was a guy called Richard Francis, a local farrier when he wasn't playing rugby. Rumour had it that he had once knocked out a horse. When you hear a tale like this as a teenager, you don't question it – ask when and where, why he didn't just lead it away or proffer a nosebag, what the exact punch had been. You accept it, swallow nervously and do exactly what he tells you to do.

I loved it there. Playing on that famous pitch, basking in what felt like a tropical sun at times, being blasted by a sandstorm when the wind was up. Rain coming in sideways off the bay, hail and sleet in the dark and stormy winter months. Tony Clement, proper Swansea legend, as your coach; Keith Colclough, old-school prop, the forwards coach.

All the time growing up, all the time pulling a little further away from my family. I would drive down from school, train until I was sick, think, 'I'm only 10 minutes from home here,' and yet turn around and drive straight back north to Llandovery. It saved me time, but there was something else going on too.

It was as if I'd left home at 16, looking back. Term time at school, evenings with Swansea, summers away playing rugby for age-group sides. And Mum remembers the gradual loosening of control, the moments when as a parent you see something and get that slight shock: they're not my little boy any more.

A big birthday bash for my dad, a hog roast the centrepiece, eight people trying to shift it around and getting nowhere. Apparently I decided to take over.

'Just stop, all of you. You do this, you do that, you sit down.'

Telling Dad what to do, Mum thinking, he's not going to like this, he's going to kick off about this. And Dad, not that I noticed, sitting back for the first time in his life. Turning to Mum, half surprised, half proud, and saying in wonder, 'He's a man now, isn't he?'

There's other things Mum remembers from that time. If there was something I didn't want her to do, I would tell her in quite clear terms. Going my own way, being my own person. Never paying lip service to someone, thinking it was easier if everyone knew where they really stood.

She talks about my eyebrow going up, how that was the sign to stop trying to argue. She says even my dad, once he realized, wouldn't go against the eyebrow once it was cocked. A big kid becoming an adult. Seeing the world as black and white, right and wrong.

Each step up, you learned. You suffered first, then tried to work it out.

What have they got that I haven't? What are they doing that I can't? How can I close this gap as fast as possible?

There was an overlap in schedules, when I first started training with the Ospreys. The academy was in its infancy, run by Gethin Watts. I could do a Tuesday and Thursday with Swansea after a session with the academy, play for Swansea on the weekend, watch the Ospreys when the chance came. I remember going to the Gnoll in Neath when the Ospreys beat Edinburgh to win the Celtic League, Gavin Henson running the show. Looking back, it felt like the last days of club rugby, when it was actually the start of something new and shiny – a proper feisty contest, a sold-out Gnoll. Noise and tight stands and the smell of beer and whisky in the air, fags and pipe smoke.

I wasn't on the radar for the senior side then. That's not how it felt to me. But when the squad was short, maybe because a player had been called up into the national squad or there were injuries or players who needed a rest, us younger ones would get a shout. I just wish I'd been more prepared.

So. I wasn't to know that Gethin had given the big sell to coach Lyn Jones, told him that I was a future Wales captain and Lions player. One of those comments that's great and awful at the same time. What Lyn saw was a kid who had never been slim who had now fatted up even further after being out injured himself. I'd also rolled my ankle and was wearing the only boots that felt comfortable: a pair of white Mizunos.

Gavin Henson may have been ready for coloured boots. Gavin Henson was winning Grand Slams. I was not. You could see them all looking at me in these white boots, my hair long over my ears. The unspoken thought obvious: who does this kid think he is?

That was the start of the nickname, thanks to Lyn. Alun Wyn Boots. Which became Wyn Togs, which became Gwyn Togs, because *gwyn* is Welsh for white and togs are boots. Not hugely creative, but simple and accurate enough to stick. Then the session began, and it got so much worse. 18 years old, 110 kilograms, all the muscle and power of a soup sandwich. The props staring at me, shaking their heads, pouring the abuse on. I hadn't jumped, I hadn't run, I hadn't done anything. Me breathing like a steam train climbing a mountain, staggering around the pitch. One thought in my head: what the fuck is this now?

You don't understand it all, back then. You don't know what training is really about, how important it is compared to games. Now? Now I think that training's as much about getting your mistakes out as anything else. Rugby is a performance-based sport. Of course training matters, but nothing like a game. You're judged 100 per cent on what you do on the Saturday. What you do during the week that precedes it matters only to you. Think about it. You care about the 80 minutes, not the other eight hours. No one's ever said, disappointing to lose to England, but to be fair that lad's trained brilliantly, so . . .

You strive for perfection in training, of course you do. But sometimes you can train too perfectly. You get a false sense of being ready. For all the work you can do on set piece and set plays, it's much more the intangibles that decide games, the emotional side of things. The margins are so tight between teams at the top of the game that it's the ones who stay in control who have the best chance of coming through. Not enough emotion and you lose the gain line. Too much emotion and you give away penalties and get yourself carded.

I always tried not to be intimidated. I'd seen enough on my way through, from Bonymaen to the big English schools we'd play with Llandovery, to know that you had to go hard as hell from the first bit of contact until you were on your knees seeing your breakfast for a second time. If you don't, you'll just be brushed aside. There's others there waiting for you to fall. There are always players waiting. You just have to make them wait.

There would be times when I was doing double days with the Ospreys. Lyn had a trick he'd drop in. We'd be driving the maul, and he'd have given us the signal beforehand to go absolutely flat-out, hard as we could, and then not tell the other team. I'd get clipped by one of the opposition, see stars. Get a bash of heads, a taste of spice. Taken off for a moment and then back in, more than happy to be in the melee again. The way I was, maybe they thought I had a chip on my shoulder. I hope not. But I had to punch above my weight. I had to fight. I had to do more than anyone else. That's what I thought.

You had to force them to notice you, force yourself to places maybe naturally you wouldn't want to go. Lyn Jones made it clear I was raw. My positioning outside of set piece wasn't great. Some of my tackling was messy. It was why he sent me back to Swansea for long periods. Work on it. Prove yourself.

In response I'd try to squeeze everything out of him too. Every Monday morning at 8.30 a.m. I'd turn up at training with a laptop and ask him to watch back footage of the weekend's game for Swansea. What was I doing right? Where was I letting the team down?

I'm not sure he appreciated it, at first. He had bigger things on. But I'd gone all the way to him, so I think he felt almost obliged to sit down with me, to give me the time and then the feedback.

Examples everywhere, showing you the real world could be complicated, that you found out what worked for you and then stuck with that. A few years later I'd be on the scrum machine in

Wales training, hear a screeching of tyres in the car park and see Colin Charvis skid to a halt. He'd got his timings wrong and missed the session. Other times in the early Wales days he'd offer me a lift in, and we'd go to the wrong place or be an hour early. I'd be thinking, oh shit, is he going to have a go now because I didn't remind him? Times when we rocked up to an empty training ground with his windows down, and a few kids spotted his car and ran over for autographs, and he groaned and just pressed the button to send his window back up, all these kids disappearing behind the blacked-out glass.

And then you watched him play, and he was incredible. He always was with Wales. He'd put it out there again and again. That was just how he was. That's what worked for him.

You see others who are all about the obsession. Dan Biggar and Leigh Halfpenny, out there for hours with Neil Jenkins, their kicking foot like a whole set of golf clubs. Now for the five-iron, now for the pitching wedge, now the driver. You stare and shake your head and wonder how they do it. Then there's the pure physical specimens, the ones like Huw Bennett who don't appear to have the tired gene. You think they're failing, and then they bang out another eight reps. Stef Terblanche, 37 caps and 19 tries for the Springboks, in the sort of shape even when he came to the Ospreys that made a pudgy kid from Mumbles realize how much fat there was to trim and how much definition to gain.

I took it from where I could. Players I could watch close up, others I could admire from afar. John Eales for Australia, Martin Johnson for England. The touch and leadership with Eales, his impossible kicking. The edge to Johnson.

It was almost funny with Johnson. He'd come out of the tunnel for kick-off looking like a growling tiger, all that reputation preceding him. Never needing to go looking for the aggro, it always coming to him. Dealing with it when it came, letting the pack deal with it if the referee was watching him too closely. I loved watching those Leicester forwards. Graham Rowntree, Julian White, Ben Kay. The crazy fitness of Neil Back, 125 tries for his club, more than one every three games; 16 for England, plus a drop goal. You'd hear rumours of how Back had completed all the levels on a bleep test before anyone else. You didn't know if it was myth or rumour, but it sounded good either way.

Maybe I was too uptight back then. I wanted everything perfect. I'd beat myself up if I ever fell short, if someone else didn't seem to be as serious about it as I was. Maybe I was too scared of making mistakes. If I could go back to that kid with the Ospreys, stepping out of Swansea, I'd tell myself to try more, to risk a little. To see where I could go rather than being scared of where I might fall.

But I never felt relaxed enough to have too much fun. Enjoyment was always okay. That came from the hard work, or finding time for a drop-goal competition or keepy-ups when the session was in the bag. It took me time to learn that the higher up you go in the sport, the more you need to keep that enjoyment. You have to let off steam. If someone wants to have a drop, let him have a drop as long as his hamstring doesn't fall off. Fun to me was disrespecting the environment. Fun was dangerous. It was when you stopped caring.

Yet part of me finds it really hard to say I should have been different. Coming in to professionalism I thought, well, I have to be professional. Maybe I wouldn't have achieved what I have if I didn't have the foundations of my approach. I couldn't see how I would be where I am now. It sounds a contradiction in terms, doesn't it? Confusion where there should be clarity.

Maybe the fun was there without me going after it. For my warm-up I used to chase Shane Williams around the pitch. I was never going to catch him. There's a reason why you've never seen a giraffe eating a cheetah. But I'd keep going until I was blowing, and both of us would be laughing by the end.

Run everywhere. That was my thinking, back then. In the Bonymaen days, particularly as I started my journey with Swansea, with the Ospreys. I did it with Wales, and it suited the mindset under Warren Gatland a treat because he was all about quick transitions and short, intense sessions. Buzzing around like a blue-arsed fly, probably without the thinking to make it count.

It would take me a while to realize the importance of clarity. Of pausing for thought, of doing moves at half-pace or walking speed. If you can get both then you're in the right place.

But you try telling that to a young man. Me against the world, me on my own. Desperate to prove myself. Desperate to push on.

When a contract from the Ospreys arrived, something changed for all of us. That's when the pride kicked in. Okay. I'm a professional rugby player now. This is on.

And, because my dad was who he was, it came with something else. Going back to the house one day, signing the contract at the kitchen table. Seeing another fat stack of papers there.

'Mum, what's this?'

'Oh, didn't your father tell you? You've bought a flat.'

Dad being Dad all the way through. Investing on my behalf. Not asking me beforehand, not checking if I wanted to buy a flat, or where, or which one.

Even in the act of me moving away, Dad holding on tight.

5

CYFLE | OPPORTUNITY

There's always a gap between you and the impossible, until suddenly there isn't.

March 2005. I'm playing for the Wales under-21 side. We've just won our own Grand Slam on the Friday night, and now Wales – actual Wales, proper Wales – are chasing the real deal. Ireland coming to the Millennium Stadium on Saturday afternoon, Wales without a Grand Slam since 1978. A mad seven weeks of Shane tries and Gav penalties from halfway. Martyn Williams on the charge, Stephen Jones off the tee.

Cardiff on a big international day. There's nowhere better to be, particularly if you and your mate get given spare tickets. If you're sitting right behind the posts. If you're watching when Gethin Jenkins charges down a kick and rumbles on to score and then chucks the ball at Ronan O'Gara's head, when Gav bangs over a drop goal, when Kevin Morgan comes racing up on the outside of Tom Shanklin and dives over the line.

And it's still so far away. These players are not like you. You might know a few now from training sessions with the Ospreys. Shane and Gav, Adam Jones and Ryan Jones. You might look at how the system works and think, they all came through this. I'm on my way. It won't be long.

But I didn't believe it, or didn't want to let myself believe it. Even when I was called into a couple of sessions by coach Mike Ruddock, being put through a load of sprints at the indoor track and leaving my lunch in the bin afterwards. Another at Sophia

Gardens, not having a great session but starting to realize, okay, I can catch and pass and do all these things that these other players can do. Walking away from that with the first little bit of hope, with ideas. If I do this a little more, if I try a bit more of this, I'll get better. And if I get better . . .

And then one day it happens. A call from the Welsh Rugby Union. You've been selected for the senior summer tour to Argentina. Can we assume your availability?

It only hit home when I took the bags of kit back to Mum and Dad's and they hit the hallway floor. Not so much how many bags there were, how many training shirts and shorts or tracksuits or polo shirts, but the badge embroidered on the left of the chest. Right, there are three feathers everywhere. A realization of who else has worn that badge. What they've done in it. How they made the nation feel. A world that already feels as if it is rushing along, suddenly shifting up another few gears.

I assumed I was going out there purely for the experience. It was Gareth Jenkins's first tour in charge. Mike Ruddock had lost his job, in the dramatic way that Wales coaches seemed to lose their jobs; inevitably, it was my dad who was looking after his legal action against the Welsh Rugby Union, but no one seemed to be holding it against me. A year out from the World Cup, a good chance to rest the regular first-teamers, to have a look at a few for a couple of seasons further down the line.

I wasn't sure what sort of player they imagined me to be. I was second row, but I was also being used at 6. I'd definitely never dreamed that a debut might come in Patagonia. Cardiff yes, London maybe, possibly Edinburgh or Rome. But that was where we were heading – a little town on the coast called Puerto Madryn, founded by 150 Welsh immigrants back in 1865, named after an old ancestral estate in Wales, still a home for the Welsh language all these years later.

It felt almost homely, if northern Patagonia can feel like home when you're from Mumbles. Shop signs in Welsh. Hearing Welsh in the street, albeit with a strange Spanish twang. Mum and Dad staying at home but, in an unforeseen twist, my grandmother – the one who'd helped put me through Llandovery College, who'd questioned where rugby would ever take me – flying over with my sister. Who had grown up a native Welsh speaker in north Wales, who had now sat on a plane for most of a day to find people who could speak to her like she was back at school in Dolgellau.

It was like stepping back in time, that place. Like an old world, lost halfway down a continent.

A hotel like a block of flats, a lift that could fit one rugby player at a time. A training pitch on top of a cliff, even windier than Bonymaen at its bleakest. The local rugby club with an emblem of a seal on its badge. Driving along a track by the beach, looking out into the bay and seeing a pod of killer whales about 20 metres away in the shallows.

Even the team announcement was retro. All of us sitting in the dark in the team hotel, someone flicking a switch, the light coming up on an overhead projector, the starting XV on a slide. Letting my eyes adjust to the light, seeing Ian Evans picked in the second row and James Hook and Richard Hibbard on the bench, and then realizing – hang on, I'm in there at 6! Walking to the front of the room with Ian, standing in the wrong place and having the words on the screen projected onto our faces, bent and distorted as we grinned with a mix of embarrassment and pride. There's the photos. You being made to stand at the front of the bus, one with all the senior players flicking V-signs at your back.

I could tell Mum and Dad were shocked when I called them. It was as much good luck as congratulations. Have a taste, son, try to enjoy it. Not feeling daunted so much as determined not to let myself down. The year before, I'd been watching some of these men win a Grand Slam. Now I would be taking the field with them, 20 years old. Okay, Alun Wyn. Don't take any of this for granted. Hold your own, when the whistle goes.

There are so many little emotional peaks when you play for your country for the first time. The moment you're given your shirt. The moment you walk into the dressing room and there's the famous red jersey on your peg. No cap number under the three feathers yet, because you haven't taken the field. It's not real until you've crossed the line. You could get injured in the warm-up.

I loved that. Even though you're in the squad, until the referee's whistle goes, you haven't got a cap number. I loved the fact that you could train in the kit as long as you wanted but none of it counted until then. I looked at that shirt, at the deep red, at the three feathers and the gold crown at their base, and didn't worry that it might be the only time I was ever picked. You never want to be a one-cap wonder, but one is a lot more than millions of people will ever have. One is something that so many would give anything to experience. It makes you part of the history of Welsh rugby, in an infinitesimal way. One leads to two and two leads to more.

You hear all the clichés about how you're just passing through the jersey. Looking back, that all makes sense. It's also the value that you put inside it. What you add to it with your performance. The older players – the ones who give you a friendly clip round the head when you get your first start, a clout on the shoulder – they get it. They're looking at you to make sure you understand it too. This is special, boy. This you will never forget. This is for you, but it's for everyone else, too.

And there's the anthem, and nothing can quite prepare you for that.

The music swells. You feel the pull of your teammates' arms either side. You try to fix on a point in the stands so the emotions don't overwhelm you. And then it kicks in, and it feels as if you're at the centre of this beautiful storm. Everyone is together, all part of one thing. You could be in the crowd, the crowd could be on the pitch. You on the inside of it all, connected to everyone on the outside looking in.

I've never lost that sense of wonder in all the years and matches since. I've never let go of the possibility that it could be the last time I ever get the chance. I might be injured, I might not be selected. And so it stays incredibly personal, even as it's a collective experience. You get some players who won't sing the anthem, who don't want to because it'll all be too much and they'll lose their focus. I think two things: the strongest people are those who are in control of their emotions, and can switch their focus on and off. And, more than that, you're not going to take away from me that opportunity to be purely in the moment. It's probably one of the only times I ever let myself get lost in it all – not thinking ahead, not worrying about the next contact or the next score, just standing there and letting the noise and the passion swirl around me and carry me along with it.

That's what I remember from that day, as much as the details of the match. How it felt inside, as well as the massive names lining up in pale blue and white against us: Leguizamón and Fernández Lobbe, Pichot and Hernández, Roncero, Scelzo and Ledesma. The 30 toilet rolls that came hurtling over the fences from the crowd when Ian Evans gestured in celebration at the stands after his interception try. The disappointment of losing when we really should have won, the pleasure in James Hook coming on and scoring a very James Hook try. Understanding how green I was, really.

Another cap a week later in Buenos Aires, a more hostile crowd again. Another defeat. That was how this grand adventure began, and it's never slowed down, now I'm on it. Coming back that autumn and coming on in Cardiff against the All Blacks, all wound up after having to perform the haka in their dressing room. Starting in the second row in my first Six Nations, losing to Ireland, to Scotland and a pile of Chris Paterson penalties, to Italy in Rome. Breathless on our own try line as we tried to hang in there at the death, trudging onto the team coach outside the Stadio Flaminio and hearing the boos and jeers of some Welsh fans who'd had enough. A rude awakening to how quickly it turns, still very critical of myself after every game.

I felt every one of those defeats. Never a sense of, well, I'm only 21, I'm the baby of the team. It's no good being a prospect in a team that's doing badly. There is no pecking order, when the losses start piling up. A World Cup in France coming later that year, wondering if we were all blowing our chances of getting there. Last one in, first one out.

And then you finish at home against England, wooden spoon on the cards, and it suddenly all comes right. An initiation into another very Welsh experience: liberated by the most intense pressure, cutting loose when all seems lost.

James Hook was pretty special that day. One of those matches when you watched him stepping and swerving and thought, he's the modern-day Phil Bennett, this kid. A win, at last, amid the bedlam. A heightened sense of being inside something special – looking up at the stands, seeing the red shirts, the flags; feeling the choirs, and the anthems, and the celebrations in the streets outside, deep into the night. Drinking off the adrenaline. Not wanting to look back too much, not wanting to dream too long of what might follow.

6

ANTUR | ADVENTURE

You play elite sport, and often it feels like life is on fast-forward.

You're playing up the road from where you were born. You're still a kid, although you've grown tall and you've filled out. You're in national age-group teams – under-17s, under-18s. You're a young one in the under-21s. To your pleasure and surprise you start being picked to play a few games with the senior side, with men who have 80 more caps than you, who've seen everything you want to see and a fair amount you have no idea about yet. And then there's a World Cup on the horizon, this competition you watched as a kid, that made players into superstars, and it hits you: I could be playing in that. It's there, in front of me.

And maybe you might blow it. 21 years old, that summer, and in for another harsh lesson. World Cup warm-up games aren't supposed to matter. Everyone says that. But every game matters. You try holding onto that when you go to south-west London to play a new-look England side, and end up being on the wrong end of a 60-pointer.

I understood what losing felt like before that summer. A compressive weight on your shoulders, a hollowness that won't go away in the days that follow. Worse was to come.

It wasn't just the scoreline, although the scoreline was horrific. It wasn't Nick Easter scoring four tries, although when you've been picked in the back row and the opposition number 8 strolls over the line every time he tucks the ball under his arm, it's never going to be a good feeling. It wasn't trying to defend their scrum-half Shaun Perry off the edges and having him use me like a power sled for 10 metres, like he was the strongest player in the world, as if I knew nothing about body position and technique and aggression. It was when Lawrence Dallaglio came off the bench, smashed over off a scrum, and you got up off your knees to see the soles of several of your teammates' boots lying on the Twickenham turf. They'd thought they'd been sent the boots to be worn in France that autumn. Instead they were the prototypes, mere models, never intended to see actual action. You try pushing in a scrum with nothing between your sock and the warm grass. You try chasing after Jason Robinson and a young Mathew Tait with no way of changing direction.

I had no idea it wasn't going to get a great deal better. Sketchier than a box of frogs that I was going to be selected, all sort of quiet pride inside when I was. Thrilled to be going to France, disappointed in a strange way that we had two games coming up in Cardiff, because it felt a little less like how I imagined a World Cup should be. The group looked testing without being brutal. It wasn't how 2011 would one day look, what we'd face in 2015.

You don't know the signs, at that age. It's all new to you. I could tell some of the senior players were apprehensive that we were going out to a little place called Marmande for a four-week training camp, somewhere in the baking countryside between Bordeaux and Toulouse, because we'd be based there again during the tournament. Knowing familiarity isn't always a good thing.

Me? I was young. I was at a World Cup. I was playing rugby with players I was used to watching on television, in a fresh batch of new kit with the World Cup logo in key visible places. I couldn't see that negativity building. What was there to complain about?

And then the tournament started, and it accelerated away in a manner that I struggled to understand.

You play Canada in Nantes. You're 17–9 down just after half-time, and the pessimists in the stands and at home are starting to worry. But you pull through, and you even score a try, bundling over when they make a mess of a simple exit, and all seems good in the world.

You play Australia, in the match that's supposed to decide the group, and it's all Cardiff noise all around and beer in the air and optimism. And then Stephen Larkham and Matt Giteau, Stirling Mortlock and Chris Latham are running sweet lines everywhere, and you look up at the scoreboard just before half-time to see you're 25–3 down and a mountain to climb, because this is 2007, and no one ever really believes you can overturn that sort of deficit, not against a side like the Wallabies. But you beat Japan a week later and it's back to the west of France and what everyone hopes, what everyone assumes, is going to be the game that takes you into the quarter-finals.

Of course it's obvious in retrospect. The lessons from Welsh World Cup history, from Western Samoa, from the whole of Samoa. The sort of rugby that Fiji can play, the players they had in that team – Seru Rabeni, Nicky Little, Akapusi Qera; the rare preparation time they'd had coming into a World Cup.

But it all seemed okay, to a kid who hadn't seen it all before. There was even an excursion the week before in Paris, going from the racecourse at Longchamp to the Moulin Rouge via a police-escorted bus trip the wrong way down the Champs-Élysées. Good times and frivolity, all in the name of team bonding. My mum and dad flying out to Nantes with half the rest of Wales, my dad bumping into a client of his named John Rees and his daughter Anwen. Remember that girl. She becomes rather important in this story.

Sitting in the dressing room beforehand, out of the bright September sun, hearing the songs and the shouting outside. An awareness there that if we lost this one we were going home, knowing that could make us more fragile, hoping it would stiffen our resolve. Looking round the room, at players like Gareth Thomas and Adam Jones, at Shane Williams and James Hook, at Colin Charvis and Martyn Williams, and thinking, look at all this experience, we should be all right here.

I don't think we took them lightly or anything. I certainly didn't. Maybe the week off didn't help. Maybe the excursion was better for morale than performance. Maybe we were better as the underdog rather than the favourites. A very Welsh idea, preferring to be the outsiders. That you find it a more natural fit being the hunted rather than the hunter.

The Webb-Ellis trophy sat there on a plinth as we walked out of the tunnel into that warm autumn afternoon. All golden shimmer in the sunshine, like a promise of beautiful things to come. You could have reached out and picked it up, if you'd wanted to. It looked small and manageable.

We fell into the trap. Walked right into it.

We were never meant to go fast and loose. We meant to be controlled, to play our game rather than theirs. But you get sucked in, in a game like that. Like a poker game where you want to give nothing away but instead let the adrenaline get to you and shove all your chips into the middle on the first hand.

The crowd were a fair way from the pitch, but the noise came in waves. Fiji crashing over from close in, Fiji counter-attacking out wide and offloading with a reckless precision, the ball bouncing between Mark Jones and Gareth Thomas to be touched down for their second try. Spreading it right again, me trying to cover too many runners, a show-and-go and them cutting through on my inside.

Less than half an hour gone, and we were 25–3 down. Australia all over again, except not against a team who could do what Australia could do.

They just kept coming at us. And as we chased, the game broke up more, and no one thrives in an open, messy contest like Fiji. It almost became a game of sevens in a 15-a-side contest.

These are the moments when you're truly tested as an international rugby player. Are you ready for this? Can you find answers that others can't? Can you take that feeling of pressure – the lactic in the legs, the lungs on fire – and use it? Be controlled.

Slow it down. Take the craziness out of it. Grind, if grinding's what's going to work.

And we had a crack. A try before half-time, Fiji with a man in the bin, the most Shane Williams try ever from Shane just after. Another from Alfie, and a rush of relief, a sense of, we might be all right here. We might survive. Martyn Williams intercepting and galloping away to put us ahead with time running out.

But it was never over, that day. Never safe. Stopping those white shirts was like trying to dam a waterfall with your bare hands.

The passing and the offloading made them untouchable. Running onto bouncing balls, not seeming to be structured, but not a sixth sense either because there was absolute method to it all. Popping passes away almost like they had air-time on the ball. Leaving it in space and letting big men run onto it.

And so they came at us again. That's when time finally slows down, when it seems to stop. When you're ahead by a score and defending for your life on your own five-metre line. You think, let's just hold them off for another 30 seconds, another 60. Don't worry about what comes next – just make the tackle you're in, get up, fill the line.

A good chunk of phase play can burn through two minutes. A great one can get rid of four. But the energy, the mental strength that takes? It's like sitting on the rower for 1,000 metres while somebody's hitting you, with a bout of wrestling thrown in somewhere in between. It's lactic acid building up in your legs, your arms, your chest. It's trying to make good decisions when you can't breathe. It's finding the precision to perform your skills when your brain is so fried that you can barely remember where you are.

Stay in the arm-wrestle. Don't be the one who lets the side down. Don't be the one who's the gap in the line, the soft shoulder in the wall.

We had nothing left, still too much to do when they broke through that final time. Unable to stop the last charge, that decisive eighth try in the 80 minutes.

The feeling? It's a long time ago now. Defeats have come and gone, World Cups with hopes and heartbreak, with wondering again if that golden trophy might be within reach. But I remember trying to push the memory away that time because it was too much. Thinking, in one year I've gone from my debut to going out of the World Cup at the group stages. Is it going to be like this every year?

So many subplots coming together in the aftermath. Alfie's 100th cap and no reason to celebrate it afterwards. Wondering what was going to happen to coach Gareth Jenkins, after a difficult Six Nations and a World Cup where we'd fallen far short. Feeling sorry for him and desolate for ourselves. Not so much shell-shocked as thinking we'd beaten ourselves as much as been beaten. Realizing it felt far worse that way round.

Not a lot of gallows humour in the dressing room. An awful lot of self-medication through alcohol. A further education that when the Wales rugby team lose, it's felt throughout the nation, and when we win you see it in the nation as well. Seeing that when someone says nothing, you know the hurt is even greater. Silence tells you more sometimes that anyone saying anything.

Learning too that when Welsh rugby wants to be brutal, it's ruthless. Gareth Jenkins didn't need to be sacked in the car park of our hotel. We thought they might at least wait until we'd got back to Cardiff. Show him some respect, think of his reputation. Instead he was seen trudging away on his own, head down, all his stuff in a Tesco's bag. The bottom of his trousers all soaked from the dewy grass as he went up the road.

There was an argument that he should have been given the job earlier in his career. That was a possible mistake. It hadn't worked. Whether it was the timing or his coaching philosophy, his standing in the game in Wales couldn't be questioned. Most of us players were still half-cut when we saw it happen. Then a meeting called by management, the official line given. Gareth standing up to it all, travelling back and leading us home even as he knew he was already out of a job.

It was a harsh wake-up call for me. Okay, this is business, not sport. It's not just about fun and good times and camaraderie. It can be dark. It can be cruel. The coach who selected me to play has gone. What will the new man think? Who will the new man be? Results up and down, selection changing, the coaching philosophy uprooted. The only constant I could see was inside me. I still wanted this. I wanted more. I just wanted better.

The only good thing in that messy aftermath? It was only an hour and a half flight home. Sitting there, hungover or still woozy, the drive back from Heathrow to Cardiff stretching out in front of us. Not much talk, no smiles. One thought in the air, from everyone: just get me home.

You don't know, in that moment, the transformation that's going to take place. You don't understand that it's the start of a new chapter. You're looking back and wondering what if, not forward to what might be. None of us had any idea how our careers and lives were going to change, what was going to happen to the Welsh team and the Welsh nation.

They didn't mess around with the appointment. We got home at the start of October. By early November the announcement came: the new Wales coach was Warren Gatland. His assistant would be Shaun Edwards.

You're selfish, as a player. Your first thought is not, how good will these two be? It's, are they going to pick me? Are they thinking I'm part of the solution or part of the problem? Am I a squad member or a starter?

They were different from the first meeting, those two. The first thing Warren said: family comes first. Whatever happens with us, that's always going to be the mantra.

It didn't get much more complicated after that. I want to work you hard. I am going to work you hard. Not said with a glint in his eye or a thousand-yard stare, but with honesty. Looking into our eyes, no edge to him. I am just telling you – it's not going to be nice, but if you buy into it, we could do well. Okay?

Warren in a grey suit and red tie. Shaun Edwards next to him in a tracksuit. That's where the glowing eyes were. The proper sparkle and glint. You looked at him and thought, if someone says the wrong thing here, it's going to get ugly.

The Edwards mantra was straightforward in a different way.

'Legalized violence.'

Those were his first two words. Then the explanation. 'Defence isn't about technique. It's legalized violence.'

As if we could be in any doubt. As if it could be any clearer. You'd heard about this sort of thing when the two of them had been at Wasps. You knew this was a thing in rugby league.

It still hit home. No smiles. No chuckles. Me with wide eyes. 'Shit, he's serious . . .'

The next line. 'We're going to be fitter, stronger and faster than any other team. That's what's going to happen.'

You realized in those first few minutes that he wasn't afraid of putting it all out there. Total honesty, no room for misconceptions or mistakes. There's a point with players where you learn to buy in with certain coaches. It can be about their track record or their reputation, or it can be how they are with you.

Gatland and Edwards had the first. Those three Premiership titles with Wasps, the Heineken Cup win. Everything they'd been through as players. You knew they understood. You knew there was no bullshit filling gaps on their CVs.

And then you began your own relationship with them, and you found it clicked. I'm pretty literal in a lot of things. If I'm asked to work hard, I can work hard. And that's what so much of our game play and training methodology was about. That was philosophically easy for me, even if the practicals of it often left you feeling broken.

Then there was the attitude. From the start Gats was on to us about being more confident, about backing ourselves. That wasn't the instinctive Welsh way. We were the underdogs. We were the ones who pulled off upsets. The hunted, rather than the hunters. But he could have that effect on us because so often his predictions were spot on. If he told us we could win a particular game, we usually would. If he told us we could come back from the sort of half-time deficit that used to be insurmountable, we went with him. And we learned something else: it wasn't arrogance. There's nothing intrinsically wrong with being confident. It doesn't make you a twat.

I understood Warren's ways, from that first meeting. I think a few guys didn't. It was easy for me because of the simplicity of it. I wasn't looking for affection or a personal relationship. I was looking to learn, get on and start winning. I'd had just over a year of international rugby. I was green. It suited me at that time in my life, in my career.

I'd change, in a good way, as I got older. I learned to enjoy having more personal relationships with some coaches. I began to realize I could challenge them a bit more on the rugby side. I could bounce ideas off them, and it was a positive thing, not insurrection. And with both you felt a deeper trust, even in those opening weeks.

You learned things about Shaun. You saw the side to him that people outside his teams never experience. He's always the first one to drop you a text if you're having a difficult time, to give you a call. He's one of the few people who always remembers what's happened to you – who's who in your family, who might be ill, those close to you that you've lost.

You know they say insanity and genius are two sides of the same coin? Shaun can be terrifying. But no matter how million-miles-an-hour he can be, he's really consistent on those sides of things.

And he protected you, too, when he felt he needed to. When we came under stress, when he felt he may have underprepared us or missed something in his prep, he would accept the responsibility. In my eyes, his mentality was, I'm doing this job because I'm out there with you all the time. That's why I like to coach the way I coach, that's why I like to see you succeed when it goes well.

If the school of hard knocks ever needed a headmaster,

Edwards would be your man. Starting as a player for Wigan aged 17, in his first 10 games having his nose broken, two teeth knocked out and facial wounds so extensive that he needed 15 stitches. But the people who just saw Shaun's crooked nose and heard the screaming and shouting never really got him. We saw the other, softer sides to him. He would sing songs with us on the bus – all right, one song, 'Saturday Night at the Movies'. He wasn't afraid to show us how much it all meant to him. In a male-dominated sport, you have to be strong, and he had an emotional force as well as a physical one. Quite quickly you realized: this man cares.

And he took enormous pride in the collective achievements. Not just the wins or the trophies. The small stuff that acts as the foundation for the things that draw the outsiders' attention. The season we statistically had the best defence of any international team in world rugby, he had a few percentage charts printed off, framed them up and gave them to a few of the boys.

Defence was his department, his obsession, his cup of strong tea each morning. If he was going to be number one then he was going to have something to show for it. You can respect that. His efforts, his commitment, the consistency of the two of them together – you couldn't argue with it. You either kept up, forced yourself to understand when things were getting feisty or the speed was going up and up, or you got left behind. That, we realized as time went by, was the challenge under this new regime.

You could also see how good the two of them were, working together. It was another step up for them, going from the domestic game to the international scene, regardless of Warren's previous time with Ireland, and that seemed to push them on. Shaun always said how grateful he was to Gats that he'd given him such a coaching opportunity. And they didn't pretend they had to be best friends all the time. In any decent working partnership, there's always going to be stress on the bonds, but often that brings the best out of people, and for a large period of the next 12 years, that's what we were going to get – whether the coaches were competing for training time in sessions, or us being challenged by Shaun on tackle completion, or Shaun wanting more time. As a player you were always on your toes. You'd see the coaches under Gats getting frustrated with each other because they'd gone two minutes over through talking too much.

'All right, I'm having a minute of yours tomorrow!'

'Sorry, we've gone over two minutes today, so we're going to take two minutes off tomorrow's session.'

All that energy would translate into our approach as players, because we'd have to be on the button all the time; Gats didn't want to roll over, but Shaun didn't want to lose his time either. You were running from one part of a session to the next. 'If you're late to my drill, I will start without you or you're gone.'

That was the rugby side of things. The fitness side of things was, well, we're going to try and break you, you know that. We're going to get you really fit, but we're going to try and break you on the way. That knowledge, those tests, gave you mental strength. We would learn we could be confronted by that pain, get through it, get up and then get going again.

Maybe the game plan was limited at the start. People might say we didn't play much rugby. Fine. What we were doing was working. Elite-level sport is about winning. I'd had a taste of the other side, and I didn't like it. They were showing us the way to something else. I was comfortable with the sweet simplicity of it all: be honest, work hard and go from there. I could be prone to overthinking things. I could procrastinate to a high level. Gatland and Edwards would cut through all of that.

And it would all be worth it, even if we had no clue at all at that point. No idea about the Grand Slams, the World Cup campaigns, the championships. The days and nights in Cardiff, the sackings of Twickenham, the madcap evenings in Paris. All of it to come. The impossible possibilities. All of us on the cusp.

7

YSBRYD | SPIRIT

The strangeness of being recognized never goes away. I'll be at the Vale, the hotel where we stay with Wales when in camp, and someone will spot me walking through the lobby. A supporter, another guest, will come up to me, not necessarily with a smile on their face, say hello, Alun Wyn, and start talking to me in Welsh.

That's when I have to tell them, in my broken Welsh, '*Dydw i ddim yn siarad Cymraeg, dwi'n dysgu.*' *I don't speak Welsh, I'm learning.* And you can see the confusion and disappointment on their face. Looking at me as if to say, am I speaking to the right person?

I'm not unique among South Walian men. But I still feel as if there's a part of my Welsh identity I need to find by being able to speak our native tongue. My grandmother on my mother's side is from Dinas Mawddwy, a little Welsh-speaking village in Gwynedd. My wife speaks Welsh; we're bringing our girls up to have that part of my Welsh identity I feel I'm missing, and to keep that connection alive. It's not about politics, for me. It's pride – the girls growing up, travelling the world, the world understanding what Wales is, who its people are, that it has its own culture and language. It's practicality – being able to talk to Mali and Efa as a Welsh dad with Welsh kids. When people from my country speak to me in Welsh, I'd like to be able to respond.

I'm better than I was. I can understand more of what's coming at me when those people at the Vale walk over. You get to know how people ask for an autograph, or a photo; when it's 'Hi, how are you?' or 'Don't spoil my weekend, now . . .'

And it's only part of what being Welsh means to me. We all have our own personal identity, our own ideas. Modesty is a big part of me being Welsh. A natural shyness, a dislike of anyone who appears to fancy themselves. You get too big for your boots in Wales, and people are quite happy to remind you where you come from. You learn early on that working hard and being modest is better than trying to stand out. You can win the Six Nations four times, you can be on TV every other weekend, but you'll be respected if you remember to behave like the kid next door.

I put a wall up straight away. You'll notice the shyness before you discover the other stuff underneath – the stubbornness, the humour, the determination. And it's a contentedness with that shyness. I'm quite happy sitting in a cafe with a coffee and no one else for company. It's not rudeness, even if some people interpret it that way sometimes. I'm just not going to force myself on you. That would be the rude part. I can go down for breakfast when in camp and sit in silence on my own, because you're in the team environment, and you want to make the most of the time on your own.

I used to think I didn't care what people thought about me, but when you're in the public eye, there's responsibilities. It forces you to listen. My wife Anwen worries about the big things, the important things. The cost of the house, the bills coming in. I worry whether I said the right thing to the bloke who wanted a selfie by the fruit and veg aisle in the supermarket.

She'll have to reassure me.

'Ans, was I rude to that man?'

'Alun, he was really drunk. He was the rude one.'

'Yeah, but when I said he'd have to stay two metres away because of Covid, he just walked off. He's going to think I'm really rude, isn't he?'

It's a constant feeling of being watched. I find that hard. Wondering if someone's going to take a photo, how it'll be interpreted if I've had a drink. Going to a friend's wedding and people coming in from another wedding across the way to ask for selfies. Anwen suggesting that it might not be a good idea to go to a funeral with her, knowing that there'll be someone who sidles up to you at the crematorium and says, all right for a quick pic, *butt*?

It comes with the job, and you're lucky to be doing a job where people feel that way. But I genuinely don't think I'll miss being asked for photos, when the day comes. Wearing a hoodie and cap and shades when I go out. Thinking about my dad, and how when he was out he'd always want to sit with his back to the wall so he could see what was happening all the time. Struggling with the vaguest idea of praise or public approval.

The week after the Grand Slam in 2019, Anwen's parents were looking after the girls. We thought we'd go out for a quick meal – Bistro Pierre on the front in Mumbles, no big deal, jeans and hoodies and let's just pop in for an hour. We walked in, sat at this tiny little table, ate our dinner and we were just about to get up to leave when the whole restaurant stood up and applauded.

I was both absolutely mortified and as proud as I've been of anything in my rugby career. I wanted the ground to open up. I didn't know where to look, what to say. Amazing, for what the Grand Slam meant to us all, horrifying in the same moment. Walking back to the car with my face burning, finding when we got there that someone had paid for our parking ticket too. A little note scribbled on the back of it: 'It was the least we could do.' A fellow Welshman looking after that kid next door.

Tribalism is alive and well in Wales. It's feeling fiercely protective of the nation, about the game of rugby here. Understanding what it means, the heritage behind you, the kids growing up into it, the players and the watchers.

It's knowing where I'm from, knowing about my grandfathers, about the life and home of my grandmothers. It's my mum telling me about her grandmother, Annie, how she was brought up in Glynneath as one of 14 children. How she was known as Annie Five-Minutes, because she would say she'd be gone for five minutes, and then disappear and nobody would know where she was. It's knowing my dad, where he was from, what he did. Trying to understand why he looked at the world as he did.

My grandfather on my mother's side cared about my academic progress – encouraged me, looked out for me. My grandfather on my dad's side was about the rugby. Long before socks were capable of staying up by themselves, he insisted on making me a fresh pair of elastic garters to keep me looking smart. This was when I was still playing junior rugby, but he made pairs for me all the way through, and I've kept the very final pair with me in a white envelope in my kitbag ever since. These two black elastic bands, made by hand.

When you play for Wales, you realize you represent your family before anything else. The nation is built around families, the bonds between them, the similarities. Welsh blood is thicker than water. You can disagree with your parents, struggle with a brother, not see much of your sister. They stay your family. There's 3.3 million of us in this country. You go most places and someone knows a relative, somehow. And your family first, not you through rugby. It's like when I went to Bonymaen. That's why I was Mrs Jones History's son.

That's good. It's a powerful thing. And it can be hard, too. It can be claustrophobic when everyone knows everything. When no one is a stranger.

Growing up, I struggled with it at times. I was shy and I was a boy; I probably wouldn't share as much as I should have done. I threw so much into rugby that there wasn't a lot else left to go round, my own worst enemy in many ways. Call it independence, call it puberty, call it selfishness. I just wanted to be left alone sometimes.

It's all connected, in Wales. You think about the heritage and lineage of your family, and you're connected too to the heritage and deeds of other men and women who have played for the country. It's almost like an oral tradition. *Mabinogion* – the first prose stories in Britain, spoken in Middle Welsh, 800 and 900 years ago. It's the same thing.

Myths and adventures and stories are told about previous Welsh sides going way back, the way they won. It's passed down from father to daughter and mother to son. What you're told when you're first told about Phil Bennett or Ray Gravell. The first time someone digs out a VHS tape and tells you to sit down and watch carefully and presses play on the Baa-Baas' try against New Zealand in 1973.

Rugby has always been the sport. It always will be. Cardiff on match day is like the lake that every stream and river in the whole of Wales drains into. Got a ticket? You're one of the lucky ones. Don't have a ticket? Doesn't matter. You go all the same. To drink, to sing, to say *I was there.*

You go to Twickenham as a player, the coach takes you through the Memorial Gates and parks up right by the players' entrance. At the Aviva in Dublin they bring you through the tunnel under the stadium. At Murrayfield you circumnavigate half the stadium following a piper.

Cardiff? It's the intimacy of a beautiful chaos. That slow, almost spiritual drive. All that week, you've been driving past people on their way to work or to home, and you get to the stadium and it's like they're all there waiting for you. It's a 200-metre stretch of road down Westgate Street with fans six deep on either side. You turn off Castle Street and it's like Moses is driving the bus. My God, we've arrived.

At Murrayfield there was a running track between the supporters and the pitch. At Twickenham you've got a gap large enough to install one. At the Principality, it's front row of the stands and then the touchline. You can hear everything they're screaming at you. You're part of them.

Driving back in the coach after a game and finding yourself alongside all the minibuses taking supporters to their own towns and villages and homes. The pride unrelenting in victory or defeat. Captain, supporter, obsessive. You and them together, in red.

*

I thought I knew all that. What it means to play for Wales. What Wales means to the nation. And then the 2008 Grand Slam happened, and I realized: it means so much more.

Gatland and Edwards hardly had us before that tournament. A couple of weeks, no time really to make big changes. Training was hard, intense, short. You went in full of intrigue and went out having emptied yourself.

It shouldn't have been enough to make a significant difference, but it was all calculated. They'd done it before. We were used to playing great rugby for an hour and then falling away. The new regime turned that on its head. Boys, you're going to be fitter than them. Fitter than England, fitter than Ireland. You're going to be the ones coming through in the last quarter of tight games, not them. You can beat anyone.

A series of tweaks and changes, some of them physical, some of them mental. With Gats it was different from that first session in January. He was breeding confidence, sometimes in the simplest of ways. We're going to go there and do this. You're fitter, better organized, better players. Forget this stat about not having won at Twickenham for 20 years. That wasn't you. That isn't now. You're going there to do a job. Here's how we're going to do it. And it's logic, boys, not some soft romantic hope.

'Bigger, stronger, faster.' Each word emphasized with a slap of the palm into the palm.

The defence. Shaun Edwards's baby, and it had teeth from birth. We're going to use the blitz. Never injured in defence. That was the other part of it for Shaun. Doesn't matter what you've done, whether you're on one leg or can't move your arms or there's blood spurting out of some massive fresh hole. You get up and you fill the line. The opposition won't know you're injured, but they will know if you're not there. When they glance up, ball in hand, they'll see a red shirt rather than a gap. That's what matters.

Then the selection. No time yet to overhaul it, so let's pick players who play well in combinations. Let's pick from a team who play the closest to the version of the blitz defence that we want to get. Pick Martyn Williams, Mark Jones and 13 Ospreys.

You couldn't argue, because you'd never been through it before. It was a new journey under a new leadership. No dramatic change of behaviour under pressure, no treating anyone different. A trust, from the start. A look and a furrowed brow from Shaun, but that was okay. You never settled with Shaun, but you began to understand what was coming, or what wasn't. That you might see him in a white vest, tracksuit trousers and black slip-on shoes. That he'd be in the gym before anyone else, boxing, on the leg-press. That there'd be times on the training pitch where he'd get sick of explaining something and we'd be chasing him to the next drill, because we were running short of time or he wanted to keep the intensity up. Him with his elbow up over his face if he was getting stuck in, to protect his face in the middle of a feisty drill, not afraid to catch you if you weren't looking out.

We sort of expected him to go ballistic when we got back to the changing rooms at half-time in that first game against England at 16–6 down. 10 points down and all the rest, because if Huw Bennett hadn't somehow got himself under Paul Sackey in the left-hand corner just before the break, none of the rest of it might ever have happened. The comeback, the history, the madness of Cardiff seven weeks later.

But there were no hairdryers. Trust, and small important details. Stick to your jobs, do a little more of this, know your roles and it will come. Keep the ball in play, kick to space rather than to touch, get rid of their attacking lineout, force them to give the ball back to us. Shaun didn't need to shout. The eyelids would roll back a little bit, and the shop front would be open. It was either come along or be shut out, simple as that.

Here come some clichés, but clichés contain truth somewhere down the line. Momentum is everything in rugby. When you've got it you want to keep it, but it's hard to hold on for long. When you lose it, it's even harder to get it back.

What changes it? One big moment. Forced, unforced, good or bad. One team doubles up on errors, the other finds something impossible from nowhere.

Huw's tackle was that. Even when England were still ahead, it suddenly felt like they were six points down. James Hook swivelling hips and pulling strings, Lee Byrne diving over in the corner, Mike Phillips putting up a kick, charging down Iain Balshaw and kicking ahead.

You could feel it. You rode it, this mad wave of adrenaline and belief. Me charging after Phillsy, right there on his inside shoulder, screaming for the ball as he appeared to be brought down just short, throwing my hands in the air and then picking him up by the shirt and dragging him up when he crashed over the line instead.

Then you remember strange little frozen moments. A big kerfuffle with Shaun when he ran down from the stands to the edge of the pitch when we were finally in front but a man down and he'd spotted some critical change he wanted to make to the defence. Rolling my ankle two minutes from the end and having to limp off, Ian Evans coming past me to fill the breach, me already thinking, am I going to get another chance here? Hearing the short, sharp explosions of noise from the Welsh fans in red pockets around the stadium, this vast silence from the home fans. How quiet it went so quickly at the end as the natives were silenced.

11 years on, in Paris, we'd start another Grand Slam campaign by being 16 points down in our opening game. That time, I would be the only one from Twickenham 2008 on the pitch. But Shaun and Gats would still be there – and Rob Howley, who of all the coaches was the one losing it most openly in the stands in south-west London.

And both times they let us celebrate it afterwards. That was the way it always was with Gats. When you win, you enjoy the night and you enjoy each other's company. You're not expected at breakfast at 7 a.m. He would put the onus on the players and the senior group a lot of the time. You're grown men, you make the decision.

We wouldn't always make the right choices in those early years. It took some of us a little bit of time to get there, on and off the field. But that night we went at it properly. Staying at the Richmond Gate Hotel on top of the hill by the park, looking down over the Thames, over Petersham, over towards Twickenham in the distance when the sun was out and sparkling its steel frame. Having a few on the coach back to the Vale and then deep into the morning.

I'd been pretty strict as a kid. I was so focused on doing everything right, being ultra-professional, driven by this fear of not making it, of falling short, that I didn't always take the enjoyment while it was there. When you're losing on tour in Argentina or not bucking the long-term trend against the All Blacks at home or witnessing Fiji make history at a World Cup, you don't particularly feel like celebrating.

Now I was ready to do it properly. Be in the moment, think about tomorrow when tomorrow arrived. Except because there was so much pent-up energy and nights out inside me, I'd go too far. Binge it rather than pace it. Get into the sort of scrapes that have you waking up thinking, uh-oh. Getting home without remembering the actual details of it.

It was always who I could keep up with rather than who could keep up with me. Rooming with Ian Gough, being put to bed by Adam Jones a few times. I was supposed to have hollow legs, being a tall man, but just because I'd discovered I liked to drink didn't mean I could drink. And anyway, I'd hope with fingers crossed I was cheeky but seldom disrespectful. I'd like to think because I'd worked hard, then people knew I was happy to be there. Whatever happened, I wasn't Shane Williams, asking Gats to step outside for a fight some time in the early hours. We thought nothing could make us happier than beating England at Twickenham, and then suddenly we had our smallest player wanting a punch-up with the new head coach. Tremendous.

That was it for me, for the next two games. Injured against Italy, injured against Scotland. Back for the trip to Dublin, to Croke Park. Feeling the expectation building, the whispers in Mumbles when you went out to get a coffee, when you turned on the TV – win this, and it's a Grand Slam decider. The nation caught flipping between the two extremes: dare to dream, and don't you dare dream.

A proper Ireland team, developing from a very good one into maybe their best of all. Brian O'Driscoll and Paul O'Connell and Ronan O'Gara; David Wallace and Denis Leamy and Jerry Flannery. Tommy Bowe, with us at the Ospreys; Shane Horgan and Rob Kearney. And a weird game, never feeling that it was away from us, not even when Mike Phillips was sin-binned for dropping a knee on Marcus Horan, when Martyn Williams got a yellow of his own for a trip on Eoin Reddan.

The difference, as it was so often in that period, was Shane. Handing off Andrew Trimble in no space at all and with no overlap, Tommy Bowe marking Tom Shanklin outside him. Trimble going backwards, because Shane was so quick and so powerful. That impossible ability to step and still move forwards at the same time.

Those last 10 minutes crawled. Hook kicking us a little further ahead, and us trying to burn time away. We'd started something in training called the minute drill, where you had to keep the ball for, yes, a minute. Maybe four rucks in that time. All about protecting possession rather than trying to punch holes. That afternoon it felt like we were doing minute drills for five minutes straight, all around the 40-metre mark on the right-hand side of the pitch. Knowing that each ruck was a potential game-loser. Aware of how time had slowed and the implications of making the sort of mistakes your brain and body want to make after 75 minutes of attritional Test rugby. Glancing up occasionally at referee Wayne Barnes and thinking, this is all going to come down to one man's interpretation of the rules in a great pile of bodies when time has lost all meaning, isn't it?

When Phillsy had scored his try at Twickenham, you were hearing about it for weeks. With Shane, you almost took it for granted – not from a lack of appreciation for what he could do when others couldn't, but because he was doing it so often.

And it wasn't just the tries he scored, although in that period he was golden: the one against Fiji in Nantes, the critical ones in Dublin and a week later, the ones in South Africa that summer where big lumpy Boks were trying to melt him from the side and he's just stepped inside and gone, when he took on Bryan Habana one-on-one. You're not supposed to do that to South Africans, particularly when they're the reigning world champions. The one against France in 2010 when he ran through one tackle, stepped inside like a rubber ball coming off a wall and then stepped inside again. It was all the ones he created for others. Making half a break to create the space a few phases later for someone else to cut through; pulling defenders to him even when he didn't have the ball.

There were times when you were trying to gallop up to find a support line and you had absolutely no idea where he was going and you'd be chasing his heels like everybody else. None of us ever minded because it always seemed to work. He very rarely took the wrong option. 90 per cent of the time he would make a dent or create critical space.

At other times it felt like schoolyard rugby. Shane, you stand over there, we'll give you the ball and you have to beat that guy one-on-one in no space. Like putting a big guy up against the smallest, except with Shane the small guy would always win. Knowing he was going to run round them. Making a complicated game look simple, all the time never acting like a superstar. A confident bloke, but never arrogant; a better drinker than the proposed Gatland title fight would suggest.

Someone too who had experience of these big games. Like Gethin Jenkins, like Ryan Jones, like Gavin Henson and Tom Shanklin, all that Grand Slam knowledge from back in 2005. Two World Cups in, threatening England in the 2003 tournament but no more. Having seen Steve Hansen come in as coach, Scott Johnson have an influence, Mike Ruddock in and out in no time at all, Gareth Jenkins. Buying totally into the new regime all the same. Sensing the difference. Realizing they could kick on again, that there was more magic to be had in their careers.

I felt lucky, as a 22-year-old still trying to hold onto a place. So many players who were redefining what their position was meant to bring. Gethin Jenkins tackling and jackalling like a blind-side, Mike Phillips a half-back but an extra back row too.

The week leading up to a Grand Slam game, you need all of that. Experience. A sense of calm. So much pressure suddenly there if you want to acknowledge it. Those who want to talk about it all the time, some who don't even want to say the words. Everyone pushing for selection, those who aren't making the starting XV not happy, and that being fine, because that shows they care. All the talk about our defence, about how we'd only conceded two tries in our first four games, us in the camp loving the simplicity of it, the clear communication from Gats, the confidence he felt and passed on to you.

I didn't want to ask for too many tickets for the France game. A couple for the family, no more. I thought of myself as a pup. How could I ask for more tickets when I hadn't done anything in the game? I didn't want anyone to think I thought I was entitled. Head down. Smash yourself in training. Wait for the week to tick by.

I wasn't a great sleeper before big games in those days. Me being a bit obsessive about what I should pack in my bag, what might go wrong and what I'd need to do about it. Always two pairs of boots, back then a third pair, just to be sure. Sure of what, I don't know. Whoever needed three pairs of boots in a game? We were playing in Cardiff, not Puerto Madryn. Had I somehow needed to source a pair on the day itself, I could have walked half a mile from the ground into town. But back then I took everything, because I didn't want to have to ask anyone else. I didn't want to show any vulnerability. Even on school tours I used to take an old lunch box stuffed with a full first-aid kit. No need to find a shop or bother the doctor. Always striving to be self-sufficient and independent.

So my kitbag was all packed the day before. Then the other traditions and superstitions. Bomb and Shane telling me I was coming to Tesco's with them for the usual pre-match activities.

'Why are we going to Tesco's?'

'Well, I need some razors, and you need to get the sweets.'

I was given charge of the trolley. And then we played what appeared to be a version of *Supermarket Sweep*, just for sweets.

'Don't worry, boy, we'll pay for it, but you've got to push it round and carry everything back to the hotel.'

That was the night before the game. What I used to call the Last Supper. Treat food for dinner, burger and chips or tempura-battered cod. Bags of gummy bears and chocolates, watching a movie in the team room. Grand Slam, what Grand Slam?

Me still so naive around what was about to unfold. Sensing the crescendo but not how loud it would be. Coming out of the team room downstairs that Saturday morning and seeing the lobby all cordoned off with red ropes and barriers, the big 'Good luck Wales!' sign in the middle of the lawn out front. Going to the gym to do my primer and when you came out, even more people being there to wish you well and see you off. Three or four deep as you walked out onto the drive, shouts and smiles and cans of beer being raised in your direction. The coach out front waiting for you, all white with a big red dragon down the side, wing mirrors adorned with ribbons. Like you're off to the ultimate rugby wedding.

A little window of tranquillity on the bus. Lads with their headphones on. Following the police outriders onto the road, the same drive you did the day before, when it was just you lot on the bus and no one else around. Hitting the M4 and seeing the flags and hearing the horns, and that illusion of tranquillity soon disappearing. Building up as you go through town, down through Leckwith, still moving, seeing the thousands walking with you, the pubs and the overflow and so much happiness and expectation.

It was like you were driving through the congregation on the way to a cathedral. It was like that feeling as a kid when you're in the nativity play at school and you walk down the aisle in the assembly hall and feel everyone staring at you and you've got to get on the stage. That times a million.

I could hear the white noise above when we were in the dressing rooms underneath the stadium. A muted sound of great steep stands filling up, bars packing out, feet marching in the same direction. Not wanting to go out too early to warm up, guessing at what would hit you when you ran out of the tunnel. When you're older, you simplify it. Worry about what's going to happen between the two white lines, not the stuff outside it. That afternoon, it was all new and fierce. Shit – hold it back, hold it back. Stay in until you want that energy to lift you and let you go.

I wasn't talking in that dressing room. I was always quiet in those early days. No one blasting music out of a stereo, because the music lovers had their headphones on. Some players comfortable in silence, the ones who aren't looking around for the others who want to chat the anxiety away instead. You don't need to say a lot when you're that far in – four games, four wins, one more to come. You've trained all week, you've been to the stadium 24 hours before to do your captain's run, walking out on the pitch, getting a fresh feel for the length of the grass and the sight lines. Gats letting it seep in over the course of those final days: if you don't know it by now, what can we say?

And we were at home. This was our place, our town, our country. You can win Grand Slams away. It's easier to lose them too.

*

0 mins: Wales 0–0 France
Hooky kick-off. Chase it hard. Get close to the ruck.
  Get in the game, don't chase it.

France in their 22. Szarzewski in front of me – get him, get a hold.

Let's get him in touch. Big effort.

Noise . . .

39 mins: Wales 9–3 France

This is a tight one. Trading pens.

The energy's good.

France just short of halfway.

Turnover, force them back with a kick into space.

Their 9's box-kicking. Read it, get back. Mine.

Take it.

Here they come, two blue jerseys, three . . .

He's off his feet, here. No? How else is he getting that ball?

Turnover.

France coming at us down the right. Defend it, just like Shaun's coached.

Pressure, real pressure. Penalty coming. Offside in defence.

Advantage.

Coming left at pace. Ouedraogo with it, he's moving.

High from Gav, high.

Another advantage. Penalty.

Élissalde with it . . . down the middle, 9–6, here comes half-time . . .

60 mins: Wales 9–9 France

Scrum to us, just inside the French half.

Tight game. We're not slowing up.

Quick ball for them.

Head up, Shanks staying connected and in the line. Filling space on the outside.

If they get this away . . .

Horrible pass from Skrela under pressure, behind Jauzion. He can't hold it.

Loose ball.

*Shane off his wing, seeing it before the rest of us. Shane booting
the loose ball. Three blue shirts round him.*

Shane pulling away.

Get there, Shane.

He's getting there . . .

*Chase him in. Chase him in. Could bounce off the post, this
kick. Got to be sure. Could be a tackle. Got to hit the ruck.*

Try!

Noise all around.

*The ref wants to check the grounding. Look up at the big screen
for the replay, heart thumping.*

He's definitely touched this down.

The roar. Try!

Jonesy with the conversion. 16–9.

Only one score in it. Run back. Get ready for the restart.

65 mins: Wales 19–9 France

Scrum France, five metres out.

*Let's have a pop at them here, boys. The scoreboard gives us the
chance to have a go. Roll the dice, it's worth the risk.*

Big shove. Go forward. Pressure building. Getting tighter.

Over the ball.

Past the ball.

Our ball!

Come on now – protect the ruck.

Phillsy stepping back. Big boot, into touch.

Another roar . . .

75 mins: Wales 22–12 France

Socks down. Cramp flickering.

Their lineout, 15 metres out.

French error. Loose ball in front of me.

Hands on it. Pop pass to Mark Jones on a short ball.

Boycey away. Going, still going.

Blue shirts after him.

40 metres out, 30 metres out.
20, five.
Brought down. Ball loose.
They exit.
Our ruck, just outside their 22. Me working back to midfield.
Martyn Williams picking up. Gap on the edge of the ruck.
Nugget is away!
Space.
Nothing ahead of him . . .
Try!

Final score: Wales 29–12 France

*

You pile back into the dressing room, and you're exhausted but filled with this mad energy. Like you could do it all again if you had to, like you're not sure whether you want to hug someone or fight them.

And then Warren sat us down, and we waited to be told how good we were. How far we'd come. How pleased he was with us. Instead he looked at us, and said, enjoy this one, and get ready to work towards the next one.

That was the approach to the media too. We're two years away from being a good side. Initially you think you've misheard. And then you think, he could have bigged himself up here. Less than six months ago we were getting knocked out in the group stages of a World Cup, and now we're winning a Grand Slam. This is the moment of triumph. This is the day to go to town.

He knew what he was doing. He knew there was the makings of a team there waiting for him when he came in. He knew what he personally had done and what he hadn't done. And he was tempering expectations, within our group and for all the supporters dancing about outside. When you make a comment and say the same thing on television and to the newspapers, you're communicating with your own people in two different ways. It always cuts through. This was Gatland for the long term – not another short-term spike, not another crash and burn. Settle in, boys, we've only just got started.

I hope I appreciated that day in the moment. I had this weird sense of disappointment that I'd only been involved in three games, that I only had partial claim to a Grand Slam. That the ever-presents should be celebrating more. Not a fraud, but a part-timer.

I know I committed to the aftermath. The official after-match function at the Hilton, then piling into town, probably Revs and Oceania, wherever the senior guys would know someone and have a word and we could all follow them in. Memories getting washed away, everyone around you all on the same wave. No one caring about the rain and the puddles and the wind.

My tipple in those days was vodka and Coke, with the caveat that anything alcoholic would work after a certain time. If you were sweating and it was going to give me a bad head in the morning, that was the one for me. Starting off on the celebratory champagne on the pitch, sticking an empty bottle away for a souvenir, hoping there would be a story in there, somewhere. Back to the Vale in the early hours at some point. Trusting in each other to get every man home. You never leave a teammate on the battlefield.

Part of me wishes I had the self-discipline not to drink anything on those special nights and so be able to remember it all, these days and years on. Scary thing is, we'd probably have drunk just as much had we lost. It'll sound like the old cliché: win or lose, on the booze. But that pressure has to come out somewhere. We were young men. We needed some sort of release, and no one was paying for a psychiatrist. Without it we'd have gone stir-crazy. It would have come out somewhere else less controlled and less benign.

The social CCTV wasn't the same then. If you had a camera on your phone it was fine for shots in daylight but not designed for videos inside dark clubs, even if the person you were trying to film was six foot six and in a dinner suit in the middle of dancefloor with everyone else in their best clobber. Certain tunes just hitting everyone the same way – the Killers and 'Mr Brightside', the Automatic. On Grand Slam night when the Stereophonics come on, then all bets are off. You may as well be back in the stadium.

As you mature and look back, it all goes so quick. Seven weeks it takes, from start to finish. From opening game in the Six Nations in early February to the decider in late March and the first kiss of spring. You glance back at that long campaign at the end and it feels as if you could squeeze those weeks of training and playing into one memory. The week building up to a Grand Slam day sort of compresses together, and the day itself is gone in the blink of an eye. Maybe that's the pressure, maybe it's the happiness at the end of it. The celebrations.

It's weird thinking about it again, watching the game back. I'd grown up dreaming of playing for Wales, being desperate to be in Cardiff for a Grand Slam. Then it comes to pass, and it's like it happened to someone else.

The strangeness too of thinking that you haven't just been a passive part of this, but you've helped make it happen. This mood across the country, the jumping around in living rooms in towns and villages you'll never go to. The absolute mayhem all around you in the city centre, spilling from the stadium into the streets and bars and clubs, the chip shops and the taxis, the late buses and the hotel rooms with three to a bed and four laid out on the floor.

When I watched the 2005 Grand Slam as a fan, I knew I wanted to be at the heart of it. I could sense the relationship between the 75,000 of us in the stands and the players on the pitch. I didn't even think of the television audience that day. It was all the visceral stuff around me. The years as a kid obsessing about playing for Wales – not just the under-16s, or the 18s, or the 20s, but the real deal. I wanted to be on that side of the white line. I didn't think I would, which is why I also studied part-time for a degree in law. Intrigue and aspiration pushing me on.

But a hope, and a desire, all coming together that wet Saturday in a wet March. Shane scoring his try, turning back round from the posts towards us, and it going sort of slow-motion so he appeared to be levitating in front of me. Running towards him, the crowd behind him going mental, Shane being lifted by the roar of the crowd . . . and me catching him.

There's things you dream of achieving, and then they happen like that. You in that moment, in a way you could never have imagined.

There was someone else on the pitch that day who could have the same impact on a game as Shane.

From someone who saw him up close, there's very few people in sport, very few in rugby who can move like they're gliding, not running. Who have so much time with a ball it's like they've pressed pause on the game and they're just stepping past other figures frozen around them.

I played with Gavin Henson for Ospreys and Wales. I saw the stuff you might not have seen. The athlete he was, the effort he put in. The skill-set he had: attacking with ball in hand, defending like a tank, with his boot. Maybe you got distracted by all the other stuff, the hair, the silver boots, the fake tan. The extra-curricular activities. Me? I felt fortunate to have been there. He was so good it was scary.

I was always young around him. I came into the Ospreys and his profile was massive – what he'd done against England and Ireland in the 2005 Six Nations. He was different – not anti-establishment, but a man of his own volition. Cavalier in some ways but in the positive sense, a maverick who did things because they made perfect sense to him.

Some people thought he was outspoken. Looking back, he was showing his experience. He'd had more time around people than me, more time around elite rugby. You play a certain number of matches and you realize how the game works, how some coaches and officials are going to behave. He was candid about how he didn't like certain senior player groups, saying that they were yes-men and all that stuff. Well, I was involved in a lot of those, and I don't blame him, because I understand his point.

With Gav, it sometimes felt like the more people told him what to do, the more he wanted to do the opposite. He looked flash, but he trained harder than most and looked after himself better than most.

He was shyer than anyone on the outside realized, too. He needed to be told by the coaches how good he was, and the whole look was part of that. A Bridgend boy whose character reflected where he came from. Alan Phillips used to called them the Fab Four – the lads who were all fond of a spray tan and a dab of hair wax. Shane, Lee Byrne, James Hook, Mike Phillips. Gav made it the Fab Five. It worked for him, so I couldn't see the problem. It was harmless enough at the time, it was funny, entertaining. If you've got five blokes like that playing that well, why would you intervene with whatever routines they feel they need to do?

Wasted talent? He won two Grand Slams. He played for the Lions against the All Blacks. And he was authentic, to me, even if that upset people. I remember him leaving training once, just because he'd had enough, but there were other times when Warren Gatland would trust him, ask him how long we should train for, and go with his suggestion.

You saw the talent, and so you wanted his approval on the pitch. We played Harlequins that Grand Slam year at the Liberty, and I broke through to throw a pretty decent 12-metre pass off my left hand to Gav before he put Shane into the right-hand corner.

For that I got an 'okay, well done kid'. And that felt good. The praise wasn't wasted on me.

8

ANRHYDEDD | HONOUR

The first time I sat down to watch the Lions was in the school assembly hall. Maybe the most popular assembly of all time: an early-morning gathering in front of a big telly on wheels. Knowing this was special, that it was up there with the World Cup and the Olympics as something you looked forward to and couldn't miss.

The dreams of a child. Maybe one day I could play rugby. The dreams of a teenager: maybe I could get a cap for Wales. And it keeps moving on, as you grow older: you win two caps, and you wonder if you might one day go to a World Cup; you go to a World Cup, and you wonder if your form and career might coincide with a Lions tour.

Back then it was all a million miles away. Seeing the black-and-white photos of the Welshmen on the tours to New Zealand in 1971 and South Africa in 1974, coming down the steps of airplanes, clutching luggage. Beards and moustaches, big lapels. Hearing the stories of the '99' call, of Willie John McBride, the Pontypool front row. Jim Telfer and his Everest speech and all the stuff that went on in '97.

I'd watched all the tour videos and DVDs like everyone else. Thinking I'd seen it all, not aware then of all the stuff you never get to see, how they manage to keep the mystique and the honesty there as well as the cameras. That there'd be players who would lean towards each other with a nudge or a chuckle when someone went off on a monologue, whispering, 'Fucking hell,

1. Lowri, always the doting big sister, with me some time in the late 1980s. These styles were very of the moment in south Wales at the time.

2. Always good to get a red jersey on.

3. Getting in a decent water-based recovery session on a family holiday in Spain.

4. Me and my dad, at his place at the kitchen table.

5. You'll have seen better lineout takes. Llandovery College at home to Millfield at Tredegar Close.

6. The top of Table Mountain, on a Swansea schoolboys' tour of South Africa in 2001. That country would become ever-present in my senior career.

7. Game-face on, and I couldn't be happier – representing Wales under-16s at St Helen's, the home of Swansea RFC, where my dad and grandfather played.

8. Lineout drills pre-match for Wales under-18s at Brewery Field, Bridgend. A proper rugby ground, and one the Ospreys have returned to on occasion.

9. Enjoying the sunshine post-match at the Under-19 World Championship in South Africa, 2005. All ended up turning professional or semi-pro: *(top row, from left)* future Ospreys flanker Tom Smith, Ricky Williams, David Flanagan, Ed Shervington, Aled Thomas; *(bottom row, from left)* Aled Brew, Tim Riley, future Ospreys second row Alun Wyn Jones, Andrew Bishop.

10. Wales under-21s after winning the Grand Slam in 2005. Me *(top left)*, sweaty scrum-cap still in place. It was a good party that night. And the next day, I went to the Millennium Stadium to watch the senior side seal their Grand Slam too.

11. My first cap for Wales in 2006, in a home away from home in Welsh-speaking Patagonia. Lee Byrne and Adam Jones in support.

12. A decent dink to the bodywork in a 2007 match against France, courtesy of Lionel Nallet's elbow at a ruck. Nothing that won't heal up with some ice, stitches and a beer afterwards.

13. 2007, with my Ospreys teammates. The great thing about winning the Magners League is that you're not short of the sponsor's product to celebrate with.

14. Croke Park, Dublin, 2008, and the Triple Crown, with the Grand Slam to come against France in Cardiff a week later. Helped along by Shane Williams's hand-off try and one of Adam Jones's more experimental hair-dos, just visible on the left.

15. With Paul O'Connell and Lee Mears *(right)*, on the 2009 Lions tour to South Africa. An education, an adventure and an opportunity to play alongside one of the best.

16. World Cup quarter-final against France, Eden Park, 2011. I'm still not over it.

that's a DVD moment . . .' Not fully aware then of the real privilege of being on the other side. What it's like to see the workings of it all from the inside.

I never had a Lions jersey, as a kid. I only ever had one Wales one. Me being a bit weird and stubborn about it: I'm only going to wear another of those jerseys if I'm actually playing in it. I had plenty of club jerseys, Canterburys, Cotton Traders. I had some nice Super Rugby ones, because you wore those round the club and in training sessions and they felt like collectors' items. 'Oh, now that's a nice one . . .'

And I never wanted to think about too much, when the 2009 tour was coming round. We had the Grand Slam the previous spring, but I've always hated it when people start making big Lions shouts too early. A year in any sport is a lifetime. Don't ask now; when we get to a few months out, maybe raise the question then. And come the start of 2009 I'd only been playing international rugby for two and a half years. I didn't have the ignorance or arrogance to think I might be in contention.

Here's the thing too. In the Six Nations that precedes a Lions, every player in every squad from Wales, Ireland, England and Scotland gets fitted out for kit. No one knows who might actually be selected, and they do it quite surreptitiously – going into each camp, oh, we're doing this for everyone. That's the first shot across the bows, the first to raise the tension. The other is when the head coach pops in to your country's training session, shakes a few hands, says he's just there for a little recce. Ears prick up, then. Performances sharpen. Walks become jogs and jogs become runs.

It can be a dangerous thing, the thoughts that wriggle into your head. You can't say to yourself, I'm going to get on that tour. You have to wind it back. Okay. I know I have to play for the Ospreys to be selected for Wales. I've got to be on it in training to make the starting XV. I've got to stay on it to stay in the team. Then I have to be outstanding for Wales, not just against one nation, but consistently, against all of them. Not a rite of passage on it but a definite process. No one has a divine right to be picked by the Lions.

Then you find out, and it's all a sudden whirlwind. We were with Wales, training at the Vale. Not in a team room or lounge, watching it come through on Sky Sports like in later years. Out on the pitch, and a quick meeting called. Boys, we're just going to let you know . . .

You're so pleased but trying not to let it all come out. Photos and cheesy grins, a fair bit more hair for me back then. And then the practicalities, beginning with a pack that comes through the post with forms to fill in that have nothing to do with romance and glamour and everything to do with National Insurance contributions and how much income tax you might have to pay under another country's fiscal system.

There are the freebies. This time it was a special edition iPod, engraved with our names and the tour details. That's still in its box. Hampers to your family, a nod to the time you'll be spending away from home.

There's the first meet-up, which is less like a rugby camp and more like trying to organize in one day the biggest wedding you've ever been to. Us Welsh boys all travelling from the Vale down to Pennyhill Park in Surrey in a minibus, all in bad bootcut jeans and the sort of shirts that suggested it was 1995 rather than 2009. Good players, poor dressers.

You're in the machine, then. Being measured up for three suits, the tailors delivering them for final alterations the next day, the props trudging round with sleeves down to their knees because they've calibrated all other dimensions from their chest measurements. Having your legs laser-scanned for compression socks for the flights. Photos taken for official programmes and marketing, films for TV, newspapers and radio and websites queueing up for their five minutes. Trying to find a moment to take a breath and grab some food. Understanding now why they'd called it Messy Monday.

There was familiarity around me as well. 12 Welshmen in the

original selection, Warren Gatland and Shaun Edwards and Rob Howley and Neil Jenkins all coaching. Phil Vickery taking the mick out of my accent, but in an affectionate way. A senior player not saying, I'll look after you, but happy to point you in the right direction. As a young player it doesn't lighten the load, but you do know you're not being left in the lurch.

And the way I was, there was no one I was desperate to be friends with. No ambition to hang out with anyone in particular. Not like the first day at a new school, because everyone knows what they're there for. A wide-eyed smile from me, a polite nervous laugh. How's it going? Yeah, okay.

I am pretty insular like that anyway. I felt respect for everyone there, but I wasn't intimidated by anyone. Not being up to the standard, making a few mistakes early on in training – that's what I worried about. Being uptight. Letting myself down. Not worrying about the track record of those watching on. Focusing on myself. Alun Wyn, can you do this?

The rugby is the comfort, in the end. So much to deal with around the schedule and build-up that you just want to stick a ball under your arm and feel grass under your feet. It's the game that is the great leveller. Once you were playing it became irrelevant who had achieved what, where they were from, what they had done.

There's things I learned quickly about being a Lion. You come together from four nations, but you need to keep your identity too. The individuality of your character. I think of myself as a Lion, but a Welshman playing as a British and Irish Lion, just as I'm an Osprey playing for Wales. It's about celebrating where you come from and who you represent, rather than just being swallowed up by an organization.

Yes, you become a custodian. A guardian of the traditions. It's a club you know you could never leave, even if you wanted to. But you are there as you, not a watered-down version. Just as Sir Chris Hoy could win multiple golds for Team GB and yet still be

Scottish, so you are with the Lions. You have a foot in both camps. That's where the strength comes from.

It's the same with all the fine words, the video montages, the new anthems. Playing together is the unifying factor, not the bollocks you chat before and after. Words are great if you act upon them. If you don't, they're empty.

The more you play, the more you see it. You pull on the same jersey with the same Test date embroidered on the chest and face the same team. That's what it's about. Rugby, not rhetoric.

I was naive in other ways. I was so focused on doing well for myself that I didn't worry about who might be ahead of me, about who might get picked. I didn't think too much about the combinations that were starting to settle, how the balance was starting to fall between midweek and Saturday sides.

You appreciate those around you as rugby players. What Paul O'Connell could do. What a great athlete David Wallace was. What a specimen Tom Croft turned out to be. You got to know others as men. Rooming with Lee Mears, him on the phone most of the time like a shorter, more athletic version of Arthur Daley. Joe Worsley unpacking one bag and then pulling from the other his own top-end Tempur mattress and laying it down on top of his bed. Finding out this destructive blind-side also had grade eight piano. Andy Powell joining in a game of football keepy-ups, chasing the ball round as the circle got bigger and bigger, eventually grabbing hold of it and punting it over the fence like Peter Kaye in the John Smith's advert. 'HAVE IT!' The front five? They're almost always decent guys. Paid to make a mess of things for the opposition. Dependable as a result.

Me? Looking back, I was green. I was going from medium fish in medium pool to a small fish in among the sharks. At the Ospreys I'd been cheeky and competitive, but respectful. When we landed in South Africa I just knew I had to make it clear that I'd always give it everything. The easiest way to show you don't care is by not trying. At the same time, thrashing yourself into the ground when you don't have to gets people thinking you're daft. Endearing, but stupid. I didn't do it to impress people, but because it was my fall-back. If anyone wanted to ask me why I was killing myself, I'd think, well, shouldn't we all be doing this?

And if you ever wobbled, if you ever doubted that approach, there was always Shaun Edwards to snarl in your face. The Lions resonated with him. He'd played for Great Britain in too many classic games in rugby league. He knew what that meant to him and he understood how you had to step it up.

With Wales, he had always been wired. Now he was prime-time Shaun. On the training pitch he'd either be running or doing the fast walk, straight legs with arms pumping the air, like a regimental sergeant major, but he was much scarier than that. Charging round sessions, blowing his whistle when he spotted anything that dipped below his standards.

'What the fuck is that, lad?'

You might be familiar with the clip from the third Test when Ugo Monye has picked off an interception and is racing away, and the cameras on the sidelines spot Shaun going bananas, trying to clench his fist while also holding a clipboard, and even though Ugo has half the pitch to run, Shaun's already lost himself totally in the moment.

That's how he coached, too. With pure emotion, with the passion of a man who's coming on to play, not advise. He'd be so caught up in it sometimes that he'd be telling us about the drill while facing the other way with a strong wind howling across the pitches. You wouldn't be able to hear a word he was saying, and then he'd turn round and blow his whistle and look absolutely furious you weren't face-down in what he'd asked for.

'GO!'

'Erm, what are we doing?'

We'd get it on the second attempt. And he had such honesty in his approach that you went with him all the way. On the very rare occasion – maybe once or twice on the entire tour – that he'd missed something, or not quite been prepared for some strange eventuality, he would say: *boys, this is on me.*

When he spoke, you went quiet. When you trained he got louder, and everyone knew what they were doing because they were listening harder as well. He didn't try to be your friend. He would go at 100 miles an hour, and you would have to keep up. And that dysfunction reflected what defence is like sometimes. In a way, it was priming you without knowing you were being primed.

You need people like Shaun when you're touring South Africa. I'd been there before with schoolboy and age-group teams, and I understood there was nowhere else in rugby quite the same.

You can tour Australia, and a lot of people you meet have never watched rugby union. But you tour South Africa and you feel it. This is their game. Invented by the English, filled with flair by the Welsh, taken to the heart by South Africans.

Taken to the gym, too. On tour with Wales in 2008, I'd tried to take Bakkies Botha on in a maul. He hadn't been slow in responding, and I left him alone after that. A national team that were reigning world champions, Botha and Victor Matfield a second-row combination that was less the spine than the pecs and lats and traps too. John Smit, capable of playing 1, 2 or 3. 4 or 5 is easy. Right across the front row is not. You switch from loose-head to tight-head and it's like using your wrong hand to do everything. Seriously impressive.

A nation behind them that would wave at you on the coach as you approached stadiums, wait until you smiled at them and then make the throat-slitting gesture. A private school system that seems to churn out huge men who have never looked teenage and never will.

On that earlier trip with Swansea Schools we'd gone to Grey College, the school that produces so many Springboks. Same age as us south Wales lads, looked four years older. That happens when you've got a strength and conditioning coach at a school, and when even the boys who don't play rugby are twice the size of your mates back home. All those farmers, strong from the cradle, same as New Zealand, same as west Wales.

You could sense the revenge in the air for the 1997 Lions tour. Almost as if they'd been counting down the 12 years since Matt Dawson's dummy pass and try in the first Test, Jeremy Guscott's drop goal in the second, the holes that Scott Gibbs knocked in them and the slices Neil Jenkins took off them.

And so you try to find strength in response. Coming off the bench in the first game up in Rustenburg, the ground a concrete bowl, the air thinner than back home. Sneaking over the try line from either 50 metres or five centimetres out, depending on the tricks your memory wants to play. Taking everything you physically can from those early matches, coming together and hoping you're going to get up to speed fast, but realizing that until you play you never really know how fit you are. There's no truer test than a bloke being there with a whistle and the other 15 blokes not wearing the same jersey as you.

You feel the combinations within the team in those first tour matches, but you can sense them in training too. It's almost knowing your trade more than vocalizing it; if someone fills a space in the defensive line or leaves a space for you to fill, you respond without thinking. If someone's doing a switch and you run a short line, you just react.

In a game of touch rugby, you can always spot the people that have played rugby in a good team. They make it look a little bit easier than the ones that haven't. That stands out even in the elite level. On the Lions you could talk through an attacking play off a lineout in 10 seconds and then go and do it immediately on the training pitch, because everyone's at that level. There will always be little anomalies or execution errors but combinations develop around you all the same.

It's hard, squeezing in the right level of prep. Two games a week and it's never the learning that's the issue, but the de-learning. You've got finite changes or calls, and it's hard to forget the ones you've already done. Some things will double over. You're okay on habit and you're the same on this new level. Others it's big jigsaw pieces to slot in, particularly in a set piece, and that's when the head work ratchets right up.

You can't force it. As the weeks went by and the miles racked up, the hotel rooms and the restaurants, I didn't try to spend more social time with players I might be picked alongside. Maybe I was a little insecure. I didn't want anyone to see me gravitating to the lads I already knew, like I couldn't handle it all. I genuinely liked having breakfast on my own. When I was eating I didn't want to be talking.

Sometimes I was just being a grumpy bastard. I've got that in the locker. Other times you just need a little alone time on a tour like that, some space for you on your own, wherever you can find it. Get your coffee, get your eggs, get your toast. So I'd play it fair the other way round too. If there wasn't a free table, I'd go up to the one with boys on and ask, *okay if I sit here?*

You have an inkling, whether you're going to get picked for the first Test. The XV they choose for the Saturday game the week before, whether you've dropped a bollock and the lack of communication from some coaches can all give you an inkling. You know the front-runners for certain positions and there's always a few you assume are nailed on.

I wasn't arrogant or ignorant enough to think I was in. There is no nod or subtle hint in advance. And then you walk into the team meeting, and the world has moved on since your international debut three summers before, because now it's not on an overhead projector but an actual PowerPoint on a proper screen.

But it's still the coach and a piece of paper that tells you first. Ian McGeechan, in his blue-and-green Lions top, popping on his gold-rimmed reading glasses and looking down at this folded printout in his hand. Us all sitting in front of him in the conference room, some in t-shirts and jeans, me in my training gear. Easier that way.

Going through it in numerical order. 'The Test 22 is as follows. 1: Gethin. 2: Lee Mears. 3: Vicks. 4: Alun Wyn Jones.'

You don't really hear the rest – Paul O'Connell beside you,

Mike Phillips and Stephen Jones at half-back, Jamie Roberts 12. Lee Byrne full-back. And no one says anything. Everyone's trying not to flinch.

It all gets very real, very quickly, from that point. A thickening of the experience. Not just the kit, not just tour games. A Test. The real thing.

You might have been together for 10 weeks. Suddenly it's all about three weeks. Three matches. Almost like a season within the season.

Durban's a nice city. The beach, the surf. The fresh air.

You don't think about any of that. At that stage of my young career I was still trying to do everything with my prep. Opposition, defence, attack. Lineout calls, targeted defence. When you gain experience, you get a better balance. Focus on yourself first. Know the core elements of the game and then slot the fine detail around it. I was still only three years into international rugby then. I was yet to work out that if you have one eye over there, then you're going to miss something over here.

And the weight of responsibility is as present as always, when you're younger. Not a Six Nations match, where if something goes wrong you've got the next week, and if you're dropped you've got the summer tour and the autumn and another Six Nations a year later. It's a Lions Test. Get this one wrong and your series is over. Then it's a four-year wait. There's a pool of four nations to choose from. The odds close off a little more every time you let yourself think about it.

I didn't really feel I belonged. I still don't, to be honest. Imposter syndrome, where one part of my brain is telling me I can do what I've been chosen to do, and another is saying, 'What the hell are you doing here?' I'm a fan first. I'm not saying that to fake humility or appear humble. If I didn't have imposter syndrome, I'm not sure I would have made four tours. I would have done that first one, felt relieved and sat back. I had so much pride in being a custodian of that jersey that I could see the dangers of it. I could see that you could do very well out of that image if you wanted to, without giving enough back. Moments where you watched an individual and thought, shit, they don't show this on the DVD. You get picked for the Lions, and it's an honour and a privilege, but it's more than that too.

No need at least to call home – Mum and Dad were out there already. Mum all maternal calm: 'Very well done now, look after yourself, hope you enjoy it.' One of the reasons why I am as I am, a parent who shows controlled pride rather than blowing it out of proportion. Never over the top, and that always helped. Although had you seen my dad in his blue fleece hat with the red Viking horns sticking out of it, you might not have sensed that vibe. You wouldn't have thought he was a solicitor. A statement hat, worn first to embarrass me, then retained so I could spot him up in the stands from anywhere on the pitch.

I roomed with Paul O'Connell the night before the game. I wasn't a good sleeper back then. I remember being impressed by his unruffled demeanour, plus his level of organization. All his socks in one bag, all his shorts in another. Everything decanted into smaller bags within the bigger bags.

I lay there and I thought about Kings Park, how we'd gone there on that schoolboys' tour and seen the Crusaders play the Sharks, us sitting in one of the open ends, looking up at the massive steep-sided grandstands as much as the pitch. Thinking, that was only six years ago. And now I'm here.

It went fast, that morning. The jerseys presented to us a couple of hours before by Willie John McBride. White hair and this charisma about him still. McGeechan's captain on that 1974 tour. All of us hanging on his every carefully delivered word.

'For a lot of you today, this is your first Test for the Lions. You've got here. Now it's about finishing the job.'

Looking round the room. Shaun Edwards at the back, foot tapping, ready to jump out of his seat and tear down the tunnel.

'There are times today when you're going to have to reach into the very depths of your soul to get to that ball. To help the guy. When you come off the field today, if you can look your teammate in the eye and say, I couldn't have given any more, no one can ask anything else.

'Go and do it now. Go and live it. Because you'll never forget it.'

And then it began, and it was rugby on fast-forward. Wild animals charging at you. The noise barrelling down from the stands. Shaun saying to us before we went out, don't let them go for it. Whatever we do, we have to beat them on the fold. Beat them on the fold. And the first scrum they get inside the 22, and we let John Smit come round the corner and score by the posts.

Oh. We didn't beat them on the fold.

Typical South Africa at the time, and that made it worse. A bellyful of angst, and they just kept ticking over with penalties. Quite happy picking up scrum penalty after scrum penalty. Ruan Pienaar banging them over.

You're hanging in there, then. Jean de Villiers somehow stopping Ugo Monye in the left-hand corner when we all thought he'd got the ball down. Roberts busting through, Brian O'Driscoll outside him, Tom Croft inside him. Try.

Penalty. Penalty.

They didn't play with a huge amount of width. Fine. Why would you, if you're always a good 10 points ahead?

It hurts when the Springboks turn the screw by doing Springbok things to you. Big scrums. Long place kicks. Driving mauls. When Heinrich Brüssow went over at the start of the second half, it felt like he was being driven over by half the nation.

We were always in there. Four line breaks from us, none from the Springboks. Croft going over again. Me off on 69 minutes, Donncha O'Callaghan on. Mike Phillips slicing over.

And we could have made it, on another day. But we didn't, and you sit there in the dressing room, listening to the coaches tell you how we had them every time we went through the phases, how their lot were out on their feet for the last 20 minutes. The breath still heaving in your chest, socks round your ankles, pulling the white tape off your legs. Leaning back on the wall under your name-plate, the hanger with your suit and tie, the strip lighting in your eyes.

The what-ifs. What if there'd been another five minutes? What if one more of those line breaks had stuck? If that ball had stayed under someone's arm rather than being ripped?

Thinking about the combinations that had worked. Roberts and O'Driscoll. The players who'd come off bigger names than they'd run on: Phillips and Croft. And knowing that you started and got replaced, and that the questions would have to be asked. At this level, you don't go to participate. You go out there to win.

You know they're going to make changes in the front row, when you've been penalized plenty at the scrum. There's no second chances when you're one down in a three-match Test series. You've got to get it right in the next.

So there's no shock, but it still stings like hell. I was told 20 minutes before the team announcement for the second Test. And knowing late was better than knowing from way out. Less time to wallow in it. Having to get on with it. Rationalize. I'm on the bench. I'm still involved.

I was given a reason. You were too late in to a driving maul. Not the first one, nor the second one that had marched half the pitch and led to the Brüssow try, but another, and that mattered too. In public, the explanation was less specific. We just feel we need the additional bulk that Simon Shaw brings.

And you have to take that. Where's arguing going to get you? The hardest job is not being involved at all. You see some players going off reservation because they're elite athletes and they're all about being at the top. You can't blame them for it, but it's a true test of character.

The players coming in are all up. You can feel the vibe coming off them. We're going to make a difference. We're going to get the 'W'.

And all around it feels different. Now you're in Pretoria rather than Durban. From the beaches and ocean to pitches where there's barely a blade of green grass. All the pitches short and burnt yellow. Another deliberate challenge from the hosts: right, you've done sea level, now come back to the veld, where the air is thin and the lungs burn and the opposition kickers can blast it half a pitch without getting a bead on.

You train for the altitude. You have masks and special training sessions. You tell yourself it's only 1,000 metres up. And then you try dragging your 120-kilogram body through two halves of 40 minutes, 15 other blokes trying to knock you back into the sheds, you trying to cut them down and wrestle them and shove them into their own stands. You can train all you want at sea level and it never gives you enough prep for altitude. It's a placebo, if you go with it. Not much more. Accept it, know your limitations, push past them.

International rugby is quick. On the pitch, when the referee blows his whistle. In the week before.

You don't get the chance to look around and take it in. You want to fix the speed after a defeat, find some way of getting up to the external pace or slowing it all down. You run out for a Test with the Lions and the occasion and intensity can feel like a physical weight on your shoulders. Meetings become more serious. The days accelerate. It's like you're running downhill to the moment of kick-off and then uphill again when it all starts.

You felt it in Pretoria. You could smell it in the air: the meat on the braais, the lager on breath. Smoke rising into the sky. The brief warmth of a winter's day sunshine giving way to a clear cold night.

Even the pitch smells different. You don't see much tweed and you don't see much champagne. Stadiums so steep the crowd are almost on top of you, as if you're the gladiators and they're the emperors and senators.

That game was unforgettable if you watched from those stands, if you were in the pub on a warm June afternoon back home, on your sofa. The injuries – five Lions taken to hospital. Adam Jones and his dislocated shoulder from the Bakkies clear-out. Gethin and his smashed eye socket. Brian O'Driscoll concussed. The indiscretion from Schalk Burger at the very start. The way it was in our grasp and then slipping, the penalty at the end against Ronan O'Gara, the long-range penalty that took it all away. Morné Steyn's kick going up, hearing the shouts from their players, the start of a celebration, then the roar of the crowd catching up and swamping it, like a great wave picking up a surfer and carrying them away.

In the midst of it all? From the bench for the first 45 minutes, head down in the madness for the last 35 minutes? You don't realize, not at the time. It's just the game. Your mate comes off with blood streaming down his face, they throw someone else on. Stretchers coming towards you, oxygen masks and medics with pale faces, and you glance at them as they go past and then look straight back to the storm itself. You're not logging it – the cumulative pain, the emotional toll. It's just you and the moment and the next ruck you have to hit. The next tackle, the next chance to suck in air.

So it sort of passes you by, the controversy that kicks on off the back. Should Burger have been red-carded? Was that definitely a try for Jaque Fourie in the corner? Did Bakkies deserve his ban, and what the hell was their coach Peter de Villiers saying afterwards?

Bakkies was a big man. He always hit hard, and Bomb had been trying to steal their ball. It was a hell of a wipe. I did think it was instructive that the players wore their 'Justice for Bakkies' armbands the following week, but there were no 'Justice for Schalk' campaigns.

I didn't blame the referee. The TMOs? The technology? That's the vagaries and vicarious liabilities of human interpretation, because it still comes down to interpretation, in the end. You could have 10 refs on the pitch and you'd get four different outcomes. Rugby is a game of laws and rules. Fine. But there's no room for empathy, and that's needed sometimes. A ref can make mistakes, just like we do – the misplaced pass, the tackle where you slip off.

And you're selfish, in a benign way. You want to get on the

pitch as soon as you can. You sit there in the aftermath and you obsess over it all. You don't move on, not for months. Years sometimes. Thoughts that are contradictory but still real: if I had fucking started, we wouldn't have been in this position; Shawsy getting man of the match, me knowing he deserved it.

But this is the thing. You're teammates but you're also direct rivals. I wanted us to be honest, to be genuine. This idea that you might pass a fellow Lion in the street in 30 years and just exchange a look – it's romantic, but it gets in the way of a better truth.

There'll be lads you don't get on with. You'll still be civil to them. There's others that you've roomed with and you develop a genuine affection for. You still won't be messaging them every week, and that's fine. You're together for a special but finite time. You go back to trying to ruin them when your nations next come up against each other. The more you respect someone, the more you want to give your best against them. You remember those bonds but you don't try to play up and pretend to be some-one's bestie. You wouldn't take any of them for granted.

It's the same as me not speaking to many of my primary school mates any more. I'm only in contact with one lad I played rugby with at college. You haven't fallen out; you're just not together any more. The Lions isn't like we're all spies and it's secret nods and winks. I don't want to erode the myths and mys-tique or the true feel of it. Maybe a more prosaic truth, but a more accurate one. There's nothing wrong with enjoying the simplicity of it sometimes.

So. That inability to move on, the pain of being 2–0 down in a series you could have won. The frustrations and the time away from home and what's happened to your teammates. All that will leak out somehow, and it happened in Johannesburg, in that pur-gatory between the second and third Tests.

It always starts innocently enough. We were offered the chance to do a day safari. One coach going to the game reserve, the other – with plenty of Welsh and Irish on board, a good few stragglers too – heading back into town, into Nelson Mandela

Square, into the bars and pubs and hours of mischief and mistakes.

A lot of the stuff that had been building up came out that night. One of the team analysts ended up in the pool with all his mobile phones in his pockets. Andy Powell can take the rap for that one, but it wasn't my finest hour either, if I'm honest. A mate who was out with us said afterwards that he could see I needed to let off steam. Fuelled by something more than booze, being relatively young, new to everything, feeling the control slipping and committing to that mood with everything I had.

I can be that man when I've had a few. I don't think so at the time, but my energy levels go bananas. I'm not a sleepy one. Adventures appear in front of me and I embrace them with enthusiasm. Suddenly much more sociable, letting the guard down. Affectionate on the gins, my subconscious enjoying its rare time in the spotlight.

And that's why there are emails flying around afterwards, and letters of apology. Youthful exuberance or being a dick, depending on how many you'd had yourself. And that's where the self-loathing comes in. What have I done? In time you'll find out the repercussions, being vaguely remembered or informed by others, depending how many you've had. You sort of hope there will always be someone who's done something worse, just as on the pitch there's always someone faster, fitter, stronger, more skilful. So I regret the way I was that night, but I also don't know how I would have got it all out otherwise. The pressure on that tour was immense. A dream, but also a heavy weight – being where you want to be, but sometimes going through things you don't.

Your memory fractures, down the years. Big sweeps of the brush that disappear from the canvas, intricate little details that stay with you. So while I remember Shane Williams's two tries down the left in that third Test, Ugo Monye's interception, it's something else that feels alive, that's there in full colour and sound. A kick-off in the second half, Paulie O'Connell shouting at me in his Irish accent. The white ball against a pale sky. Going up and seeing the ball rotating, spreading my fingers, softening the hands. Bringing it in to my chest. How strange to remember something as simple as that.

There's something Brian O'Driscoll says. 'The Lions is a drug, and you can't get enough.' And after that summer out there, I did understand what he means. It is everything you'd ever want from rugby, what rugby can really mean. Almost like the A-Team; you start with nothing, you come together and you end this band of elites, together not for personal reward but in both a traditional and authentic way.

But like a drug, if you have too much of it, it can chew into you. It can create paralysis if you think too much about what you're part of. You get home and you pull your Test jersey out of your battered kitbag. You hold it creased in your hands, the dirt and sweat still on it. And you can feel everything that has gone before, all the players who have worn it.

I'd realized it when I played for Wales. You think of all the Welshmen who have run out onto a green pitch in that jersey. And there's never as many as you think. I'm Lions number 761. Even with Wales there's fewer than 1,200 men to have been capped. It's a remarkably low number, across the continents and centuries.

It's not a spiritual thing, being a Lion. But it is close to it, and there is something profound about it. It can be hard to explain it to outsiders, to those who haven't been there. On a professional level it's everything you aim to be. You're a custodian, but of something that lives and breathes, not an idea frozen in history. You can add to it as well as reflect on its past.

And it can never be taken away from you. Anything you achieve in the game belongs to the game. Someone else will come along and beat the numbers, but they'll never take away the memories. They'll never erase those series I've played with the Lions. It's a massively precious thing to me and I won't let anyone else say it isn't.

It takes time to realize that. To reflect on it. When a tour is whirling around you, you don't stop and look around. Halt time, do a 360, write down the details. You're always facing up to the next challenge, the next game, the next training session. There are times to enjoy yourself and decompress towards the end, but for the most part you're training, packing, eating, sleeping or playing. There's always something filling the day. Always a new hotel to move to, always more packing, always a coach ride.

You can find yourself consumed by the disappointments. Wondering how different it might all have been had you done this or your teammate done that. When you win, you bask in it and you enjoy it, and then it's a steady decline off that peak. When you lose, it's like full stop, bang. Straight into the first debrief and the questions. The doubts. Never forgetting.

Back to the famous Lions DVDs. So you find out, on your first tour, that you don't see everything. So it's not the bits that you see that make you watch the DVD, when it comes out, but the bits you know you're not going to see. For the feeling of once again being in those corners, in the shadows, in the nitty-gritty – in the dark places, the corridors of stadiums, the taxis, the shuttles. The little moments no one else cares about but you and those you shared it with. You know you won't get those moments back, but you want to hold onto them.

There is playing for Wales, and playing for the Lions. Those are the things. They say dreams don't come true, and they're wrong. And when those dreams do become real, you never want them to slip away. They're part of your journey, your story. And you take solace in knowing you've written a few lines in one of those unforgettable Lions chapters.

9

CYDBWYSEDD | BALANCE

Pain and regret. Sounds like an album, doesn't it. Maybe an indie band, maybe an old bluesman. Not a way to live your life.

And it's not what's defined rugby for me. You get the highs, with rugby. Days when you're exhausted but you've come through. Away in a stadium where they're screaming everything in the dictionary and a lot of stuff that isn't, and you silence them. Nights with your arms round your teammates, singing favourite songs. Telling old stories.

But when you accept all that, you have to reconcile yourself to the darker side of the bargain too. Fighting to find the equilibrium.

You get the epic highs from winning the biggest games but also from winning the games you think you've lost. Wales against Scotland, Six Nations, 2010. Us still 10 points down with three and a half minutes to go, and then Leigh Halfpenny's converted try, and Stephen Jones's penalty with 10 seconds left, and Shane Williams diving over with his left arm up in the air to send the whole of the Millennium Stadium into a beautiful sea of red shirts and beer and hugs and chaos.

And the low? I'd dislocated my elbow an hour before. Going hard on a kick-chase with Tom Shanklin, both of us going in to tackle Thom Evans at the same time and my arm getting hyperextended, and feeling a pop.

I looked down and I saw my elbow had gone three-dimensional. It's why I failed to bounce straight back up. A double-take, and then I got back into the defensive line and tried to tackle one of their forwards with one arm.

It probably wasn't the cleverest thing I've ever done. The elbow popped back in, but it was still useless. I couldn't bend it, let alone scrag an 18-stone man with it. But that was the Shaun Edwards mantra once again. Get back up, get back in the line. Unless your leg is hanging off, you can keep going. Even if you can't run, get back to your feet. The opposition won't know.

You're never injured in defence. Shaun had hammered it into us. And my way of interpreting things literally must have helped me, even if it took me a bit longer in Shaun's eyes to get back to my feet than it should have done.

You crack on. Make the next ruck, step into position again. Ignore the pain, because the pain will find you quite happily on its own. Get it strapped up, rely on the adrenaline. And before you know it, you're back into it – jumping for lineouts, hitting rucks, tucking the ball under your arm and charging into contact. It's amazing what you can do for the team when you really want to.

There's a simple truth behind all that drama. If you haven't got some sort of niggle, you're not playing enough. It becomes an unwelcome addition to the routine. Some need injections to get through matches, or painkillers plus a pill to protect your stomach from the painkillers. Some condition that isn't quite enough for an operation but has to be managed through training. The accidental cuts, the lacerations, the stitches done quickly in the dressing room. Souvenirs you're happy to own.

And all that physical pain – the dislocated elbows, tendinopathies, the broken bones – none of it hurts as much as losing a World Cup semi-final. The physical stuff heals faster than the memories. I've felt my shoulder pop into my armpit when I was competing for the ball against France in Paris in March 2017, and I'd take that every time compared to losing to them by a single point at Eden Park in October 2011.

Here's another obvious point we forget to acknowledge. The

fitter you get, the harder it gets. Why? Because you do more. You're making more tackles, at the bottom of more rucks. You're going for longer, the GPS unit between your shoulder blades showing more impacts, greater speed, more metres covered.

And it's cumulative. You have to go through walls to be able to prepare for matches where the walls are thicker and higher. Doing drills on a pitch in Poland pre-tournament training for the 2011 World Cup, living with a state of permanent muscle soreness for two weeks. Doing scrum drills in an oven, known locally as Qatar, before the 2015 World Cup, the heat at eight in the morning already past 38 degrees. With added Shaun Edwards.

Pain is temporary. The rewards last. The adrenaline, the endorphins. The ability to control body and the mind; when it's hurting, being able to come out the other side. In rugby, it's the highs of those wins. The camaraderie. Yes, the silverware, but also what it means to you and everybody who has contributed to you being there, who cares about you.

It's a shared goal. I don't think you can underestimate what that allows you to do, the sense that you're all doing this together, that it's something bigger than just you. It's the difference between pushing yourself into lactic exhaustion on a rowing machine or doing it as part of a crew. You realize at times you'll miss that shared pain. It can define the group. It's the nails in the tight joints between you all.

Warren Gatland would enjoy pushing us to the limit. Some of us enjoyed telling him 'that was an easy one today,' even though the truth was quite different. Gats with a wry smile, as if to say, I know how you really feel, and that's why we'll go again. Always be careful what you wish for.

Our fitness, our collective ability to get through those training sessions and the pain they brought, was our not-so-secret weapon under Gats in the early days. When you know you're going to be in the battle for as long and probably longer than your opposition, you start to believe you'll always come through. He would learn pretty quickly about the ones he didn't know. Try to break us all so he could see who would be the ones to complain, the first ones to blow up or question.

I never take too much pride in an ability to work hard, because that's my job. I'd be sensible enough to stop if I was close to injury, but the struggle is why you're there. I don't like coming off the pitch. It's pretty simple in my eyes. I don't want to work in an excuse factory. It's not a good place to be.

Rugby teaches you its lessons. You accept the game has its potential for pain and the longer you play, the less the laws of probability favour you. Harder, stronger, faster.

You can see the lads who appreciate the balance, when you're coming through. You work out which are the ones who will get taken off in apparent agony and yet somehow recover miraculously for the next game. The ones who'll get nicknamed The Phoenix. You'll see others who go through injuries and then have the resilience and strength to push themselves through all the shit you have to do to get back and do it all over again. That's real toughness, the stuff you see in the gym when a player is rebuilding, and the stuff you don't see, the mental battles. The changed schedule, the loneliness, feeling as if you're alone on an island even when you're not.

You hear about things that get you through and you use what you can, if it works for you. I tried a B-vitamin jab once; it felt like a horse had kicked me in the backside, and I never went near one again. I've used quinine to keep cramp at bay. We've gargled quinine solution on the pitch after training – not one you could ever drink, one to swill around your mouth and then spit out. I've used co-codamol, overloaded on it after my shoulder injury and found it impossible to pass anything solid for a week. On some occasions I've had to rely on anti-inflammatories regularly when needed and while I might not like that, it's not going to change.

There's an increasing awareness of concussion and its impact on players and the game. What it does now, what might be lurking in the future.

Having the responsibility of family heightens your awareness of the potential implications. Being aware of things in the future, not getting them involved in something they didn't sign up for – it would be irresponsible not to acknowledge it.

For myself? Should my health deteriorate, I know the first thing that some people will say is that it's from my rugby. But until science categorically proves it one way or the other, I don't believe you can necessarily blame the game alone. More than 400 professional games, and I'm okay now. I'm fully aware that things may change. Then obviously my search for answers will deepen.

You push on, in rugby. Because you want to, more than any coach or team putting pressure on you. Before we played South Africa in the World Cup semi-final in 2019, I needed 100mg of anti-inflammatories for 10 days. That was my choice. It was how I could play on after tweaking my groin.

It was a World Cup semi. I couldn't run flat-out and I couldn't do much of the warm-up for the team run, but I could do what I needed to. And it wasn't as problematic as after the previous World Cup, when we came back and played Ireland and I was moving like Quasimodo on account of having plantar fasciitis in one foot and Achilles tendon issues in the other.

I look at the volume of games I've played and the number of minutes on the pitch in those games and maybe it's miraculous that I've had as few major issues as I have. I've never tried to protect myself on the pitch. I've never hidden or shirked the contact. What I have done is everything else around it to get to that place – the mobility work by myself, the nutrition when it's just me on my own and no one's watching.

You play the sport, but you live the profession. That's how I look at it. People will say, you're getting paid, you're supposed to. Yes, but would you commit day after day, year after year – not the glamour stuff on the pitch, the fun with ball in hand, but the dull sacrifices, the repetition, the being boring at home with sensible food and extra stretching sessions in the garage when you could be on the sofa watching Netflix with a beer.

I've always done the research into training and nutrition, hunted around for anything that might help. Asking myself, what's next? What I could learn from other sports? It's why I started doing hot yoga. Anything to improve performance, even if it's marginal. It goes back to the idea of investing in yourself. Critics might say, ah, it's easy to do that when you earn what a pro player earns. But would you?

Don't get me wrong. I've got plenty of physiological deficiencies. I'm never going to be the fastest or the strongest. But I don't think that longevity and consistency are dirty words, as some people subscribe to, depending on which way you use them. You give me a choice between jogging three miles and smashing it for one, I'll take the fast one. There's nothing worse than that somebody who wins the last rep when they've been coasting for the previous ones. I'm comfortable coming last in the final one if I know I've gone as hard as I could in all the others.

So that's the pain, physical and emotional. And then there's the regrets.

Those highs, those days and nights you couldn't experience any other way? With all that comes the other side. The times you're up against it. When the crowd are giving you everything and they never stop. When it's you making the errors, and it costs your team and you know it and they know it.

A lot has slipped away from me down the years. But I can still remember the Test against Australia when I dropped three kick-offs, or the time against the All Blacks at Carisbrook in Dunedin where I had the chance to put young Tom Prydie in at the corner and I didn't get the pass away. The lineout option against England when they won back possession and went over for the try.

All these things. Memories that flare up. As you mature you try to move on, but it's not natural for me. You have the next game to think about; you have more games stretched out behind you.

The unforced errors are the ones that frustrate you, because it's nothing the opposition have done. Back in the day, I used to go straight home after a game and watch the whole thing back.

Straight into it, facing it down. Now I try to at least leave it from the Saturday to the Monday. Hold it back to the working hours, keep the family away from it. You can get swallowed up in it – your game, the opposition's game, the other stuff that's going on in your world. You end up watching too much rugby. That's your life gone. We all take our jobs home now, but you have to be free of it somewhere. If you can't ever switch off, you can't ever switch on. It's the balance, once again.

When I was younger, I couldn't let go of the mistakes because I believed otherwise you couldn't improve. That was always what I thought – if it needs working on, work on it. Now I know mistakes are a learning process. If I'd been the sort of person to feel content with where I was, I wouldn't be where I am.

I've never been comfortable. Thinking about what I could do to improve keeps me going. I don't think I'm passing through. I still train with a purpose. You should know where you are yourself, as a player.

There's been times when I've played well and I've tried to reinforce it too much. As a young lad at Ospreys, full of youthful exuberance, a bit cheeky, a little cocky, beating Bristol and then going up to our coach Lyn Jones and asking him if he could sit down and go through my performance with me. Getting the right reply from him: 'Fuck off, Alun Wyn, you know you did well . . .'

So I'm always harsh on myself now. The only thing worse than playing badly is playing badly and people telling you that actually you've played well.

There's frustration there – over my mistakes, my flaws. The emotional control was lacking in my younger days. An ultra-competitive streak getting me into sticky situations. I probably didn't ingratiate myself with everyone at that time. My self-regulation is probably better than it used to be, but every now and then that streak will resurface.

I wouldn't take other stuff that was going on in my life and let it bleed into rugby, not unless I could use it for inspiration. Nothing

I thought would interfere. All of it was for competitive reasons: could we do this better? Can we be honest about where we've gone wrong?

But it happened, and it wasn't always verbal. It got personal at times. An anger inside: 'I'm going to get him back.' If a teammate puts a big hit in on you in training, you don't like it, but you usually respect them more for it.

And there's back in February 2010 again. England v. Wales at Twickenham, the week before the crazy Scotland game, the ridiculous comeback. The game at 3–3 with half an hour gone, opening round of the Six Nations, Warren Gatland's third campaign in charge. Memories of our win there in 2008 and how it had jump-started our Grand Slam campaign. Full house, England in a swanky cream kit to celebrate their centenary. A contest to be at your absolute best. To make your family proud.

And then me rolling out of the side of a maul, the ball bobbling about. England's hooker Dylan Hartley picking it up at the back of the messy ruck and setting off.

Shit, he's going to get through here.

Me on my knees, seeing him picking up pace, sticking out my right leg.

Hartley going down.

Roars from the crowd. Shock, outrage, delight.

I knew as soon as I did it. Referee Alain Rolland was right there. I tried to feign as if I was stretching the cramp out of my hamstring, but he knew. We all knew. The most obvious yellow card you could ever imagine.

There was nothing premeditated about that. Desperation mixed with some deep-rooted instinct. Stop them at all costs. Not gamesmanship, not cheating, not even a brain-freeze. Pure reaction.

I was on one leg. Technically I was out of the game. I could have dived, put out my right arm. 39 international appearances by that point, and you should know better by then. You're not a kid. A Lions tour and a Grand Slam in the past two seasons.

And so you see the card coming and you see the yellow. A lurch in your guts, like you're an egg-timer and the glass has smashed and all the sand has suddenly dropped out.

Maybe the action and its repercussions are two separate things. You could be sent to the sin bin and your team don't concede a point. No one remembers. A footnote to the game, a word from the coach afterwards, a load of piss-taking on the coach home.

When you're binned and the opposition score 17 unanswered points as you sit there, in a form of solitary confinement, it's different. First the slow walk off the pitch, pulling your scrum cap off, damp with sweat, looking straight ahead. Right on the far side of the pitch, the longest, slowest walk you'll make. Thinking back to when I limped off in the same direction two years earlier, a rolled ankle two minutes before the end, us ahead then after that beautiful comeback. Thinking, this is very different: 80,000 people in there and yet you're suddenly very aware that you're all on your own.

England landing the subsequent penalty and then crashing over for a try. The clock suddenly slowing down for you on the bench – the clock slowing down, but the play speeding up. How are they scoring so quickly? Feeling even more helpless, even more lonely than before. This is all my fault, and I can do absolutely nothing about it.

Going into the dressing room, staring at your feet. I always tell players now – don't feel you ever have to apologize for mistakes, partly because they're done, partly because it could have been anyone. You want to play, pass, offload. You don't want to stop your teammates doing the good stuff. If it comes off, you're a hero; if it doesn't, there's no point worrying. You can't get it back.

This was different. Shaun Edwards coming up to me. No bawling me out, just the clipboard tight in his hands, his eyes on you like binoculars. You're almost pressed up against the wall without him even touching you.

One sentence.

'I hope you never do that again in your career.'

A little part of you, when you do something that stupid and useless, would almost rather you'd done something stupid but effective. Something sensible, in a strange way, that helps turn the game your way. Something that stopped England scoring, not opened the doors.

Another thing. As I sat there on the sideline in the early part of the second half, watching England go over for their second try, I felt torn. One part of me saying, Alun Wyn, you're not good enough to be worth 17 points to this defence. You're not that important. And the other part going, this is all your fault. All of this.

You go back on and it's all brewing inside you. Trying to make up for it – hitting rucks harder, knocking their big runners backwards, bouncing up like tiredness just wasn't a thing.

And I didn't get away with it. Taking the ball 10 metres out and spotting Adam Jones out to my left, passing into his hands, watching him dive over the try line almost in slow-motion. James Hook having one of his Phil Bennett days, stepping between Mathew Tait and Tim Payne, handing off Danny Care, reaching out for our second try. All that stuff you'd hear back in Wales about how what the nation really needed was a 10 like Jonny Wilkinson, a calm controller; and then Hooky doing stuff like that from outside centre and everyone going, ah yeah, you've got to have a man who plays what's in front of him, right?

Three points from parity with time on the clock. England on an almighty wobble, like 2008's happening all over again. Us deep in their half. Come on, boys, save us.

And then an intercepted pass, and Tait going away, and Haskell on his outside once again to kill it all off.

Warren Gatland didn't mess about in his press conference afterwards. I soon heard.

'It's huge, isn't it? It's absolutely stupid what he's done and to be honest it's probably cost Wales the game today.

'You need 15 players on the field, particularly as it's an issue that we highlighted during the week about making sure that we don't give anything soft away, trust your defence, trust the system, trust your teammates. And unfortunately on one or two occasions we didn't do that today.'

That was the headlines made. Gats understood, because he's smart that way, and came up to me on the bus to explain why he'd said what he'd said, that he hadn't meant to blame me. But much as I was thankful he made the effort, I also felt I had nothing to complain about. It was an honest appraisal of what I'd done.

There's times now, looking back, when I wonder if I should have lived on the edge a little more. Flirted with rugby decisions that might have got me a card. Would it have helped? Would it have driven on the rest of the boys? Maybe there were times when a cynical penalty might have saved a try.

I ask myself the question, and I think: nah. Rugby is about discipline too. About understanding where the line is and staying just this side of it. Anyone can get themselves carded. It takes a better player to stay on the pitch.

And I wouldn't want to feel the way I was that week ever again. Glad that the social media world was quieter then, learning a lesson from it, seeing others learn from Gats's reaction too. But also having to go through the whole review process when you know your negative incident is coming, and the impact it had on the game. You think that 10 minutes when you're off the pitch is long. It's nothing compared to sitting there on the coach going back west down the M4. The silence around, the staring out the window and seeing your own pale face reflected back off the dark glass. The whole of Sunday at home with it sitting heavy on your shoulders. Going back into camp on the Monday, thinking, is it worse if they spend the whole morning highlighting what I've done, or talking about other stuff because everyone already knows how big my fuck-up was?

They always rumble on, these moments. I did a TV interview the following week. The guy asking the questions kept repeating the same one again and again. 'Is there a rift between you and Gatland, after what he said after the game?'

I watched the edit back, when it went out, and it looked like he asked the question once. It looked pleasant and balanced.

In that room, bright lights in my face, black screen between my legs and my face, it felt like an inquisition rather than an enquiry, like it was personal rather than professional. It felt like he was coming after me.

I knew he had to ask the question. It's his job. He didn't need to afford me any respect; I hadn't earned it then. It was the way it felt like a police review. There's a tone to take, and a point to realize the damage you can do to a young player within five sentences.

A more senior player than me, more miles on the clock, saw it. And he stepped in afterwards, said, *That was wrong. You don't need to do that.*

I was civil to the guy, when I saw him again. But maybe that's where it started to change for me, getting a bit more closed off. I thought, are you being asked barbed questions about your own job? I'm not a politician being held to account; I'm a 24-year-old rugby player who made a mistake. I wish I hadn't, but I did, and I'm paying the price, and I won't forget it.

Three days on, we played Scotland. We came back from the depths. No one was talking about my trip. I ruined my elbow.

Rugby never stops. Never lets you go. You look up one day and think, how did I get here?

10

CARIAD | LOVE

Some people think playing rugby is just about winning. It's just about trophies. Just about glory.

As a professional it's the only thing, because for those three or four seconds you lift a trophy above your head to the packed Principality Stadium, it all makes sense. All the rest of it falls away – the baggage, all the negative reverb from others who never have and never will. For those moments, you're free. Nothing can touch you.

As a person it's more, so much more. I wasn't great at rugby as a kid. I found some photos of me a little while ago, and I didn't realize how tall I was, how fat I was. I looked at them and thought, how the hell have I ever made it? I literally look like someone's smaller dad playing with them.

But it worked. The game was a good fit for me. It gave me focus and it gave me satisfaction. I got the chance to try all those other things – football, sailing, kites, buggies – but rugby became my thing. And I don't think you realize when you're young quite how much you love something. I loved the training, never complained about it. I loved watching it on TV, I loved looking the part. I was fascinated by how you could play and how you could improve.

Part of me wishes I could go back and join the dots and tell my younger self actually how much I was enjoying it. You don't know, then, how fleeting it all is. How brief the lifespan of a team is, of a period in your life. When you're a kid, there's always another game. Always another session. The seasons never seem to end. You're just alive to the sensations of it all. To the moment.

I look back, and the funny thing is that I still feel the same way as I did then. You grow, leave home, travel abroad. You move through the age ranks, find a summit, realize there's another summit beyond and set off again. And the one thing that doesn't change in all of that is the game. Tweaks to rules around the fringes, to interpretations of the laws, but not to the fundamentals. Run hard, tackle hard. Defend space, create space. Impose your physique and your will on another team.

It's not rugby that makes it hard. It's the stuff all around it. So when people are complaining – that I've gone on too long, that I've made mistakes – I find it quite hard to compute, because I still feel the intense draw of the game. In my mid-thirties, with some guys who have known me on a professional level for more than half my life. A career but also a vocation. A way of life, a calling.

There's only a few occasions when it ever feels different. When you're injured, and there's no outlet for everything you've poured into all this. And then, for me, the stuff that comes with professionalism – the requests for your time, for interviews, for exposure. It's a lot easier when I push all that shit away. I've always done it, always shut the door and said, no I can't do that. It makes everything easier; it keeps it simple. I am not going to deny that the game has been kind. But I don't regret any of that at all. It's always been about the game for me.

You could almost plot on a graph, as I matured, with my level of ability versus my size. Early on, low ability, high size. As I played at Bonymaen, at school, better ability, others catching up on size. I was fortunate, the kids and then boys and men I had around me. They were always two, three, four times better than me. I remember names, and I see people even now around me and I think, You were unbelievable at 15 . . . Was I that lucky, or did I work that hard, or were you unlucky, or did you just fall out of love with the game? I've always had to work at it. I had to lose the weight and I couldn't just rely on my size. I had to get better with the skills stuff. Because when you come on the scene as a pro, there's always someone better, and there always will be. Whatever the level, there will always be someone bigger, stronger, faster; someone who can beat you in one of those departments. There is now.

There's one thing I'd like to think. I was always consistent. Always durable. Even at a young age, not just consistent playing, but consistent trying, consistent turning up, because I wanted to be there, I wanted to get better. And all that goes back to having that focus and that relationship with the game.

Consistency is not one of the sexy attributes. People much prefer the idea of raw talent. They'd rather see someone do the miraculous thing one time out of 10, than someone do the right thing most of the time. It's the same with durability. There are guys 10 and 12 years younger than me who are already having their injuries and appearances managed. Guys that have to be strapped every session.

And I appreciate it all. How special it is to be able to have lived the life I have. You use words like *privilege* and *proud* and *honoured*, but those words can be throwaway these days. It's hard for people outside your world to understand the strength of your feelings, the sincerity in what you're trying to say and elucidate. They read those words and think, yes okay, but it's supposed to be, isn't it? Well, I speak a lot of nonsense sometimes. But there's some things I don't fuck about with.

There were a couple of friends of mine who had a bet with each other when we were 15 that I would be a British and Irish Lion one day. Only a tenner on it, but I think about that still. How far I still had to go, how quickly it seemed to come around. You want to explain to everyone how special that feels, but you worry that no one cares. Stories from the heart that become a swipe or a click. Something that feels profound, turned into a quick headline or online bait.

Here's something else. Rugby worked for me as a release. I was definitely never quick as a kid; I'd be at the back of most kick-chases. But it suited my mentality – the energy you could ex-pend, the physical impacts you could find. Part of me would love to have a time machine, to go back and see whether it was the sport or the boy. Had I been bitten by the bug for a different sport, for golf or for tennis, would I have done what I've done in rugby? The success we enjoyed at a young age with Bonymaen must have made a difference. You can enjoy things that are tough and not successful, but when you're winning district cups and the odd tournament, the game holds onto you tighter. The no-nonsense nurturing from the people there was like the hard core in my foundations.

There's being part of a team, of relying on others, on others being dependent on you. In football, one superstar player can drag a team deep into a World Cup. One brilliant batsman can transform a Test series. In rugby, you can't do a thing without the players doing all the stuff you can't. Nothing comes without the collective. Props need second rows need back rows need half-backs need centres and wingers and full-backs. Props can't run fast, not all of them, although there's few sights in the game as glorious as a prop going flat-out. But they don't need to. They can do what wingers or full-backs could never do. Despite all the changes, it's still a game for all shapes and sizes, still a game anyone can play.

Some people think of me as grumpy, as angry. I am, some-times. But a lot of that anger, particularly in my younger days, came from frustration. At myself, first of all, for my own inac-curacies, my own insecurities. When I got to a certain level, it became with others – with their commitment, their inaccur-acies. That's when the stare would come out. 'What the fuck are you doing?'

Yet it was always balanced by the secret pleasures the game and the team can conjure up around you. When your team scores a try, and you've been the one digging for possession at the start of it, or been part of a passing phase, something that looks so fluid and involves so many individuals. Creating something beautiful from nothing. It's wonderful to be allowed to go around hitting things in a way you can't in most jobs, but it's those magical moments you do it for. That's what you want to be involved in, or a driving maul that keeps marching on, metre by metre, or a scrum that's shoving them backwards and going over the line.

And it's belonging, on so many levels. To a group, to an identity. A way of seeing the world. Of where you don't belong and you don't fit in, too. Rugby is about not letting your teammates down. It's about being your best for you and the expectation that you're going to work for other people.

I don't know whether I am actually more insecure than I think I am, or whether I care a lot more about what people think than I'd like to admit. But I do not ever want to be the guy going in the other direction to everyone else. Better the devil you know. Not someone who talks about all those values inherent in rugby yet does it all for show, or fails to live up to them.

So I think about belonging, and there's Wales, and there's Mumbles. And in between the two – the essential link that takes you from one to the other – is the Ospreys.

Some people imagine regional rugby doesn't resonate with the players. That it's too new, or too artificial. Welsh domestic rugby is about the historic clubs, the old grounds, the old battles. Right?

Maybe you have to be a player from this past 16 years to understand. To have lived other battles, redeveloped and new-built grounds, fresh competition. It resonates for us. It resonates for me. I grew up with the Whites; I matured with the Ospreys. I stayed with them, too, when the opportunities were there to travel, the very enticing offers further from home.

It's Llandarcy that I think about, when I think about the Ospreys. More than the Liberty Stadium. You spend so much more time at your training base. The Liberty is our home pitch but shared with Swansea City FC; ours, but not that pure sense of ownership you get with the place you go four days a week, most weeks throughout the season.

St Helen's in Swansea was my development. Going there as a

kid, taken by my parents. The link with my father and my grand-father. The Liberty will always be my Ospreys debut, the very first game we ever played there, a preseason friendly against Wasps at the end of August 2005. The next weekend, my official competitive debut, coming on as a second-half replacement in our Magners League win over Leinster. 19 years old, a lot of hair and a lot to learn. Players in that team I still couldn't believe I could share a pitch with – Stefan Terblanche at full-back, Sonny Parker at outside centre, Andrew Bishop inside him. Barry Williams at hooker, Steve Tandy on the open-side. The bench wasn't bad either: Paul James, Huw Bennett, Ian Evans.

It joins the dots, for me. The regions in Wales haven't replaced the old clubs. They represent them still. We're Swansea, Neath, Bridgend. The romance and the history hasn't been wiped away; the threads have been woven together. There is no Ospreys without the clubs. There's no four Grand Slams in 15 years for Wales without the Ospreys, Scarlets, Blues and Dragons.

Swansea was always going to be the team I played for. Then it changed, and I can't regret it, because I've seen the inside of the machine. You can't run a professional sports team on a million quid a year. Not when you're up against the wealth of the French clubs, or the clout of the big Irish provinces.

Rugby fans have always been tribal. I understand that. There's arguments too that the switch to regional rugby could have been handled better. The sums still don't add up all the time, the crises still never feel that far away.

I think how close we came, with the Ospreys. The successes we had: the three Celtic League wins, the EDF Cup win over Leicester at Twickenham. Winning the Pro 12 in 2012, beating Leinster by a single point in the Dublin sunshine with that late Shane try and Dan Biggar conversion. The superstar signings like Justin Marshall and Jerry Collins. The 13 starters for England against Wales in 2008, the six British Lions in 2009.

The Heineken Cup quarter-final against Biarritz in San Sebastian in 2010 still hurts the most. Losing by a point, convinced we should have had a penalty at the death. Scoring 28 points away from home and falling short. A third consecutive defeat in the last eight.

That was our chance, that year. And it wears you down, in the end, all the hoping, all the pushing to make things better. You pull off those sorts of successes, those near misses, and it sends expectations soaring.

We should have done more with the squad we had. We also did a great deal. We provided more internationals to the national side than any other region.

There's a lot I feel grateful for. The relationships with coaches like Lyn Jones, Sean Holley and Steve Tandy. You get close to some of them. Sean was an assistant before he was head coach, and you form bonds that endure. He understood that I didn't suffer fools, that I had opinions, that I'd want to share them.

When you're a younger player they can nurture you. Me in my white boots for the first training session I was called into, christened with that nickname to follow – Gwyn Togs, White Boots. Going hammer and tongs in training – first out, running on my toes, up for it. Playing at 6 at Bristol away at the Memorial Ground, yellow-carded at 6 again up at Borders. I got lost at times, in the back row, but that was all part of the education.

Scoring against Leicester at Twickenham in that final of 2008, running on to James Hook's pass in my grey scrum cap, going over and then jumping up to slap my hand against the badge on my chest. A roar to reflect how we all felt at the moment, a try in keeping with how we played. Chasing back with Shane Williams and Sonny Parker, trying to catch Alesana Tuilagi at the end of the game, hauling him down before the try line.

Winning that second Celtic League title, against Borders in Gregor Townsend's last game. The celebrations in the changing room, feeling the bonds and the camaraderie. Pushing in Europe, battling a low seeding, always against the champions.

You become captain, and you have to develop. You don't know then that you'll end up with 115 appearances as skipper across nine years, twice as many as the great men who came before and come afterwards. You realize over time that leadership isn't about making all the decisions. It's finding other leaders and giving them the freedom they need. It's allowing everyone the room they need to grow too.

You can show commitment in other ways too. Sean Holley's fortieth birthday one evening, a big party at his house. Me playing for Ospreys up in Newcastle. An open invite to anyone who could make it back from the north-east. 10 o'clock at night, me managing to make it to Sean's house with a bottle of champagne. Amazing what you'll do for a free buffet, isn't it? Meeting Sean and Shane Williams after the third Lions Test in Sydney in 2013, several sheets to the wind, so happy to see them that I gave Shane the biggest hug I had in my locker and broke one of his ribs.

Fun is not a bad thing. It might be the most potent motivation of all. And you need to chuck money at training and kit and systems, but it's too easy to lose the balance. When I think about all the training and prep and analysis you do as a professional player, some of the best rugby I ever played was probably in the school-yard. Not the most technically perfect, but the most enjoyable stuff. When you run in three tries in five minutes. When everyone's throwing the ball about and trying crazy steps and offloads. When it's all just a game, all over again.

My wife tells me sometimes that I've never really grown up. She's right, really. I'm still playing games. But why would you want to grow up? Some of the greatest times of my life have been that pure playing. If you can find that sweet moment where it's all fun, where you're not thinking about the aggression and bullshit, why wouldn't you?

It doesn't mean you're not obsessive. I always pushed as hard as I could. Early on, coming off the pitch and going straight up to Sean Holley. How did I do? What could I have done better? You told me this or that was going to happen – why didn't it? An insatiable appetite. A slightly unhinged level of desire.

I went through a phase, earlier in my time with the Ospreys. I'd have a plan at the start of each season. Sometimes they'd be real samey; sometimes they would only be a single line. But I'd have this plan of what I needed to improve upon, what I could do as a captain. What the club should do.

And the sad thing is, I gave up on that because I realized over time that certain people didn't want to listen, and I didn't have any influence. I could bang down the door all I wanted, but the money wasn't there. Wanting to do more, like all the senior players, and coming up against walls. If you're putting energy into something and people aren't listening, you withdraw that energy and channel it into something else. People then come back to you – 'Oh, we still want your input' – well, you didn't listen before. You still provide the honesty, the feedback, but now you wait until it's requested.

So it's the rugby that is straightforward, and the bullshit that goes with it that's hard. That inhibits you and constricts you.

Straightforward and easy. The pleasure is in knowing that there's always something to work on. If I was perfect, I would have finished a long time ago. The love affair still rages on.

11

HER | TEST

I'd had a warning, before we went to Spała for a training camp ahead of the 2011 World Cup. A few words about the challenges we might go through. Challenges beyond even those you might imagine from an old-school set-up in the middle of a Polish forest.

My Ospreys teammate Tommy Bowe had been out there with Ireland. And the headlines I had from Tommy went a bit like this: it's roasting in summer. There's no air-con, there's no WiFi. If you're in one of the good rooms it's like a hostel. If you're in one of the bad ones it's like a prison.

Which just goes to show that you should take these things with a pinch of salt. There was WiFi as soon as we arrived, and it worked a treat.

The rest of the Bowe TripAdvisor review? Spot on.

Warren Gatland had been out there with Wasps. It was his idea. And it was a very Gats kind of place. No frills. Lots of different ways to exercise extremely hard. Absolutely no distractions, if you ignored the WiFi. All manner of elite athletes doing all manner of elite things.

I'd describe the food in the restaurant as stark. There was definitely some meat, and as long as you were okay with not being entirely sure if it was pork, chicken or beef, all was well. The vibe as you walked down the corridors around the centre was municipal hospital from the last knockings of the Soviet Union: shiny magnolia paint, blue steel doors, the odd steel staircase leading to places you probably didn't want to go. The gym was like something out of a 1940s high school. Wall bars and free weights and long ropes hanging down from the ceiling. You'd pass big high-ceilinged rooms and glance through the glass panel in the door and there'd be a load of angry-looking wrestlers who were all four foot tall but looked like they were going to eat you.

And you were perfectly happy to be there. Partly because of Gats, partly because no one in Poland was going to upgrade it if some rugby players were missing their morning coffees. And also for the logic staring you in the face: this is good enough for Olympic athletes, so how can it not be good enough for me? You bought into the plan and the outcome it promised, and you stayed in your strange Spała mindset.

An indoor running track, an outdoor running track. A 50-metre pool in a building with vast windows along one side. Grass pitches, artificial pitches. Trees, everywhere you looked – around the accommodation block, out of every window, in the foreground and away in the distance. All of that, and the near-ownership we took of the cryotherapy chambers.

I'd done it before, on a so-called romantic getaway with Anwen as I recovered from that elbow injury I'd sustained against Scotland. I'd sold the weekend as a nice spa break and then dropped in on arrival that I'd additionally treated her to a cryo session. It's all about the element of surprise in a long-term relationship.

And for something where you're immersed in air that's dropped to minus 120 degrees Celsius, it was relatively pleasant. We dressed as if attending a Covid slumber party: face masks, dressing gowns, knee-high socks, headbands. Not your standard treat from boyfriend to girlfriend, but it got the conversation going, and the elbow got better quicker than it might have done.

Spała was different. It became clear on our first day that I had barely dipped my toe in the world of serious cryo. Three intense training sessions a day, a cryo session after each one. The only upside was that it was over quicker than an ice-bath. We would be in and out within two minutes. But the intensity of the cold, and the repetition, were worsened by the knowledge we would have to step out of the chamber in our wooden clogs (touch the metal floor with bare feet and you'd burn your soles), then immediately get on the exercise bike, or the treadmill, or – by the end – walk fast in circles round the recovery room.

You have to do it to get the blood flowing. It's an accepted part of the process. But it was the single most difficult aspect of training, made harder still by the sight of various Polish Olympians doing significantly longer sessions without any outward sign of discomfort.

We considered ourselves in good shape. A decent amount of muscle mass, not a great deal of body fat. And then five distance runners would come in with absolutely no body fat, bang out three minutes at minus 140 degrees Celsius and then add on a cheeky extra minute at minus 10 degrees. They would walk out without a whimper, be sprayed down with a heat treatment to keep the ice burns manageable and then disappear out onto the track to jog it all off. I saw a race walker do a full double session as if he was popping in for a coffee.

A mildly painful, boring routine, and everyone complained about it at first. The novelty wore off pretty quick, but then the confidence in all began to grow. If the chamber had been going for a while, you walked into the thick cold, unable to see more than a couple of inches in front of your face, and a teammate hidden in the fog would blow on you, which meant a direct jet of frozen air hitting you somewhere exposed. And we braved it, because it became our routine. If part of you wondered if the sessions really worked, if there might in fact be a large dose of placebo about it all, you pushed that away. A commitment to do everything possible to make us fitter and faster.

The message came down from the top. None of our rivals are training as hard as you. A part of you stayed logical – do we know that for sure, maybe they are – but the larger part went with it. It simplified it: okay, I'll go until I can't do any more. And then I'll find a way, even if it's a jog or a walk or a crawl. The mindset we all knew we had to develop if we wanted to make a serious challenge in the World Cup in New Zealand.

You found your pleasures and compensations where you could. The main road in Spała is not a long one. It's not really a bright lights and cutting-edge eateries place. So when you wandered those magnolia corridors and couldn't find many of the boys, you knew you'd find them in the small pizzeria across the road, jammed around the small tables, tucking into a margherita and Coke like it was something Heston Blumenthal had slow-cooked for days. You knew which of your fellow forwards to approach for contraband, the biscuits and chocolates smuggled in under the radar to keep us going in the short evenings.

And you were shattered. In that big old swimming pool at 6 a.m. on a couple of mornings, before breakfast, never pretty because there were very few natural swimmers in that group; dense muscle mass can be a bit sinky. Then the actual serious stuff – weights, cardiovascular, endurance. Warm-ups in bare feet sometimes to work on your proprioception. Whistles going for sessions you were in, whistles going elsewhere as your teammates were put through other horrors. A punishment lying in wait, the joker in the pack: the sandpit.

The sandpit was where you went if you messed up. If you hadn't weighed yourself, or done the daily questionnaire about the quality of your sleep, or been foolish enough to have a lie-in. Press-ups and tuck-jumps and burpees in this thick sand, absorbing all your efforts, sucking away your energy. Wrestling if you were in there with someone else.

You tried not to admit you were tired. Gats enjoyed seeing the immediate results. It would have told him who was working hard. He'd stick that particular session in the memory bank and roll it out again as a special treat. And when he thought you'd banked enough, he'd wave the pay-off under your noses. Look how hard you've trained, boys. Look what you've done. Use it, believe in it, and the rest will take care of itself. Know that you can go to the edge and then go again.

You need total trust in your strength and conditioning coaches, when you're hurting like that for so long each day. That's why the little things from the rugby coaches, supporting in those sessions, made a difference: Shaun going around putting water bottles out for you when you were blowing, Rob Howley with a thumbs-up and slap on the leg. 'Come on, boys, get through it.' Never anyone too big to do that, too high up the pecking order to get stuck in.

There were rockets. Of course there were. Motivations to push you to places you didn't know you could go. The reaction would show how well you coped with having your tail pulled. Watching someone wind themselves up if they made a mistake, which could be gratifying for everyone else.

There's always a trade-off on those camps; you have a finite amount of time, and it's how you split it between physical conditioning and pure rugby work. You get to a big tournament and you can see early on the different trajectories of the teams that have leaned more towards fitness and those who have done more rugby. Gats was always pretty candid. Boys, it's harder to get fit than it is to adjust your game. This is how we're going to do it. This is our base camp.

We even had a session the morning we flew home. Watching the sun come up at 5 a.m. A test for us, as much as for any specific benefit. Shower, back to bed for half an hour and then off. But you felt good, once you'd recovered. An extra confidence in your fitness. Thinking, this is an environment where it's hard not to improve.

Training that way suited me. Go out there and do it all. Perfect. Not trying to set an example to anyone, happy to focus on myself – making the most of the time out in Poland, using it to progress. Selfish, but done too to improve the collective.

But we weren't for panicking, any of us. A few weeks on and that opening game of the World Cup against South Africa in Wellington, a single-point loss in a game we could have won, had James Hook's penalty at the end gone over, had the one that did go over in the first half been given. Going toe to toe with a team who were the reigning world champions or had beaten some of us on the Lions tour two years before. Thinking, our set piece let them back in a little there, gave them some territory they probably shouldn't have had, wondering about my decision-making before Francois Hougaard's try, thinking, do I step in or go for the man at the back and instead him cutting a line under the sticks.

But you almost want a harder pool at a World Cup. It tests you early, gets you ready for the challenges the quarter-finals and semis will bring. There's plenty of teams have cruised through their first three matches and then run into a wall in the knockout stages. That Springbok game pushed us hard but left us knowing we had more to bring. And when Ireland beat Australia in their group, a direction was appearing in front of us. Okay, it's Ireland in the quarters, then England or France or the semis.

It didn't bother us that we were being written off in the media. Ireland had won the Grand Slam two years before. They were the ones on the winning streak. You could see what the world thought of us by how sparsely attended our press conferences were before the quarter-final.

And none of it made any difference at all to Warren Gatland's attitude. There was no sense of pressure that this was his first World Cup, just a few straightforward statements from him to us players. If we win these games, this is what's going to happen. And we will win these games. A puff of the cheeks and a wry smile as we got past Samoa and then Fiji, in his home town of Hamilton.

There was nothing personal with him against Ireland. Not the way some people on the outside thought. A confidence in us because domestically we'd been doing well against the Irish provinces. The year before, Ospreys had beaten Leinster to win the Celtic League. Gats was always about keeping it simple. We're going to beat these guys if we do this, this and that. And in so many games I played under him for Wales and the Lions, he was right. You never thought he was taking a punt.

Some coaches change before big games. With Warren you didn't see the nerves. You might see a little fidgeting, a leaking of the pressure into his hands, but he had a good poker face. Boots on the pitch, catching the ball at the back of the line if he thought it was going over. Short, punchy messaging. No long meetings. This is what we're doing. You know how to do it. Let's go. He'd let you know if he wasn't impressed with a performance, but he'd also praise you in defeat if he felt you'd done everything you could.

He thought about everything around the games. The stuff a coach doesn't have to bother with, the stuff that can make a real difference if you do get it right. It was his idea that we form a choir in the squad, practising each week, working on songs on the bus between hotels and venues. He knew we would be greeted with a haka in a lot of the places we were going, and that you're expected to have a response to give back. To show your appreciation of the welcome they're giving you.

Our impromptu male voice chorus brought us together and it created a warmth from the Kiwis we met. You'd walk around town and be stopped by random people to be told how much they'd loved the Welsh teams of the 1970s. You'd look around the stands at the Waikato Stadium in Hamilton and see the neutrals that wanted us to win. New Zealand's a friendly and hospitable country anyway, but it felt like we were adopted as the locals' second team everywhere we went.

It reminded you of home, in lots of ways. Everyone wanted to talk rugby. You'd get in a cab and the driver would engage you in a detailed discussion about the art of jackalling or the outside break. Everyone was down to earth, laid back. And you got the sense of community that you get back home; someone knows someone who knows someone who knows you.

You definitely felt it in Wellington, that day of the quarter-final. A word from Shaun Edwards in our ears about Ireland's love of the choke tackle, how Munster had been doing it and how it had carried into their national team. Simple messages again: tackle the tackler or tackle our man too. The things that don't change, whether you're trotting out in club rugby in south Wales or in a World Cup quarter-final.

Shaun may have appeared eccentric at times. But he was a smart man around tactics and defence. If you were up against a running fly-half, a little word in your ear – 'I don't think he's got space to go, but always close it up.' Same with the choke tackle: get in first, tackle our guy if he gets held up, get a knee on the floor. Muscle-up and double-up.

It all came right, pretty much. One of those games you win by 12 points that could have been 20. Shane doing his beautiful Shane things. Mike Phillips showing his pace and strength and hand-off to go over in the corner. Rhys Priestland settling in at 10. Jamie Roberts and Jonathan Davies as a partnership where you're suddenly thinking, write these two into the team sheet for years; Taulupe Faletau matching anything the Irish back row could throw at him.

There's games where you're almost like a machine. All the parts working together, the cogs all meshing. All with one purpose, one plan. You're not overthinking it. It's just happening.

And it happened that afternoon in that shiny circular stadium. Luke Charteris with 16 tackles in the first half alone, six foot 10 inches tall and with a wingspan to match. You're doing well if you can get around that. Looking up at the scoreboard and being certain this one wasn't going to slip away. Not caring about the margin in a World Cup quarter-final. It's just, win.

Stay fit. Recover. Go again. And then the press conference the next week, twice the size, twice the number of questions. Okay, taking an interest now, are we guys?

It all speeds up, then. Travelling up to Auckland, both the semi-finals to be played at Eden Park. France beating England the evening after we'd beaten Ireland in the afternoon. Checking into our hotel in the middle of town, close to the Sky Tower, looking out of the window of our team room and seeing their base two flights up in the hotel opposite.

You don't quite understand the jeopardy, when it's your first World Cup semi-final. You don't know yet how much it hurts if you lose, how you won't be over it a decade later. The intermittent memories stuck in your mind on nights still to come.

So I kept myself to myself, like normal. An outlier or selfish, depending which way you looked at it. Thinking about the key focus areas: the breakdown and the jackal; the speed of our defensive line; what I should be doing on kick-offs. Critical moments and championship minutes, that's how we used to think of them. The first kick-off after a score, when you're riding high after sticking seven points on the scoreboard, and so instantly vulnerable to a mistake and an opportunity for the opposition to strike back.

You could feel the weight of it all. Trying to get that balance between topping up your fitness and not taking too much out. All the Welsh supporters piling into Auckland, reports from back home of what was going on back there. Trying to listen to Gats and his simple messaging. *Boys, this is why we're here. You're going to be fit, you know what we're doing.* And it felt special, too. Something in the air at a meal, in a training session.

If you do it enough, you know when the feelings are right. You take comfort in your routines. Not superstitions. Not ritual. The real stuff – the things you want to get right in training. Spending the right time on them. Practising something you know you'll need.

And it's magic. The heightened sense around everything you're doing. The camaraderie within the team, the trust in the coaches. You can enjoy that week before a semi-final, if you get it right. It almost becomes like Christmas Eve, but a more private, intimate one. There are sensations you have that you realize won't make sense to other people. Stuff you want to explain that only works if you've been through it.

It was a rainy late afternoon, the Saturday. Your classic autumn in Auckland day, showers coming in off the sea. Fans outside the bars, marching down the Karangahape Road from the harbour and the city centre. The floodlights bright around Eden Park, lighting it up from miles in as you drove in on the bus. Wanting the match to start.

I wasn't shouting and screaming in that dressing room. Trying to be in control. Knowing I wasn't. Trying to embrace that too. Sometimes it can feel good not being in control, if you go with the flow and the game and the occasion. If you try and force yourself into a mental state where you should be but you're not, you're in the wrong place.

You have to be real. And that's not the same as riding it out. Riding it is being a passenger. Going with the flow is being in it, letting the game come to you rather than chasing it. That's the killer – chasing it, trying too hard. Then it doesn't feel right.

*

6 mins: Wales 0–0 France
Cross-field kick, Hooky to George North. Get over the ruck, protect our ball.
   Dusautoir coming through, offside.
   Penalty Wales.
   Hooky on it.
   Lovely strike. Three points up. Good start.

20 mins: Wales 3–0 France
France lineout. Parra running it. Holding his man.
   Clerc's on his shoulder here. Warby has got him.
   Shit – has he tipped him there?
   Blue shirts in our faces, shoving, shouting.
   Dusautoir calling them off. He knows what's coming here.
   Card.
   Watching the replay on the screen down the far end.
   Knowing it now. Turning back to the ref.

Seeing the red card in his hand, in the air.
Right. It is what it is. Can't dwell on this for 60 minutes . . .

57 mins: Wales 3–9 France
Lineout to us. 25 metres out.
We will get opportunities, let's take them. We won't get many.
Me up at the back. Taking the ball in front of my face.
Down to Phillsy.
Doc down the middle. Pick and go from Jughead. Charts with the tip to Toby.
Good clear from Charts and Paul James, Assey.
Me there for the pass, four metres off Phillsy's left shoulder.
Defence set.
Dummy – Phillsy's going!
Following him through.
Try!
One-point game, 20 minutes to go.
Conversion for Jonesy to give us the lead . . . misses it.
Is that the moment?
20 minutes. Will we have another chance?
They're calling me off. Brad Davies on.
Don't take me off. Not now . . .

74 mins: Wales 8–9 France
Sitting on the bench, Bomb there with me, injured, Warby there, quiet.
Melon and Charts on halfway. Charts on the deck, setting the ball back.
Mas . . . is he offside there? Not sure . . .
Penalty! Mas, hands on his head.
Leigh stepping up.
This is the game.
The ball up. He's bang down the middle.
The French boys, leaning, like they're trying to make it fade away.

The ball falling, falling . . .
Looking for the flags of the touch-judges.
It's fallen short . . .

Final score: Wales 8–9 France

*

Right. The red card. So many thoughts at the time, and so many since. You ask a Frenchman if it was a red and he'll probably say it was 100 per cent the right decision. Maybe Alain Rolland was never going to win. He doesn't send him off, he gets in trouble with the head of referees. The memorandum sent out to all referees six months before instructed them to start at red and work backwards from there. Did he take Clerc beyond the horizontal? Did he drop him? If that's a yes and a yes, the fact that there was no malicious intent shouldn't make a difference. You want the letter of the law? It's right there for you. It's done. You can't change anything.

We had a few beers that night. A hollow feeling. And there's no going home to get away from it all, either, to start the long process of recovery, because there's the third-place game to play. Me being me, I wanted to be picked for that one. I almost needed to play, to finish things off somehow. Give myself a sense of completion. Instead I was on the bench, on the basis that another member of the squad deserved a start. Fine, but I wasn't going to be happy about it. I even messed up the warm-up, by mistake. The starters on one part of the pitch, the subs in another. I'd automatically gone with the starters, until the shout went up: *hey Alun Wyn, the subs are over there.* Thrown on for the last 27 minutes, thinking – just give it to me, let me try and put it right, let me finish as high as I can.

Australia beat us 21–18. That made it three defeats in the tournament by a cumulative margin of five points. And if that hurt, and made you wonder, and kept you awake on nights ahead, so too did the final.

It would be disrespectful to say you watched it and thought, we could have won that. We didn't win our semi, so we didn't deserve to be there. France did. And they nearly won it, too. Everything on the line for the All Blacks players because of the expectation on them, more pressure on their shoulders than on any other team in the tournament, and they got across the line, in the end.

A campaign for us built on hard work and belief. Going close, but not close enough.

12

DYCHWELIAD | RETURN

So. Three games lost at a World Cup by a cumulative total of five points. It doesn't matter. We still lost. No silver lining. A sense of pride in what we'd done but a more lasting recognition in what we hadn't. You understand pretty soon in international rugby that it's about fine margins.

Great players having great days. Little moments of inspiration that have their roots in far longer hours of training and obsession. An afternoon that ends in silverware and glitter cannons and wild nights that happens because of the work you put in far from the cameras and watching eyes.

That's the story of the 2012 Grand Slam, really. 2008 couldn't have come about without the 2007 World Cup the autumn before. It was the long shot in the new dawn. And without the oh-so-nears of 2011 in New Zealand, 2012 couldn't have been. It was all logic and momentum. A team gathering pace, a balance between the fresh new faces and the wiser, older heads. That fitness, and confidence in what the fitness could bring, still there; a shared understanding of our way of playing the game, of what our coaches wanted now they had been there for four years, of what we could give them back.

The stuff you do that no one sees. I'd fractured and dislocated my big toe in the autumn. Not much of an injury, you think at first. It's a toe, not a leg. One down, nine functioning. Then one doctor tells you it's going to keep you out for four to six months, and another one tells you it's three to four months. I decided I could give myself a more positive timeline and see if I could make him look retrospectively pessimistic too.

I'd miss the first two games of the Six Nations. I'd manage only a game and a half for the Ospreys before the third. But I got back sooner than anyone thought, and I learned another lesson: your mind can take your body where it needs to go.

Meanwhile, I watched the narrow margins and the difference that great players make. The lead changed hands five times when we beat Ireland in Dublin in our opening game. We lost Bradley Davies to the sin bin. We were down with five minutes to play. There were 10 seconds left when Leigh Halfpenny stood over his match-winning penalty, 30 metres out.

Now there's always one of these games in a Six Nations. Sometimes it's at the start, sometimes at the end and often in the middle. Think of Scotland in Cardiff in 2010 or us in Paris in 2019. But what always tips them your way or the other is the player who doesn't get fazed by the scoreboard or intimidated by the occasion. They're just playing without fear. Without consequences.

George North was still only 18 months into his international career on that afternoon. And he was coming off his wing to bust through two Irish defenders and put Jonathan Davies away with a cat-flap out of the back of his hand, staying out left to break through three green shirts when we desperately needed a try at the death. He was unstoppable a lot of the time.

It was similar to the effect Shane Williams had already had for years, done in a contrasting style. And there's the scoring of tries, the easy things to see and clip up for highlights packages afterwards, and there's the tries you can create when you've made a break to set up someone else, or not even touched the ball but attracted the defence with the angle and timing of your run. The decoy, the threat, the space.

When you're that age and you're playing like that, it's confidence. It's not over-complicating it. You'll get better as a player as you soak up the education that tournaments and tight games bring, but you might never be quite so unshackled. You're right in the sweet spot between trying too hard and not trying enough. You don't chase the game; you're just immersed in it.

The more you play, the more you understand what happens next. You've got more to process. You're reading it and breaking it down. Studying it in real time, working out how you can influence it, what you need to help those around you. You'll get accused of being robotic, of lacking instinct and flair, but you're responding to what you know. How organized the opposition defence actually is, how fit they are across 80 minutes, the strength they have to bring off the bench. The factual, tangible stuff, in other words.

George was 19 years old in that Six Nations. Jon Davies was 23, Leigh Halfpenny the same. You didn't see fear in them. You could see the talent and the hard work, but the pure satisfaction too. The freedom.

Taulupe Faletau was 21. So was Alex Cuthbert. They both played critical roles as we beat Scotland the following week in Cardiff.

And then we come to Twickenham, and another 21-year-old, Scott Williams. 12 points apiece with five minutes to go, England with a nice quick ball off a scrum, Ben Youngs feeding Courtney Lawes, Lawes crashing over halfway and into this young replacement centre.

All these little things. You practise ripping the ball off players, but most of the time it doesn't come off. You might spend a career with that practice and never get one until it matters.

You think about why Scott was there. On as a sub for Jamie Roberts, Jamie getting on the wrong side of referee Steve Walsh and then struggling with a knee injury after tackling Manu Tuilagi. You think about the opportunity he had a few minutes before, breaking through with George outside him and getting caught. You very rarely get a second chance in the biggest games. You watch the clock ticking down and try to take comfort in the opposition's discomfort. Okay, they're at home here, they feel the pressure of going for the win, we can sit tight and wait for their mistake.

But it's not really luck, when you're inside the tent. You pick your cliché on this one: when it's your day, it's your day; the more I practise the luckier I get; the more I drop, the more I catch. You make the mistakes in training to be good enough for it to come right when it matters. You're brave enough to push yourself to the point when you seem to be failing. Mauling and scrummaging for the forwards, kick-off takes for those of us in the second row. The backs with endless grubbers, garryowens, spirals and box-kicks, incense and candles and massage when they're done having their fun. And if you kick a ball like that enough times, you know which bounce is the big bounce. When it sits up so you can run onto it without breaking stride, like Scott did when he kicked ahead and gathered to dive over the try line. It's the instinct of a player at this level.

The other elements to Scott's rip. Would I have attempted a rip had I been there? Maybe I would have just tried to get Courtney to the deck. Maybe Courtney would have fought more in contact had it not been a centre trying to stop him. Maybe if he'd seen a forward coming at him he would have gone to the deck rather than try to make those extra two or three yards. If Scott hadn't come off the bench, would he have had the legs to chase his own kick and get there before Tom Croft?

You can keep going. He can make that rip because of the hours he's spent in the gym. He makes the right decision because he's watched endless hours of rugby. He has the speed to get to the loose ball because he does sprint drills again and again in training.

And, if you're Welsh, you think about the historical aspects of it too. We win at Twickenham on emotion as well as ability. Great swings in the balance of the game. A refusal to accept it's over. 2008 and Mike Phillips and Lee Byrne. 2012 and Scott. 2015 and Dan Biggar and Lloyd Williams and Gareth Davies, but that one's for later on.

You wonder, looking in from the outside, if everyone in English rugby can tap into the same things you can if you're from Wales. I'm sure plenty can. In Wales, the majority of the men involved in the sport down the years have always worked. There's a difference, and I think it's a stark one. I could be wrong, but you're brought up on it. A deeper connection. Something driving you on.

There is luck in sport. You just do everything in your power to prevent it from having a decisive influence against you. You take it out of play by doing as much as you can everywhere else. It's making sure there are no excuses. You create the right environment around you, get your prep right. You watch the video analysis, you sort out your nutrition. You go to bed early and build on simple things.

It's taking three pairs of boots to a session or a match, because one pair might go and a second could, conceivably, but a third won't. It's taking two sets of shoulder pads so you can handle whatever session might arise. It's talking to the referee so you can understand that one man's interpretation of the game.

I wasn't lucky that my toe healed in time to get me back for the England game. I did everything I needed to do to recover. If you do all of that – everything in your power to win – and then you're beaten by the better team, then there's no real luck involved. If you've done everything on the pitch you said you were going to do, and you look back at the possession stats, the penalty counts, and you've got that right, then your performance has taken the element of chance out of it. It's not going to come down to one instance.

It's the same with superstitions. When I was younger, I had many more. I was like a surfer looking for the perfect wave. You know you'll never find it, but when you get close, you think, what was I doing? How can I replicate it?

The list when I was starting out. I didn't like to put my feet on the floor of the changing room. I'd lob a towel down instead. Sometimes I'd wet my socks and stretch them out, even if it was freezing outside. I wanted my feet clean going into the socks and then the boots. And the boots were always clean. I like to get as much of my strapping done as possible before going to the stadium – do my ankles, my shoulders, my ears. Only my legs and wrists to do on arrival.

You can grow out of some superstitions. Others you keep entirely for yourself. To share them would be to feel like you're exposing them to the light. And you continue with them because they're part of the routine. They're habitual.

After that win over England at Twickenham, after the win over Italy a fortnight later that set up the Grand Slam decider against France, it reminded me of our trajectory through the World Cup. It's different as a fan. For most, there will be another opportunity. You will be supporting Wales in four years' time, in eight. You can wait for a new dawn.

There's something you realize as you get older. The opportunities to do anything you love are finite. You want to hold your kids when they're tiny because they won't be babies forever. You want to take them to the park on a Wednesday afternoon because they'll soon be at school. You want to play with them when they ask because there'll come a point when they'll want to stay in their rooms on their own.

And international rugby is not parenting, but you're constantly made aware that the clock is ticking. You know what it takes to reach a semi-final. You know all the things you have to put into it. The commitment, the work, the skill.

So that's why it's hard to move on. That's why you have to get away from this feeling that it wasn't meant to be, that luck played a part. We all know negative people who'll say they're born unlucky. It never comes right for them, in the big moment. But if you have that mindset, you're going to be forever tired. You'll imagine you live in a world where everything is against you, and you'll be unhappy as a result. Better to appreciate the good things that took you there. To be grateful for the chances you had. That you made a World Cup semi-final at all.

With seven minutes to go in the France game there would be

a mere four points between the two teams. It's the easiest thing in the world to worry at that point. To glance up at the scoreboard and stop playing. And you can't stop playing against the best sides in the world.

But Gats had trained us for these moments. Telling us, we're not leaving the pitch until we've finished off four tries. A live session where the opposition had fewer numbers but they would all compete as hard as they could at the breakdown, so you'd have to be accurate – trying to create space. He might throw a scenario at you – right, we need two tries in the next five minutes. Constantly testing you, covering different scenarios so you were prepared for matches. The reinforcement of messaging too. Reminding us we had the fitness for when games got tight, for when they became an arm-wrestle. Understanding when to dig deep.

There was a collective belief under that coaching regime. We had been told in simple terms: if you do this and this, you'll win. If you lost a game, they'd keep it just as straightforward. Some would perceive it as harsh, but it was always honest. We didn't do this, so this happened. We trusted them because they were seldom wrong. They trusted us because they'd seen our blend of youth and experience. They'd seen us in Spała and in New Zealand.

They'll always go one of two ways, those Grand Slam deciders. It's either a blow-out or uncomfortably tight. You don't suddenly become uptight, but you lean towards the conservative. You'd rather stick to the plan in the early exchanges and wait for your opportunity than give them the ball cheaply. You think about the core details, about having the best of the territory and possession. About discipline and control. It doesn't need to be made into science. Sometimes it's not even your most challenging game. That might have been game two. That one back in mid-February might have been the decisive one, the one where you came closest to defeat. But that makes it the most dangerous.

And in 2012 we had plenty of players who had won a Grand

Slam before. We had a few who'd been around in 2005, too –
Gethin, Adam, Ryan Jones. You ask yourself the existential
questions in the days before the game, and the answers are easier.
Are you more equipped to do it again? Yes. Have you been here
before? Yes. Can you do it? Yes. Are you going to do it? Well, we're
going to find out.

When you're in the dressing room, and the minutes before
kick-off are accelerating away, it's the difference between being
nervous anxious and nervous worried. Those feelings are good.
You're aware of what's to come. If that stops, then you need to be
worried.

I knew what the team could do. I knew what I could do. We
had been here before. I wanted to do it again, so I just wanted to
get on with it.

And we controlled it, just. Alex Cuthbert's try. Leigh's conversion and two penalties. Dan Lydiate outstanding in defence. Me
there for 63 minutes until I left the field.

It's strange, watching minutes like those from the bench. I've
always hated being subbed off. Usually it means you've blown a
gasket and left it all out there, you're injured or you've played
badly. I'd like to think I don't blow a gasket. I'm not often injured.
So if you're off, it's a pretty significant tap on the shoulder. This
was different; I'd missed the first two games, so I had no divine
right to be on there at the end.

It was still difficult, sitting there. The same tension but without the ability to affect the game any more. Watching the clock,
watching the giant screen rather than the game in front of you
because it's easier to see the full picture of the play, not just
where the ball is on the pitch and who's got it. More able to see
what's coming, to read the turnovers, screaming and shouting
when you know something's going to happen and you can't do
anything about it.

When it's over, the tiredness leaves you. You stand on the
podium they've hurriedly built on the pitch, and you roar up at
the heavens as the fireworks go off and the smoke goes up. Me

on the middle row, Matthew Rees to my left, Adam Jones to the right.

You go to the post-match dinner at the Hilton in your black tie and you can't wait to get changed and head into the more vibrant part of town, only to return some time in the morning. A Super Sunday session to come the next day, on with the drinks and the good times. Thinking about how the nation had been starved of success, the 25 long years between Grand Slams and now a third in eight years. All the disappointment and negativity in the years when we weren't winning anything, everything that was happening around the country when Rhys Priestland booted the ball into the stands and Craig Joubert blew his whistle for full-time.

How the World Cup had been three defeats by five points, how this Six Nations had been a late penalty against Ireland, a late steal against England and a squeaky one at the death. Tiny margins, and this time on the right side of them. Luck does matter, when it's on your side.

13

CYMYDOGION | NEIGHBOURS

Wales against England. You'll know the history, the good times and the bad times. You'll know the clichés, the memes, the gifs. Everyone has their own feelings. So this is how it works, on the inside.

You learn early. When you're watching on TV as a kid, when you're there at Wembley in 1999 with your dad and thousands of people looking happier than you've ever seen anyone looking before. When you're playing for Wales under-16s, when normally no one outside the team knows you're playing, and you go into a corner shop a few days before and the shopkeeper winks at you and says, 'Good luck . . .' When you're strolling about a few days after and a stranger in the street grins at you and says, 'Good win at the weekend, that . . .'

Is it more than just rugby? You can get swept away in it all. It can churn you up inside. You're a fan before you become anything else.

But here's the thing: you can enjoy it too. Knowing it's coming, with its own place in the calendar. By the summer of 2021, I'd made 23 consecutive starts against England.

The occasion. How close so many of the games are. How it feels when the result slips away from you; how it feels when you keep hold of it. That day, the next morning, in the weeks that follow.

There's the geography: England on our border, our doorstep, in a way that no other nation is. There's the stereotypes, even if they're hollow when you turn them over: valley boys against the city slickers, the small towns against the Big Smoke. I don't know if it means more to Wales supporters than the English, but I know we're not afraid to show it. You only see how much this game matters to English fans when they lose. Us? We're as elated with a win as we are devastated by defeat. The English are reserved in victory, maybe because of their expectations, maybe previous history. I could be biased, I could be wrong. But that's what I've seen.

We were underdogs, under Warren Gatland, at the start. The psychological strategies he would use. And then, as we won Grand Slams, it changed again. They could call us what they liked. Sticks and stones. England with the overall edge in my time as a player, Wales with the edge in the biggest games of all – championship deciders, Grand Slam nights, World Cup epics. Each side happy to play the role when it suits them.

The week is magnified, leading up to Wales v. England. More press, more attention, a speeding up to the days that come before. The subtle digs and barbed comments from the coaches some-times lost on the media, everyone else preferring something blunter.

Apparently, if you beat England, as a Wales supporter, all else can be forgiven. Just as the Stereophonics told you in the song. And I can understand why some people subscribe to that, yet it doesn't ring true for a player. You recognize that Wales winning will lift the nation. You also know as a professional that you've got to think bigger. You want to win the tournament, not just one game within it. Where do you go next if you feel you've already peaked? You can play England first up in a Six Nations, third, or fourth. If you're drained by the emotional excess of that one game, it makes it that much harder to build up again and go just as hard a week later. It's not just England and it's not just one game. It can be used as a springboard, not just the sole target.

I've learned to try to control the emotional side. Never losing touch with it, always tapping into it, but not letting it overwhelm everything else. Focusing on the performance side of it: what you need to do, when to do it; the patterns and the play and the simple targets. In the early part of our success under Warren Gatland, England were often the team we had to beat to win a championship. Then it extended to France, and Ireland, but there was a hard, practical edge behind the romance and patriotism. There's always a team to beat.

You use all that good stuff for inspiration and motivation. To dig from within everything you can find in yourself.

You feel it all right, on the way to the game. You always do. The same journey to a familiar destination that's also subtly different every time. The past, the present. The hopes and dreams. The ride to the stadium on the bus, a special place to be.

What's it like in Cardiff when it's Wales against England? You go if you have a ticket, you go if you don't. You might be lucky enough to get a hotel room, and if you can afford it, you'll be in prime position. You might be one of five kipping on a mate's floor. It's packed in Cardiff when it's Wales–England at Twickenham. When it's at the Principality, it's like nowhere else in the sporting world. It's going to be a good night, win or lose. But if you win, it's going to be memorable. And a lot else besides.

It's an occasion for everyone. The ones piling on the trains from the west, the ones coming out of Paddington, coming home for the weekend with carrier bags full of cans of beer. Standing in the aisles of the Great Western train, finding old friends, making new ones. Thrilled if you're getting inside the stadium, thrilled if you're in the streets and pubs all around. You're always within earshot, in Cardiff. You're always connected.

You feel the privilege of being one of the few who can do anything about the result. And you can feel it in the air, too, that day. Almost like an invisible mist, heightening your primal senses. Test rugby, filling the air. Hard to explain, unless you've been there. Unforgettable when you have.

You like to think it's all timeless, too. That it feels the same to us as it did when Wales were winning three Grand Slams in the 1970s, as it did in the 1950s when Cliff Morgan and John Gwilliam were winning theirs. The stadium has changed, grown with the game in the city. The stands have switched on their axis and grown taller. There were no fireworks and flamethrowers when you walked out back then. But it's still a pitch, and two sets of posts, on the banks of the River Taff, in the middle of the capital city. It's still the Angel Hotel and Westgate Street. It's still Cardiff Castle and St Mary Street and the arcades.

The game against England in March 2013 was all those things. From that heritage, rooted in that history. And another chapter again, another to add to the myths and legends.

Not much had gone smoothly since the Grand Slam game against France 12 months before. A summer tour to Australia where we'd fancied pulling off a series win, only to go down 3–0. Beaten in the autumn by Argentina, by Samoa, the All Blacks and then the Wallabies again, at the death, to a Kurtley Beale try that had started deep in their half with less than a minute on the clock.

That last one pushed us out of the top eight in the world rankings, into the third band of seeds for the World Cup draw made a few days later. Setting in motion another Wales v. England clash that could prove to be unforgettable, a Saturday night at Twickenham to maybe match Wembley '99. We had no idea back then. How could we?

2013 coming around. I'd missed the home defeat to Ireland at the start of the Six Nations, when we had been 30–3 down at half-time, and then the start of the fightback, the win in Paris when George North's dad celebrated his son's try in rather public fashion and ended up in the gendarmes' cells. On the bench as we won in Rome, back starting as we beat Scotland at Murrayfield in a game of endless penalty kicks – 18 shots at the posts in total, 13 successful, eight of those for us.

England? They'd won all four. It was their turn for a shot at the Grand Slam, a decade after their last. There was trying to beat them. Then there was trying to beat them by enough to make it our championship, not theirs. A winning margin of seven. That was what we needed.

All that week, all we heard was that points difference and how we would never do it. And there is nothing as galvanizing as everyone telling you what you can't do. I had nothing against the people of England or any individual opposition player. But when a narrative is assumed, it gives you nothing to lose. You're coming to our home to win a Grand Slam? We haven't got a hope of turning you over? Okay. Okay.

You know, after a few years of this fixture, that anything you say publicly can be taken out of context and used as ammunition or fuel. For that week, we said nothing. Rob Howley didn't drop a single grenade. We just prepared. And thought about what it all meant.

You don't always need to talk, before a game like that. Sometimes you need to elevate your own performance and your own ambition, rather than compare with dramas in the past. Absorb the week, enjoy it and the sideshow that comes with it. You can get a lot of energy from emotion, but sometimes emotion can be the most tiring thing there is.

You don't need an updated version of the famous Phil Bennett speech from the 1970s. We're professionals now. It's too insular and insecure a perspective to have, saying you hate another nation. I don't hate the English. I don't obsess over England. I want to beat everyone.

You felt it that afternoon, that night. The bus journey in was quiet, until a montage started on the video screens. Us making big tackles, big runs. Scoring great tries. Eminem pounding away underneath it all.

Rumours were going around about how many English supporters had bought tickets. Where the debentures had gone, how much the touts were making. You couldn't see it on the streets, where it was red shirts and flags and dragons on faces.

But you never can. It was out on the pitch where you noticed –
the white shirts, the songs.

You wondered, for a tiny moment. And then 'Hen Wlad
Fy Nhadau' began, and your doubts just floated away. I'd
never heard it so loud. The brass band dropping away and the
whole congregation sang it *a cappella*. It was there in your chest,
in your heart. It was everyone with you. It was all of us, together.
Belonging.

*

0 mins: Wales 0–0 England
Noise. Noise.
   It's going to be a big one.
   Phases, early on. A scrum for us on their 22, good attacking
platform.
   We're going wide, familiar pattern.
   Keep playing, keep playing.
   Go wide, not wide wide. Wait for it to come.
   Penalty. England not rolling away.
   Leigh will have this. Yep. Come on . . .

8 mins: Wales 3–0 England
High ball from them. Leigh under it. Penalty Wales.
   Phillsy with the tap and go.
   Fend, acceleration.
   Go on, Phillsy . . .
   Get with him!
   Tom Croft over the ball. Get into him. Shove him backwards
and away.

18 mins: Wales 6–0 England
Feeling the pace. Take a knee at this scrum, breathe.
   Scrum cap off, too hot.

40 mins: Wales 9–3 England

We need to win by seven for the title. We're up by six.

Got to kick on here. We're not even a full score ahead, let alone comfortable. A slim margin.

If we're nine up, 11 up . . . but even then, it'll be real dangerous if we relax.

50 mins: Wales 9–3 England

English maul, our 22. Got to stop this.

Good set for them, if they go right here we're fucked.

Good outcome here, they're down.

Compete for the ball.

Now get up.

Scrum to us, our 22. Bomb looking for the early push – so strong, pinning his opposite number, them folding in.

Right side. Scrum penalty!

A roar so intense it's almost like the crowd are coming on . . .

53 mins: Wales 12–3 England

Legs filling up.

Heavy legs.

It's hard running normally. Each step getting heavier.

55 mins: Wales 12–3 England

25 to go.

England trying a short ball against the grain. Me going down in the tackle. Get back onside. Get back in the line.

Ken Owens disrupting it nicely. The ball squirting out the side.

Tips on it.

Phillsy there for him.

Fuck, there's a narrow four on two here . . .

Foxy, he's passed that early . . .

Pass to Cuthy, Cuthy accelerating, Mike Brown closing in . . .

Great hand-off! Go on son, you're in, you're in . . .

62 mins: Wales 19–3 England

Time stretching. Not long now. Still danger.

Toby Flood in space. I'm third man. He's going to attack my channel.

He shows for the pass to Lawes, dummies.

We've got a disconnect here. Trouble . . .

Got to catch him.

Past me.

Leigh on him, stopped just short.

Close.

64 mins: Wales 22–3 England

Great drop goal from Bigs. We've got to use this momentum now.

Restart from Farrell. Knock-on from Tom Wood, we'll have it back.

Toby with the ball. Fuck, what a sidestep. Fuck, another one! He's Phil Bennett here . . .

Almost through two more.

Warby in front of me at the ruck. England are short of numbers. Warby scooping the ball up, he's away . . .

Chase chase chase.

Half the length of the pitch under my boots. I'm not getting on his shoulder for the pass, but we need speed of ball here, I've got to get to the ruck.

We've just got to make this big hole work. This is the moment. It's there for us . . .

Phillsy to Bigs to Jamie.

Tips on his right.

Blue scrum cap. Knees up and driving.

Brad Barritt coming across on the inside, Mike Brown the full-back.

Going between them, showing the pass, cutting back inside.

Cuthy on his shoulder. Holding the pass, holding . . .
Brown committing. Pass perfect.
CUTHY!

Final score: Wales 30–3 England

*

They can be strange, games that end that way. With the result nailed on long before the final whistle. With the crowd celebrating even as you're sticking your head into another ruck. Dancing in the stands, heavy lifting on the pitch.

It could never be an anti-climax. Seven points needed, 27 found. A record-breaking margin of victory over England – bigger than the 27–3 of 1979, the 25–0 of 1905, the 26–3 of 1899. Back-to-back titles for the first time since 1978 and 1979. All that old history and something new and extraordinary from the here and now.

A presentation on the pitch, all the lights dropped except for that podium at the centre of it all. Each player called up individually, their name announced to the crowd, the crowd roaring its approval. Ryan Jones, injured, in his suit, with one hand on the Six Nations trophy; Gethin Jenkins, captain for the night, on the other side. Me on the back row, Mike Phillips to my left, Ken Owens to my right. A nation before us, a nation behind us.

When you begin your career, you want to be involved in the big ones. As you go through, you realize that if you want to win things, you've got to do it properly. You've got to beat everyone.

14

HUNAN HYDER | BELIEF

Each tour with the British and Irish Lions is different, each squad, each game. And that's a good thing, that air of discomfort. When you're picked for your second tour, you don't want it all too familiar and *welcome back Alun Wyn, nice to see you, come on in*. It needs to feel challenging. To feel on edge. To be thinking, this starts all over again, now. Nothing I did or didn't do last time makes the slightest difference now.

I felt excited as we set off for Australia at the start of June 2013. People might say that's a juvenile emotion to have, but I play a game for a living. And we're all kids inside; of course you're excited. Rugby, even at this level, is the easy bit. You've been given the opportunity to travel round a beautiful country, with an elite coaching and training environment around you, a shot at being selected. Everything is ramped up. Why wouldn't you feel excited?

Expectation, too, amongst the travelling support for the Test series that traditionally has been the most likely to end up in Lions success. Familiarity everywhere you looked on that plane to Hong Kong: Warren Gatland head coach; Rob Howley and Neil Jenkins in his coaching team; Adam Beard doing strength and conditioning; Bobby Stridgeon on fitness. Me now 27 years old, but no thought in my head about a leadership role just because I was more experienced, who I was, what I'd done, having only featured off the bench in the last two Tests on the tour of South Africa four years back. Taking confidence from the way Wales had come back into the Six Nations and won the championship 10 weeks before, from the players who had been part of that and were going to be part of this adventure too.

There were 15 Welshmen named in the original tour party, although Gethin Jenkins would pull out with injury early in the tour. And me with the same sort of attitude I'd had in 2009, the way I naturally was: not thinking about trying to be mates with anyone, pleased to be reconnecting and playing in the same team as my fellow survivors from South Africa, but no one in my cross-hairs. You know a little about me now. I don't like people, do I, I like rugby . . .

So as we travelled around Australia, from Perth to Sydney to Brisbane to Canberra, I listened to the speeches and the lovely words about what it means to be a Lion, and I enjoyed them, but I didn't need them. I didn't need to be told. I said a polite no thanks if I was offered the handheld camera for the tour DVD footage. I didn't want to be a monologue. I didn't want to perform for an audience. I just wanted to be me.

It's different on the inside. That first Test was a spectacular game: 52,000 fans inside the Suncorp Stadium, a clear winter night in Queensland, the air still warm. Brilliant tries from Israel Folau on his Wallabies debut, after Will Genia had tapped a quick penalty inside his own 22 and stepped and accelerated away; from George North, taking Berrick Barnes's overhit high kick and scorching away on a long curving run into the corner, skipping past James O'Connor, stepping Barnes, leaving Genia chasing his heels. Another from Folau, the explosive pace to hit a small gap and blow it open into a bigger one; Alex Cuthbert running onto a pass from Johnny Sexton and past four sets of Aussie hands to go under the posts. People forget how fast Cuthy was. Three of those defenders thought they had him, and he just burned past them. Only one got fingertips on him. Another just waved an arm at his back.

It's hard to enjoy it when you're in the middle of it all. We were seven points down right at the start. When we led, it was never by enough to feel safe. But even if you're winning and the score-board looks pretty, you can never sit back and allow yourself to appreciate a game. As soon as you slip into spectator mode, you're in the most dangerous place to be.

Things happen that are talking points if you're watching on TV. Christian Leali'ifano gets knocked out in the first minute and is carried off; Barnes gets stretchered off before half-time; Pat McCabe goes off the same way just after half-time. You barely note them when you're on the pitch. You don't have time. Formula One drivers don't win races by slowing to watch every time a rival goes into the pits.

Nothing matters but staying in the contest. I'm on the ground in a ruck in the third minute, and James Horwill either stamps on my face or accidentally treads on it, depending on your opinion. I had to do the citing afterwards, and the defence was that he was off balance. The judicial officer said there was no conclusive evidence he had acted recklessly. Now I've never seen anyone off balance who is falling one way and puts their leg the other way to stay upright, but that's rugby. And I'm not going to slate James, because he drove all the way down to Cardiff from London to my testimonial dinner, and that's rugby too.

It's more about how you react. If I stand up and retaliate, then I miss the rest of the series. Equally, you're not instinctively ready to trot away. I've had to check if my eye is still there. I've had stitches put in.

Why didn't I react? Some people will say I should have done. There's not many yellow cards on my Test record. And there's always those who tell you it's worth getting one in.

I'd rather stay in the series than have a few brief seconds of anger and satisfaction. There were 77 minutes left in the game, two more Tests to come. In what occupation is it worth putting yourself out of work for a month for one moment of gratification? I might have liked to. I don't profess to be an angel. But even back then, the disciplinary system had a responsibility to the game, just as much as the players.

I was subbed off in that game with 70 minutes gone and two points in the game. That made me angrier than being stamped on, to be honest. Not because I don't like Geoff Parling, who came on, but because I felt fine. I sprinted off the pitch, pretty much to show the coaches I was still fresh, and then almost passed out in the dugout. The heat, the exertion, the sprint – it was as if someone had pulled the plug out of me.

And there is a sense of incapacity when you're suddenly cast away on the bench. Have I done enough? That's the question in your head. Enough to win us this game, enough for your standards, enough to get picked to start again. Nothing you can do, as the scrum starts creaking. Nothing you can do, as referee Chris Pollock starts giving the opposition pack penalties. You may as well be sat in the stands, when Beale is lining up his penalty kicks to win it for them.

You take the recovery shake they've handed you. You start drinking, out of habit. You're getting ready for the next game even as this one is in its crescendo. You're watching the big screen at the end of the stadium, so you can see those patterns, the shape, and then when Beale is crouched down by his kicking tee in the final minute, you stare directly at him with the 50,000 others in the silent stadium.

You start preparing yourself. Right, if this goes over, and they win it, it's only the first Test. This isn't the end. And when he runs up and slips, his boots not getting the grip in the churned-up turf left by the scrums, and the ball cuts a low arc, falling short of the posts, bouncing and dribbling over the dead-ball line, you try to keep some of that relief and happiness hidden for the same reason.

You don't worry that Beale missed two penalties to win it. You don't worry about the two penalties and one conversion that James O'Connor missed too. No one remembers how you win, for very long afterwards. You ask nine out of 10 people on the street, they'll give you the headline rather than the small print.

From within, you know that detail. You analyse it all with the coaches afterwards and you analyse your own performance like the opposition would. What did I do okay? Where could I get better? And you remind yourself: this is just the first rung. The same way as when you're two from two in a Six Nations campaign, or in the quarter-finals of a big cup competition. This means nothing unless we win the next ones too.

You try to settle into the rhythm of a Lions series. A lighter training day on Monday, Tasty Tuesday as the kick up the backside. Wednesdays off if you're in the Test team, a half-day Thursday, captain's run Friday. Busier for some of the guys who might be involved off the bench in both the Saturday and midweek games.

You have team outings on down days, you have team meetings in the early evenings. You pop out for coffee and appreciate the Aussie love of a flat white. You enjoy the breadth of Aussie love for sport, and the little pockets it gives rugby union players to sometimes stroll about without being recognized. 'What are you lads over for, then?'

I saw John Eales in a cafe and got properly star-struck. Fuck, it's John Eales! A man who has won two World Cups, a lock who captained his country 60 times, a second row who could kick goals like a full-back. I caught up with my sister, and spoke to my mum and dad on the phone back home, not as often as I should have done. Getting woken up at three in the morning by the journalist back in the UK who was ghosting a newspaper column for me. *Mate, do you know what time it is over here?*

And the second Test came around in Melbourne, and it was just as tight as the first one, and this time it went the Wallabies' way. Not a lot of the sparkle and flair of the game seven days before, scrum penalties all over the place, Adam Ashley-Cooper going over for a try on the left off O'Connor's pass with a few minutes to go. Leigh Halfpenny's penalty from halfway to win it with time up falling short.

It's often the way, in these second games. It's a decider for one side. We were trying to lock it in; they were trying to be conservative. And you don't have time to look back and worry about it, because the critical match is almost upon you straight away, and there's so much weight on it that you know something's going to have to give.

It was the Tuesday when it changed for me. One of the later guys down for breakfast that day, sitting there eating my porridge, when Gats came over.

'Alun Wyn, Sam's obviously injured. We need a captain for the weekend. Do you want to do it?'

You might expect there were trumpets and blinding lights and an overwhelming sense of pride and joy. But it was just a team room of a big hotel in Sydney. I was eating porridge. And I knew Sam was injured, Paul O'Connell out too. Brian O'Driscoll must have been a contender, but still. So I just said, 'Yes', and nodded, and went back to my breakfast.

That was it. And I knew I didn't have much to do, apart from an afternoon training session, the team run on Friday and then the game. I hadn't even allowed myself an idle thought in the previous two days – those two lads are out, might I be next in line? I hadn't gone out there to be captain. I wasn't aiming to be captain. It would have been selfish to start thinking of myself as one before anyone had even asked.

And there was the other stuff. A third Test to decide a Lions series for the first time in 12 years, a team announcement on the Wednesday that seemed to upset a very large number of people. Not just 10 Welshmen in the starting XV, but an omission that no one had seen coming: Drico dropped, not only from the team but from the entire match-day squad.

The numbers of Wales players first. Gats had previous when it came to putting in lots of combinations from one team, the 13 Ospreys he'd picked for his first game as coach in 2008. Combinations make a lot of sense in tight games, on Lions tours.

Drico? Here's a few things that will sound like clichés but are actually true at the elite level. The margins between starting, being on the bench and being dropped are incredibly fine. For all you've done in the past, all you've shown on tour, selection comes down to one person's decision after a discussion with a couple of others.

I'm not sure Drico's display in the second Test defeat had a great deal to do with it. It had nothing to do with his legacy and what he had achieved in the game. Gats wasn't bringing in some kid from the cold; it was Jamie Roberts, playing alongside Jon Davies, a pairing that had been outstanding for Wales, and with Fox moving to outside centre rather than the 12 he'd been playing with Brian outside him, a more natural fit.

Everyone who loves the Lions has their own starting team. It's one of the beautiful things about it when you're on the outside. You pick on preference, nationality and whim. And sometimes a little unconscious bias.

As a player? Anyone can be dropped. Anyone can be picked. You understand that, when you've been around it. And while Brian had never been dropped by any coach in 16 years, sometimes you get more answers when things go wrong than when they go right.

So it was less of a story to us in the camp than it appeared to be for everyone back home. It had happened to me four years before, and I'd hated it, but the train rolls on. It wasn't going to do him any good if I went round to his room, asking him how he felt. He had enough experience of how the game works. He did maybe the hardest job of all: prepping the team, with the others who weren't selected.

You also have to be selfish about it. Rugby is a team sport, but you feeling sorry for another player or worrying about their selection isn't going to help your game, and thus the team's. It's not that you don't care. It's not as cold as that. You just have a job to do. I was fine with the fact that no one else gave a monkey's when I'd been dropped. You don't look back in international rugby.

Even when it happens to someone you're really close to on a personal level, you can't carry that with you. I'd display the disappointment for them but I wouldn't let it affect me. And I hope that, had it happened to me that week, no one else would let it affect them either. There is a definite line, too, between the professional side of things and the friendship or family part of your life, and sometimes you have to keep the two separate. It's easier when everything is going well, but even when it isn't, you have to remember how this world works.

Simplify it. That's often the best way, in these mad few days around a huge game. The messaging from the coaches, the drills in training. When people are making errors, as we seemed to do in our final session.

That would be me as a captain. As soon as I knew I was going to do it, I made the decision that I wouldn't change anything, wouldn't try to say anything different. We had been together for six weeks. The style of rugby, the tactics, were done. We weren't going to alter our fundamentals in those final few sessions we had.

And I had the utmost respect for my fellow professionals. I didn't need to inspire or tell them what was at stake or where we were or what we were doing or what it would mean. I was very aware that the more I tried to do, the more unsettling it would be for everyone else. I trusted the squad and I trusted myself. I didn't feel I needed to be anything else.

Here's something to share with you, having done captaincy for a long time at different levels, domestic and international. Depending on how long you do it for and how long the players around you have been playing for, a high proportion of them will have already heard a lot of what you might say. You have to read the room, and that's an instinctive feel thing, not something you're doing consciously.

You know now that I was a shy kid. That I'm quite happy on my own. I don't feel the need to speak all the time. You might then wonder why I'd want to end up doing something that seems like public speaking.

But that's the thing. It's the opposite of public speaking. I'm not standing up in front of strangers. I'm not addressing a business conference or some vast television audience. These are my teammates, players I've hurt myself against to get here but now play alongside, and who now want exactly the same outcome as I do. And as you do it, and you learn what works, you understand that knowing what not to say and when not to say it is more important than what you do say.

Communication is the hardest part. Not in the game, when it's like passing messages on a battlefield where your carefully laid plans have already been detonated on first contact with the enemy. Through clarity you get accuracy. On the way into a game, to create a line or to create a play, to create so you get everybody on the same page and then find the emotive stuff.

You need to work out which players need a lift and which don't. You must realize you can't raise everyone. If you try to carry too many, you're going to drag yourself down. It's sharing that responsibility with the senior guys who have been through it before, with the younger guys who are switched on and ready to have a say too.

Don't do too much. That's the golden rule. It's there with some coaches too: the desire to cover every base, to find some magic. To exert some control in a situation where people are throwing up with nerves, a situation where for 80 minutes you might feel as if you have no control at all. Three words can be enough. It doesn't have to be a lot to get you to the right outcome.

There would be 82,000 people in the Sydney Olympic Stadium that night. Intimidating in theory, but only a couple of thousand more fans than we were used to at the Millennium Stadium in Cardiff, always a huge travelling support with the Lions. You sit there and acknowledge the nerves and the excitement and the pressure and the expectation, but you try to welcome them. Alun Wyn, this is what it's all about. This is why I do this. This is why we play.

I had listened to Andy Farrell in one of our last meetings before the game. It was what you might know as the Hurt Arena

Speech. The one where he told us there was no tomorrow. His way of sharpening our minds.

It sat with me afterwards. And I thought, but there is a tomorrow. There's only one day in your life when there isn't a tomorrow, and that's when you die. There's always a tomorrow until that happens.

So in the dressing room that July night, as we held the huddle before walking out, Conor Murray under my right arm, Owen Farrell under my left, that was what I returned to.

Not shouting, not ranting. Not even a swear word in there. Looking round at the calibre of player, holding pauses, looking into their eyes.

'I've got no apologies for saying what's already been said. We will be physical, we will be aggressive, we will be disciplined. Every facet of the game.

'And the final thing. Faz said there was no tomorrow after today. There is. There is a tomorrow.

'There's one with this jersey, and it will remain on you until you finish playing. Until you die. From today. And there's a tomorrow without the jersey.

'We've got 80 minutes to choose which one we want. Let's go.'

You don't always need to swear in moments like that. You read the room, and you can see that to a man the guys around you are already at the right level for the game. You can say too much, spill them over or lose them just before they are about to go out. When you look around and you see the eyes are ready, they don't need much.

It only became slightly surreal as we walked out of the tunnel and I was carrying Bil, the stuffed toy lion. Knowing the names of the men who had had the honour before. Okay, this is pretty cool now. Reminding myself, there are guys behind me that have won Grand Slams, captained their clubs, captained their national sides. I'm only pushing the rudder right or left here. Nothing I do on the field will matter any more or less than the stuff these men do too.

And you look around, at the supporters and the lights, the cameras and the green grass and white lines, and you absorb it all. You know it's all going to help you somehow drag more out of yourself. Maybe that's the same for the opposition, too. They're open to all the same intense external stimuli you're feeling. But you also know it's the end of your season. They can take you back home in a body bag if they have to. Everything you have done in your rugby life has led to this moment.

*

0 mins: Lions 0–0 Australia
Sexton with the kick-off. Here we go, get after it.

Knock-on! Genia dropping it. The first into the game, 17 seconds. Not great for them, that – unforced error, our set piece in their 22, prime location.

Clap for the boys. Momentum momentum.

Early engagement from them at the scrum, free-kick. Standing up to see Phillsy going right, Tommy Bowe charging.

Three metres out, their right-hand corner.

Hibs taking it on. Got to get there, my wipe – head down, clear out, get ready for the next set.

Seán O'Brien going now, Corbs and Bomb latching on and driving forward. Folding round behind him. Phillsy hitting me on the short ball.

Driving driving driving. There's the yellow padding on the posts right in front of me . . .

Nah, not there, don't risk reaching, don't turn a good carry bad. They're so stretched here, and they're honeypotting, all piling in for the ball.

Present it back. Phillsy. Corbs steps inside Benn Robinson, rolling . . . try!

Fuck he's done well there, stepping and rolling.

Leigh with the conversion. Perfect start.

'BOYS! Let's go again! It's still 0–0!'

38 mins: Lions 19–3 Australia

Penalties piling up. Scrum dominant. Leigh kicking everything. Benn Robinson in the bin, coming back now.

Come on. Hold them 'til half-time.

Aussie lineout. Genia going down the blind-side, got to get him – arm out, hand round his hips, sliding down, taking his legs.

Penalty coming, they'll kick this to the corner, they need the points.

They're going to the back. Palu to Mowen, coming back to take it again, five metres out, three, one . . .

Stopped him. Come on. They score now and it's 19–10. It's a one-try game.

Stopping another charge. Tackle, tackle. Fill the line.

Wallaby scrum. Collapsing.

Bomb's not happy here. Reassure him, last thing we want to do here is piss referee Poite off in a tête-à-tête.

Decent scrum from them. Genia to O'Connor. Stepping Sexton. Seán picking up the inside runner, tripping.

Boys scrambling. O'Connor stepping through the corridor.

Decent try. Decent footwork.

19–10. No point in saying anything under the posts. Let's get into the sheds, reset, regroup.

It's loud now, going in. Yellow and red everywhere you look.

Game on . . .

55 mins: Lions 22–16 Australia

Sexton dinking a kick over the top. George running onto it, Foxy inside him.

Lions lineout, just outside their 22. Dan Cole taking it on. Me picking and going.

No hole, find the floor, recycle quick.

Tommy Bowe coming off his right wing. Sexton pass out the back – checking the pass, carrying on his run.

Foxy. Leigh into their 22. Genia has to push in, George has kept his width out wide.

Johnny there in Leigh's inside. Bread and butter, boys – half-backs chew up those positive lines on the inside.

Great try!

Fuck, you can see Johnny knew as soon as he passed it – shit, this is the one . . .

63 mins: Lions 29–16 Australia

Another souvenir here. I've got split on the head. No time for stitches, just stick on some Vaseline and a scrum cap.

Lineout inside their half. Fox kicking long. Genia and Beale letting it bounce in back field. Genia running out of time. His kick isn't finding touch . . .

Great ball-tracking from Leigh to field it.

Missed tackle! Tomane's let him go, two v. one . . .

Leigh drawing Beale. George outside him.

Clear space.

Try!

Not trying to calm anyone down now. Recoup for the kick-off – 18-point game, 14 minutes to go. The momentum with us – and they have to risk it now, they . . .

Short kick-off, knock-on. Different level here.

Scrum pen in our own half.

Lovely nudge – a forward nudge – from about 35 to their 22. Go on son, boosh . . .

Defenders sucked into maul not really going forward, but Conor Murray's going – Hooper held on the inside, Jamie on a lovely angle – through O'Connor . . . fending Genia . . . go on Doc, go on . . .

Conversion going over. 25 points ahead, 11 to go . . .

Final score: Lions 41–16 Australia

*

You're still breathing it all in for hours after a game like that. When you're interviewed live on TV and the noise from the fans is so intense you can barely hear the questions you're being asked. When you step up onto the plinth they've erected in the centre circle and you stand in your sweaty, bloodied kit next to Sam Warburton in his Lions suit and tie, and they hand you the Tom Richards trophy and you exchange a little nod and a smile before hoisting it high. When you take it over to the team, lined up in messy order by the big advertising boards, and you raise it again after the comedy tease of the 'ohhhh . . ' and the red confetti gets blasted up into the air and you're all jumping around and feeling like you could go all over again, if you had to.

It's not the photos you're bothered about. Not the frozen moments that'll be sent back home. It's the real stuff, the things you see, the looks and the hugs. Seeing Gats, a handshake turning into an embrace, dropping my forehead onto his shoulder for a rest. Realizing, as we walked around the perimeter of the pitch, waving to our support, that I didn't have a Welsh flag with me, and then somehow spotting Kevin Brooks, my old age-group coach from Bonymaen, waving one at me with 'BONYMAEN RFC' stencilled across the top in big black letters.

Thinking, had I not gone up the hill to Bonymaen that time, would any of this be happening? Putting that flag across my shoulders, feeling the pride and the pull of my roots. I'd take it into the dressing room that night, drink with it, wrap it round me. Then I'd fold it carefully, stash it in my kitbag. Take it all the way home, and then, when I got back to south Wales, go back up the hill to find Kevin and present it back to the club. From you to me to you again.

It's a hard feeling to describe, the stuff that fizzes through your head and heart. There's disbelief, even when you've won by 25 points. There's the sense of relief: we made it. You don't actually want it to be over. You've poured so much of yourself into it. The adrenaline you used during the game slowly dies away and the endorphins carry you through.

It's a beautiful thing to experience, even if you know there'll be a downer to follow, a few days on, when you start to come off this high. It's emotional again in the dressing room, when you all gather again and the songs start, and the beers. It's surreal, when you find yourself chatting to Daniel Craig. It grabs at you, as you fold the Bonymaen flag away.

So of course the night beyond is magical. I think that was the night Tommy Bowe and Alex Cuthbert ended up in the swimming pool in a nightclub somewhere. Well, if they will put swimming pools in nightclubs . . .

The all-dayer the day after is almost more enjoyable than the immediate celebrations. You can take your time. It just unfolds gently in front of you. You recover from your first hangover by doing the same thing all over again. You try to appreciate all you have around you, even as it all draws to a close.

You look around and see the lads you've got to know better than you thought. I'd roomed with Manu Tuilagi early on, another man of few words. Alex Corbisiero, another exemplary roommate. Then there was Stuart Hogg, who'd stunned me by claiming never to have seen *The Karate Kid*. I bought him the DVD after that.

You can't single players out after a Lions tour. Equally, you're always glad you've got someone like Leigh Halfpenny on your side rather than the opposition's. Those penalties he knocked over in the third Test were absolute momentum-killers for the Wallabies, and that's without thinking of the pressure it puts on a rival's attack, or defence, or discipline, when they know you have someone who will punish any mistake or misjudgement. You've got a place-kicker you can rely on from 45 metres? Then they're worth their weight in gold.

And none of it happens by accident. Leigh is properly obsessive with his kicking. A brotherhood, with the other kickers, with kicking coach Neil Jenkins. When they headed off with a bag of balls and their tees, it was like watching a bunch of mates go off to the driving range. All they want to do is kick and talk kicking.

19 penalties, 21 conversions. A record number of points for a Lions player in one Test, breaking Jenks's own record for most points across three Tests. Man of the series, in case he needed anything else. That's all outside of the other things he did for us as well. Without denigrating other sports, there are some professions where your job is to do one thing only. Leigh kicks, and then does everything I do bar the set piece. There's the yards he makes with ball in hand, and there's the last-ditch tackles he's made. He's put his head on the wrong side a few times, not through lack of technique but through sheer courage. I'll remember him as much for when he's put his body on the line as when he's banged over a kick from the halfway line.

He's quiet off the pitch, Leigh. He goes into Test mode early in the week. Like that mood with hackers when they're locked into some coding, like there's nothing else in his world.

That's the way it should be. Add up those individual obsessions across a squad, across a tour, and you'll be okay. That's why the satisfaction sticks around. And when it's the end of the season, it's different to a Six Nations campaign in March, when you've still got domestic games and maybe a summer tour to come. You know how quickly the next one comes; how fast you'll be jumping back on that train.

15

SIALENS | CHALLENGE

It was a crazy old day, the final Saturday of the 2015 Six Nations. Three teams in with a shot of winning it, us stacking up tries on Italy to go top, Ireland sticking a load on Scotland to overtake us on points scored, England needing a record-breaking win over France to come past in the final game and just falling short. Third place for us, an overthrown pass or missed tackle away from winning the thing again.

And it was a crazy old late summer, preparing us for the World Cup that was to follow in the British autumn. Not the cold of Gdańsk this time, not the empty forests of Spała. This time, the desert heat of Qatar. You don't know how much more you can hurt, after you've survived Gdańsk and Spała, but that's only because you've never done scrum drills in 40-degree heat.

Tough? It might have been the most brutal training camp I've ever been on. When you see ambulances parked around the pitch for each session, it sets a certain tone. Players with oxygen masks strapped to their faces, laid down on the cool tile floor of the changing rooms. All this sandwiched between two training camps in the Swiss Alps, sleeping 2,250 metres up at Fiescheralp, training at 1,050 metres in the resort of Fiesch.

Two warm-up games against Ireland, and then into the tournament. Uruguay up first, then England, Fiji and Australia. A pool of death again, after a summer of feeling you were close to it, yet we didn't feel that pressure. We'd play two games in Cardiff, but it was England's tournament to host, and Warren Gatland used that from the start. And there were murmurings about what was going on in their set-up, about how relaxed ours was in comparison.

We were seven years into the Gatland/Edwards axis. We'd won two Grand Slams, another Six Nations title, made the semifinals of the previous World Cup. We knew what we were doing worked. We believed we could win the whole thing, not just get out of that group. And that confidence came through in how we behaved. We didn't need our coaches to act like teachers on a school trip. We were allowed a drink if we'd been training hard. We were trusted to have a couple and not go bananas.

Psychology in plain sight from Gats: I told you I'd work you harder than everyone else, and now all the other nations are playing catch-up and trying to get to the same place. In those final weeks before the tournament began, you couldn't move for head coaches saying how fit their teams were. You couldn't move for talk of the culture around teams.

Now 'culture' to me is just a label. A buzzword. It means nothing on its own. Someone sees a player putting a bag on a bus and it's as if no other player in history has ever tidied up the dressing room, picked up a bottle or put a bag in the hold. You get four or five years into elite sport and the moment a coach sits you down and announces you're doing a team meeting about culture, you roll your eyes and think, here we go again. You can't manufacture culture.

Be honest with each other. Treat people well, the places you go, the facilities you use. Live your values. That's all you need to know.

When teams get it wrong, when it's coming down from above in schoolmasterly fashion, it's like having a big red button in front of you and being told not to press it. Suddenly everyone's obsessed with the big red button. At 21 years old you might need some guidance. At 23 or 24, you're old enough to make your own decisions. You've been around the elite environment long enough to understand what it takes. If you want a few pints one evening, fine, as long as you turn up and do your job as well as you would have done without a drink. Some players do. It works for them.

We were missing three big players through injury. Leigh Halfpenny, Rhys Webb, Jonathan Davies. We won one of the warm-up games and lost the other. But we were in a good place.

When you hear how many tickets their fans have compared to yours, it sets a challenge. Fucking hell, you lot all think this, but we're going to do that. Tickets? This is 15 men against 15. It's 80 minutes of going at each other, not an evening in a corporate hospitality tent.

It can be wonderful being the hunted when you know no one's going to catch you. It's what New Zealand were able to do for years. When you're that imperious, you can be hunted all you like. They're not going to kill you.

Yet you enjoy that challenge. Twickenham can be an intimidating place, I'm not going to lie about that. But it's not more intimidating than any other big stadium on match day, whether that's the Aviva in Dublin or the Stade de France. And it's not the stadium itself, the white concrete and the dark green seats. If I walked round it in the middle of the week, I wouldn't feel any of it.

It's going there representing your country. It's the occasion. And you relish that intimidation, feel glad you have the opportunity to respond. It's like jumping off the 10-metre diving board at a swimming pool: all your senses tingling, endorphins raging . . . and when you make it, pure enjoyment, pure satisfaction. Let's do it again!

There was the messaging too. Boys, we won here in 2012. We won here in 2008. You know we can, and we will if you want to.

When it's reinforced, you believe it. You do what you say you were going to do, and it happens.

We'd beaten Uruguay easily enough in our opening game on the Sunday. Then it was onto the coach for the journey west. Staying at Oatlands Park in Weybridge, just down the M3 from Twickenham.

You understand, after a while. What you need to do to get ready for a game of that size. Whether you're better using the Jacuzzi or the pool, the day before. When you want your massage. What to eat. You constantly tinker with the blend to find something slightly better. The big decision: chocolate or sweets?

You go to the ground the day before for your team run, look up at the empty stands. Remember what the changing rooms feel like, the walk up the tunnel to the pitch. Picture how it'll be a day later, when every single seat will be filled. When the bars will be heaving and the floodlights on bright. Nervous in my early days, feeling the stress of it all in your stomach. Better as I matured, as I took enjoyment from the same forces instead. And then you drive back to the hotel, have a chilled day, make a few calls, and then have what I always thought of as the Last Supper. You might get injured that next day. You might not get picked again. Appreciate it while you can.

The morning? You've done most of your analysis. Just a little top-up of some set-piece stuff, particularly around the kick-off and the restarts, the third set piece. It's a cliché, but you drop a restart after you've just scored or taken the lead, and it's the worst sort of self-inflicted blow.

*

9 mins: Wales 3–0 England
Good pen from Biggs, let's back it up.

The noise is real.

Our lineout just inside our half. Scott Baldwin to me. Parling knows it, but if we time this right, doesn't matter.

Down to Gareth Davies. What's Garces blown for here – not straight?

First lineout, fine margins. Not sure about this. Big screen confirms it.

Scrum England.

Penalty England. Ref likes what he sees?

15 mins: Wales 3–3 England

Bradley Davies on the carry. Bit exposed there, Dan Cole over him, could be turnover ball here.

Garces with the whistle – ooh, he's done him for hands on the floor. We've got away with one there.

Biggs with the penalty.

Over from Biggs. Get ready for the restart.

20 mins: Wales 6–6 England

Lineout to us on our own 22.

Fuck, Parling taking it off my fingertips.

Scrum coming. Big shove again from them – carbon copy of the first one. That picture's getting in the ref's mind now. Farrell's not going to miss this kick . . .

25 mins: Wales 6–9 England

We're getting a lot of possession, not much territory. Two metres forward, but not enough. Reset, back into another tackle.

Toby. Warby. Jamie Roberts, straight at Burgess.

Me having a go. Ball back.

Lyds burrowing low, he's going to get caught on his back here, Robshaw and Lawes over him . . .

Penalty England. Farrell kicking to our 22.

England lineout. Parling off the top to Ben Youngs. Billy Vunipola, passing it left to Farrell, not charging.

Watson. Brown outside him.

Bobbling pass. Brown stopping, going again.

Defence out of place. If that goes to hand, Sanjay's got him covered, George inside on Watson. More boys inside.

Youngs sniping. Two v. one down the left, pass to May . . . try England . . .

38 mins: Wales 6–16 England

Lineout to us, just inside our half.

Let's go front ball. It'll work. Keep it simple.

Bradley Davies with the catch. Quick ball. Sam Burgess up too fast, dummy runners. Scott Williams into the gap on his outside shoulder! Accelerating, curving, into their 22 . . .

Nearly the offload to Biggs. England off their feet. Penalty coming, go right to George . . . Back for the penalty.

Biggs in front, easy for him.

Okay. Half-time, the difference only a converted try.

Plenty left in us. And this.

67 mins: Wales 18–22 England

Injuries mounting. Scott stretchered off, Cuthy on. Sanjay off, Hallam Amos off. Lloyd Williams on, scrum-half, out on the left wing. Rhys Priestland to fly-half. Biggs to full-back. George to centre.

We've got to get on with it.

Look at Biggs, back there. Three things you need at 15: defence, aerial skills, kicking game.

69 mins: Wales 18–25 England

Okay. Farrell penalty to stretch the lead for them, but that could have been a try. May and Wigglesworth down the left. Scramble defence.

Ford on for Burgess for them. Lineout to us, quick ball off the top, Jamie running straight down Ford's channel.

The game speeding up, opening up. Noise getting louder.

Ruck short of their 10-metre line. Me ready to carry, Gareth with the pass into my chest.

Space outside. Pass left to Rhys. Rhys to Biggs, miss-pass to Jamie.

Jamie committing Watson. Lloyd Williams free on the touch-line.

Think where the breakdown will be. Sprint there.

Gar past me on my inside. Cutting a positive line.

Lloyd running out of room. Kicking cross-field off his left foot.

Wigglesworth trying to cover. Gar in space. Haskell trying to get there.

Me trying to get there.

The ball bouncing low. Gar sprinting, stooping.

Crazy pick-up . . .

Try!

Breathe. Take in air . . .

Watching the replay on the big screen.

How does Gar pick that up?

Biggs with the conversion; 25 all, nine to go.

Here we go.

73 mins: Wales 25–25 England

Not thinking fitness. Not thinking of World Cups. Thinking, where's the ball going?

Be brave. Shift to Doc, he can kick it clear. Be brave.

Ford kicking it back, Rhys under the high ball. Biggs clearing kick, Ford again.

Rhys kicking. Mike Brown under it. Running at us on half-way.

George stopping him. Melon jackalling.

He's holding on . . .

Warby in there. Brown still holding . . .

Garces's arm up. Penalty . . .

A metre inside England's half. Biggs'll have a crack from here. This is what he was made for.

Pre-kick routine.

Bang on target . . . three points!

75 mins: Wales 28–25 England
Discipline. Defence.

Pressure mounting on their lineout.

Coming at us down their right. Massive hit from Charts, off the bench for Bradley.

Brown running hard. Dip my shoulder, slow him, stop him. Can't roll away, trapped – make it obvious I'm trying.

Warby after the ball, digging. Whistle – infringement at the ruck – fuck, penalty England.

Okay. They going for the posts here, or kicking to the corner?

To the corner. An English driving maul, on our five-metre line.

Charts, six foot 10.

Ken Owens defending in the middle of lineout. Watch them.

England going front. Robshaw going up for it. Let him come down . . . and go!

Charts in early. Long arms.

Now we go through. Now we pile in. Don't give them a chance, don't give them anything . . .

Driving. England in touch. Emotion taking over.

Still two minutes to go . . .

Our lineout.

Hit Charts at the front.

Clean take. Still pressure on us. Keep control, get a good little nudge on.

Take it in, big clearing kick from Gar.

One more England lineout. Under pressure, is that a knock-on?

Take the scrum. Focus.

40 seconds to go.

Big England shove again, feeling the pressure build.

Pressure telling. Toby brilliant at the base. Support quick to him.

Glance up at the clock on the screen.

79.56.

Back to Biggs. Kick it off!

79.59. Biggs leathering it.

Ball out.

Glancing back at the board. At the ref. At the whistle going to his mouth.

That's it. It's over . . .

Final score: Wales 28–25 England

*

It went so quiet in the stands at the end. Us hugging, celebrating maybe more than we should have been for a group game that didn't even guarantee we were going through, but a reflection of the bullshit that had gone before. What we'd been told was going to happen by everyone outside the camp; what actually had.

You're not gloating. I realized what England's players were going through. I've had days that should have been landmarks but ended up being unforgettable for all the wrong reasons. Days that others are telling you will be career-defining, where you end up losing and then carry it with you.

I did think, as we walked back down the tunnel, as we sat there in the dressing room with the beers, pulling off damp shirts and peeling the strapping from shoulders and legs, how serendipitous sport can be. How the man who isn't your first-choice scrum-half ends up on the wing. Whether, had it been a winger on the end of that Jamie Roberts pass, he would have cut back inside and carried the ball into contact for the next phase, rather than kicking ahead. Whether Gareth Davies would have kicked for Lloyd, and Lloyd made the supporting run to get to the loose ball. How Gareth hung onto a ball that was spinning and bobbling and only brushed against his middle fingers, not into his palms.

We'd beaten Uruguay, England and Fiji. By the time we came to play Australia back at Twickenham, we knew we were through. It was just about whether we came first or second. First, and a route onwards that would take in a quarter-final against Scotland and a semi against Ireland or Argentina. Second, and it was South Africa, and then New Zealand or France.

And we should have beaten them. Not because we took them apart, but because we didn't in the seven long second-half minutes when they were down to 13 men.

The regrets when you look back, the elements you still can't quite understand. Camped on their line with a two-man overlap out wide, and we kept doing short balls. Toby's rare mistake, knocking on when it looked like he was over, George North held up over the line.

Why? Maybe because we'd had it drummed into us about keeping the ball and not going too wide. Sometimes simplicity can be your downfall as much as your friend. This isn't criticism, this is reflection. Sometimes when games are that close and you're chasing, you just instinctively go safe. It's easier, on a sub-conscious level. When under stress, you default to your comfort zone. But you also climb back to your feet from a ruck, see the space out to your right and think, opportunity missed.

You don't want to be the one making the mistake, not when in a game of that magnitude, not when you know how critical that one score could be. That's what's in your head. Then there's the defensive effort a team can summon up when two of their team-mates are off the field and the world feels like it's crashing down on them. A team gets one yellow card, it galvanizes them. You get two, and no one completes a single-man tackle. The team at full strength commits an extra two men, and you've lost the numbers game on the rucks alone.

You try to control the frustration. The question keeps nudging you – will the dam ever break? – but you have to push it away, otherwise the answer will be no. You go looking instead for the sweet spot. Where you can execute your skills without trying too hard, but still trying enough. When all 15 blokes on your team are feeling the same way.

We weren't far away. We were getting to the right areas of the field, we were staying there. It was literally just the final pass. And once the Wallabies got through that period, they could take all that momentum and belief into the remainder of the game. We'd had our shot, and we'd swung and missed.

But we were through, and the victim of the group of death was England. From the outside looking in, you got a fresh appreciation of the pressures of a home World Cup. Of what expectation can do to you. How a team culture can't be manufactured, but is lived, created, born. Of what happens when you lose after everyone has been told you might win. The criticism, the endless reviews, the way some careers come to an end and others never recover. The scapegoats, the victims. The fickle nature of elite sport.

You look forward rather than back. Not back to the Amex Stadium in Brighton, and the Springboks being beaten by a last-minute try to give Japan the greatest moment in their rugby history. Not at the way Heyneke Meyer's side had ground their way past Samoa, Scotland and the USA. Not at the fact that we had lost nine senior players to injury.

Forward to a quarter-final at Twickenham, forward to an alternative reality. Not thinking, ah, we can't win it now, we've lost too many lads. Not thinking, we don't have to win it now, everyone will understand. Instead, the sort of deliberate benign delusion that only makes sense if you've been there. Right. This has happened for a reason. The guys coming in are going to do something special. Not consciously turning it into a positive, but trusting the competitive instinct of those coming in. Knowing that if I were the next cab off the rank, I'd be charging into this game. Every campaign you go through, you lose friends to injury. There's always a player to replace them. Everyone will keep going. Nothing will change. Someone new will be in the red jersey with the white number 5 on the back. The train rolls on.

You don't question the strength of a South Africa team. You know what you're going to get, and that's why they've been so successful. Rock-solid in the foundations of the game, the set piece. Always in the high 80s, early 90s, mid-90s percentage success rate at the scrum and lineout. Always a decent back line, always a great place-kicker. It's a cliché of Springbok teams throughout history, but any team with a decent set piece is going to get more possession and more front-foot ball. Because of the set piece they're winning in their half, they're going to create a set piece in your half and then work it hard to try to turn it over. It's not rocket science; it's what England adopted for a long time, it's what New Zealand do a lot of but add in a better counter-attacking game on top than anyone else.

It's the rugby blueprint, with the physical stuff underlined and in bold. Simplicity consistently works for the Springboks. That's not a derogatory comment. It creates clarity. That's why they've reached three World Cup finals and won them all. You know what they're going to do, but so do they. There's a big difference between seeing that a runaway truck is about to hit you and being able to stop it.

Simplicity from Gats to us as well. Keep our pattern. Get the kicking game right through Dan Biggar. We've made good chances, just crack on.

That was the way he was around big games. As a player, you feel like you've already mentally downloaded everything you need. As a lock, you know your lineout calls, you know where you want to be on the restarts. You know the set moves. So sometimes, in those intense moments in the changing room before you went out, it would just be three words. When you're running out into a World Cup quarter-final, you don't need *War and Peace* buzzing through your head. There's time for Tolstoy in retirement.

Here's a secret, in those big games. You don't have to psych yourself up more because the team you're coming up against has a reputation for being physical. Every team at the top end is physical. Within that team there'll always be one player who is even more physical than the rest. That's fine. It's a familiar challenge. It's the day job.

And your game will naturally rise to the occasion. A World Cup quarter-final, the high-wire of knock-out rugby. You do your tactical analysis, you get yourself physically right. That's enough. Under Shaun Edwards, we had learned to take pride in our own physicality. We never thought, we're playing England this week, we can take a step back. Never, ah it's France, let's step it up. Knowing instead exactly what we were about, and what the expectation was. Understanding you would need to do it more accurately, the bigger the game, the greater the pressure. Stay the same, but do it better.

It's still rugby, the stuff you experience when you run onto the pitch and the whistle goes. You're not conscious of shouts in Afrikaans, of a different accent. You can hear yourself blowing out of your arse, when the ball's in play. When you're head down in a scrum, you can't hear much at all, because you're locked in so tight. That's where the cauliflower ears come from. That's why you'll sometimes see me asking the referee, as we pack down, to give us his instructions in a louder voice. It's all too easy to miss the jump on the scrum.

We expected that game to be tight. It was. Early penalties for them, a try for us worked off Dan Biggar's kicking game. Up and under, Dan going up to reclaim it, Gareth Davies there on his right to take the pass and slide over the line.

They're always won by a single score, these sorts of games. You know it's going to come down to one piece of brilliance or one tiny misjudgement, a knock-on somewhere or a penalty given away when you move beyond that sweet spot and try just a little too hard for one little moment. You're so conscious of it on the pitch. It's why the game ends up being played between the 22s. It's not that you lack ambition, but that you cancel each other out. The margins aren't there to risk any more. Why go wide if that man's going to get isolated, if the space is so limited that there's more around the fringes for the heavy artillery?

But it's dangerous, wherever you are. You're both waiting for the opposition to make a mistake. You're both almost happier without the ball. Play for containment rather than ambition. Dull? It's a World Cup. You're on the brink of a semi-final. Another chance won't come along for four years, when some careers may be over.

So you wait for your opportunity, knowing they're few and far between. You think you have one, and it's shut down almost instantly. The internal dialogue trying to find some calm in the storm. Fuck, another one gone!

You need to show the referee the pictures he wants to see; don't give him any reason to give that decisive penalty against you. All the time recognizing that his perception would have come from the game before, because that's the one he will have studied to try to work out where the issues in this one will be. Is your scrum under pressure? Does your defensive line push it on offsides? The paint's dry on that picture. That's the one he's had time to look at. Not now, in the midst of this, with 80,000 people screaming at him, with players piling into rucks from both sides, on the far side, with defences creeping up in front of you but behind you too.

Us ahead by a point at 13–12 at half-time, us ahead by a point at 19–18 with eight minutes to go. South Africa rumbling at our 22. Middle of the pitch, going left, coming back, going left again.

10 phases, 11. Me tackling, marking on the edge of rucks. Us

going in to compete, stripping the ball, it bouncing past my ankles and being picked up by Lloyd Williams, back on as a replacement, this time in his proper position at scrum-half rather than out on the left wing. Their forwards scragging him, the ball not coming out, a blast from referee Wayne Barnes's whistle . . . and the scrum put in to them.

You know how important that is, when it's happening in front of you. Me with my hands on my knees, lungs at full capacity. Pointing at the picture I could see in front of me. Barnes shaking his head: 'No, they won the competition. Green ball!'

A long wait, Biggar walking off for a head injury assessment. Rhys Priestland on. The front row binding, us second rows locking on. Ready for the impact, for the squeeze. Knowing: we've got to win this one. We're inside our 22. They're maybe 15 yards from our line. Thinking: we cannot let them do us here.

The shove. The front rows burrowing down. Coming up out of my bind to see Sam Warburton round from the open-side and clapping. Pen for us! Is it a pen for us?

Shake of the head from the ref. 'Fellas, one moment, I know it's really noisy, let's just respect each call, okay?'

Reset time.

Left arm around Bradley Davies, on for Luke Charteris. Down to one knee. Sticking my head between Tomas Francis and Ken Owens.

Here we go.

Barnes louder this time.

'Crouch! Bind! Set!'

Pressure coming through your shoulders, your neck. Down into your back, your glutes. Quads burning, calves locking. Feet digging into the green Twickenham turf.

Can't give. Must hold. Hold.

I couldn't see Duane Vermeulen picking the ball up at the back of the scrum. I couldn't see him begin his charge, see Alex Cuthbert come in off his wing to try to help Lloyd stop him. I couldn't see Fourie du Preez's supporting run round the back, or Ver-meulen's offload from contact.

The ball popping up, straight into Du Preez's arms. An acceleration into all that space down the blind-side, his run curving, Cuthy chasing and diving but too late.

Du Preez diving into the corner.

Try.

You walk back under your posts. You fight to get your breath. You watch the kick from Handré Pollard missing the left-hand post over your head, and you start your calculations.

Okay. The kick, the wait, the re-gather from us – that's all taken a minute out of it. You jog back up the pitch for the restart. Look up at the scoreboard. See the numbers. 23–19. 75.35.

Okay. Four and a half minutes to score a try.

Trying to forget the past. Keep your body language positive, for yourself and for those around you. Don't think about the try. How you couldn't do anything about the actual score, as a forward, with your head where it was. How did we end up there? Could I have done anything in the phases before? Could I have stopped it getting to that point . . .

Nah. No room for this. We've genuinely got time on the clock. Other teams have done it from here. They've done it to us. We've been trying to keep it tight for so long, now we're going to need more. Find something to keep the legs going. Keep the belief. We could go short with this restart, try to compete for it. We could go long, they could drop it in their own 22. Then we've got a scrum as far from the try line as they just had. It doesn't happen often, but it might. Come on. Let's go.

We're going to need to get this ball back. Priestland kicking deep to Vermeulen, me charging after him, bringing him down.

Clearing kick from them. Lineout for us, 30 metres out.

Quick ball off the top. Into midfield. Jamie Roberts on the crash ball. Me taking the ball up, trying to spin out of Damian de Allende's arms.

Us going right. Their back row all over the ball. Lloyd with his arms up, wanting a penalty for us. Wayne Barnes putting his own arm up, blowing his whistle.

Penalty . . . South Africa.

Now the sums stop making sense. They boot the ball deep into your half. Two and a half minutes to get the ball back, Du Preez popping short passes to his forwards, them going down and recycling.

A long-range drop-goal attempt from Pat Lambie. Gareth Anscombe taking it. But now we've still got to go 80 metres, in a game where no one's gone 80 metres. You either go wide or you've got to go through South Africa, and hardly any teams ever go through South Africa.

We got close to halfway. That was it. Back and across, them stripping the ball this time. Time up, Du Preez gleefully booting the ball into the stands.

I was on my knees when the final whistle went. Everything gone. Hands on head, then to the grass in front of me. Floored by the realization of how close we were. Thoughts flooding in – gone in the World Cup group stages in 2007, a point away from the final in 2011, a late score from the semi-finals now. A little part of me, aware of the overwhelming regret, the pain, saying, why do I do this to myself?

An emptiness, more than anything. As if everything solid inside you has been tipped away. You know you're going to fill up again. The self-esteem will return. Your partner will still be there. When you have kids, they'll fill you up more than anything else.

But in that moment there's nothing else. A feeling that will never truly wear off. It's only a game, but it isn't, as well.

It's almost surreal. You can't quite accept that it's over. Du Preez's try like a strange cat-flap in time. One side of it you're winning. You're celebrating, you're hugging everyone, you're bursting with happiness. This side of it, you've got nothing.

When you win a big game, it's like you've opened a door. Everyone lets the air in. Sweetness and light and joy. When you lose, it's like a vacuum. Everything sucked out of you.

You don't want to leave the pitch. Not only because you almost want to stay at the scene of the crime, but because you want extra time. You feel you deserve it, even when they've won fair and square. The game's been too tight for too long to be over. We've worked too hard for too long for this to be the end. All those sessions in Qatar, at altitude in Switzerland. All the times in the cryo-chamber. The early nights in quiet hotels, the eating right.

Gats was phlegmatic to the media afterwards. 'We don't want to make any excuses. South Africa won . . . and we weren't good enough to win. At the end of the day South Africa did what South Africa do. They got one chance and they took it and that was the result.'

The stats pointed the same way. We'd now lost 17 of our last 18 Tests against the Springboks. Back to their consistency, the basic elements of the game, their set piece.

Yet you think about the sliding doors. What happens if they don't win that scrum. If we boot the ball clear rather than getting trapped at the bottom of a ruck. What happens if Vermeulen flips the ball at Du Preez's hip, rather than into his arms, and the ball goes to deck.

None of it helps. It's not constructive for your state of mind, it doesn't teach you anything for next time.

It's not fact. The other stuff is. You look at a lot of the great individual tries, and they almost all start somewhere. Unless you're a Shane Williams or a George North, the beautiful tries usually come from team effort, from something the opposition would love to do differently if they had the chance again.

So that's what you think about. What if we'd kept that scrum dead straight. Would we have given a back row the space to make that break?

You try to process this stuff there and then. But you have to live with it, until you get to another World Cup quarter-final, which you might not do, and then win it to go into the semis, which might not happen either.

They become more distant, the disappointments, but they never dissipate. You don't remember the exact feeling or the emotion of the moment, but you look back and you think, fuck, that was a close one. And you can never watch the game back, not unless you have enough whiskey to get through it.

There's not much sleep, on nights like that. Too much caffeine going through you from the gels you've taken, your guts churning because of the strange things you've eaten and all the stranger things you've drunk. You're going to be running the whole game through your head again as soon as you lie down, so you stand up and drink more instead. The gloves are off. There aren't as many answers at the bottom of a pint glass as you would hope, when your World Cup comes to an end.

I was lucky to have Anwen. I was lucky to have my daughter Mali. They'd come up most weekends; Tom Jones, Rob Brydon and Prince William with the jersey presentations, Mali getting to meet one or two. Ans would always send good texts at other times. Understanding what it's like in elite sport. What to say, what not to say. That I wouldn't call her, unless I was in real trouble.

But that's the thing. When I play I am quite emotionally involved. Rugby is a game you have to commit to physically. I think you have to commit to it mentally and emotionally as well. Train harder, play for longer, even when that feels like pushing the tide out.

You still carry that belief, even after feeling crushed in defeat. How many games have you seen, particularly in World Cups, where teams win when they shouldn't? But it's the commitment that takes it out of you afterwards. That brings the pain. When you don't win, you have nothing tangible to show for everything you've given. They don't award certificates in international rugby. There's no marks given for coursework. It's just the exam. Just the final mark.

16

CARIAD 2 | LOVE 2

You think you know yourself. And then you share your life with another person, and the two of you bring into the world two other new creations, and suddenly so many of the things you've done without thinking are no longer quite as straightforward as you imagined.

It wasn't entirely accidental, Anwen and me meeting. Her father had been a client of my dad for years; they had known each other through Swansea Rugby Club. And then out at the World Cup in 2007 – the game against Fiji, in Nantes – they bumped into each other again.

'How's your son doing?'

'Very well, how's your daughter?'

I found out about it when we got home in the aftermath of the loss to Fiji, doom and gloom across the nation. Now, me being me, I've Googled her straight away. Not to see what she looked like, because there weren't any photos, but to see what her times were. I knew she was a 400-metre hurdler. Fine. But how good is she?

Sitting at the kitchen table of my mum and dad's house, digging out these stats. Comparing them to elite-level times. Seeing that she was a multiple Welsh champion. Working out that she probably should have gone to the Commonwealth Games.

Of course it was ridiculous. But it did sort of matter to me. Someone who would understand who I am and what I do. Who was really good at something. Now, I didn't know we were going to get married and have two kids and be where we are. Most of it was probably tongue-in-cheek. But not all of it. There was definitely some of my obsession in there. How good are these genes going to be?

We met properly at an Elton John concert at the Liberty Stadium in Swansea, at the end of June 2008, when Wales had come back from touring South Africa. Both of us in the same stand, a slightly stilted opening conversation – 'Ah, you're John's daughter!' – 'Oh yes, you're the one I've been told about . . .'

I wasn't an expert at dating. Not the most polished of operators. I was always training and I was always away – games in Ireland, Scotland, England; travelling across Wales. There may have been sushi involved in the early days. A cinema. Possibly a shared tiramisu. I'm not a fly-half.

I'd been living on my own since I was 18. I was used to being selfish. I always put my rugby first. But we got there, gradually. Ans got a flat in Llandarcy, to make her commute from Swansea to Cardiff for her lecturing work slightly easier, which had the fringe benefit of being over the road from the Ospreys' training pitches. She moved in with me in 2011, and I proposed in 2013 – being a rugby player, just before the British and Irish Lions met up for our first get-together before the tour of Australia.

I just had to get my backside in gear. It wasn't a case of now or never. It was more, if I don't do it now, by the time I get back from the Lions and roll on into another season, it's going to be another year, and it's already been four or five. Not so much a fear of commitment from me in the early days as total commitment to something else: my sport. But she understood. She knew I'd been married to rugby before I proposed to her. And it's the same now, probably. That's not fair, and it'll change. But it works for us. And it's mad when I think of all the things we've been through together; not the length of time, but the depth of the commitment, the understanding between us.

I think Anwen feels some people have the wrong idea about me. That I'm grumpy, rather than shy. That I'm intimidating, just because I can be serious, because I'm so guarded when you first meet me. That because I play rugby for Wales I don't have to do the things everyone has to do: push a trolley round the supermarket, take the car to the garage, have minor domestic confrontations about whose turn it is to stack the dishwasher.

There's a selfishness, when you're a professional sportsman or woman, because there's a selflessness required at work, in a team sport. Sometimes that looks like laziness. Sometimes it is laziness. You get paid to put your sport first and you're conditioned to put your sport first. There's always an excuse not to do the ordinary things a husband or father is expected to do.

Anwen used to leave me Post-it notes in the kitchen. 'Please do the washing up, I've done it all week.' Those led to too many arguments, so now she doesn't leave notes, and I don't do anything, and there's an argument about either the fact I haven't done anything or that I haven't been told what to do.

There was another note, when Anwen was having a rare weekend away with her friends. After a discussion around how I never wrote little messages for her whenever I went away, she left me a lovely one in our bedroom – 'Miss you lots, love you so much . . .' When she came back on the Sunday night, she found the same note on her pillow, with the 'To Alun' bit scribbled out and 'To Anwen' written underneath. It's the effort that counts.

She had to tease me out of myself, in those early days. She'll say she's made me a more confident person, a more rounded man. When we first got together it must have seemed that I couldn't actually admit we were together. I referred to her as a 'special friend'. Partly due to a typically male fear of commitment, more because I was afraid of what the impact was going to be on my rugby.

I'm aware that's not normal. It's weird. It's probably not your world.

But you think differently when you do what I do. The old joke in my sport: I was with rugby before I was with you. Anwen remembers me telling her that rugby came before her. I don't remember it being that bad; I think I phrased it as, rugby has been in my life for longer.

I was living in my flat, by myself. I'd been an independent teenager. I trained when I was told to and when I wanted to. I ate all the things I thought I should eat and did nothing at all the times I thought I should be doing nothing.

And Anwen was okay with that. I hope there were only a few points when I inadvertently referred to the love of my life as a distraction. She began to mellow me. When you're on your own, you consider it perfectly acceptable to pack big tubs of protein powder when you go on holiday. Subconsciously, I still want to. But she's helped me realize that a few days without supplementation will not see my physique wither away like an old vine.

And she understood. She came from the same place. An elite athlete, multiple times Welsh 400-metre hurdles champion. Someone who trained not for fun but to win.

When she first moved into the house with me and I said to her, you know we can't sleep in the same bed the night before a game, she got it. She still gets it. It turns out there's room in my life for both rugby and a wife. Who knew?

She sees me when I'm pissed off. She sees the emotion at home as well as the emotion on the pitch. When we go out for food, when we take the kids to the beach or the park, the guard goes back up again. I'd hate a kid to go up to Mali in school and start teasing her about her dad losing a game. I'll never phone a restaurant to book a table and give my full name. I instinctively feel a bit panicky at the idea of Anwen being on a flight to a game, chatting to the other rugby travellers on board and someone finding out that she's married to me. I'm too private. Too shy.

They've been to big games now. On the pitch when we won the Grand Slam in 2019, on the pitch at the World Cup later that year. Part of me didn't want to share those moments with people we didn't know. I didn't want them in the papers or on websites. But I wanted to show them both what I did. I wanted to share my moment with them. And I'm aware I can sound like a walking contradiction, but I didn't want to cut my nose off to spite my face. They're my girls. They are my family, and nothing comes before family, nothing will ever be as important. When I play rugby, I'm representing Anwen, Mali and Efa before anyone else. Why wouldn't I want to freeze that moment and take it with me into the years ahead?

You pop into the supermarket and someone clocks me and says, what are you doing here? And I have to say, same as you, doing my shopping.

Mali sometimes can't work it out. 'Why does everyone want a picture with my Dadi?' Sometimes she won't want to let go of me. I don't want photos taken of her by a stranger, she doesn't want her dad to put her down to tell her to go to mummy. I don't really want to let go of her either. Before they came out to the World Cup in Japan, we hadn't seen each other for six weeks. They arrive, we pop out, I'm in a shop trying to pay at the till and someone wants a photo. I don't want to let anyone down, but I don't want to hold up the queue, and I don't want my daughter to think she should walk away from me when she's getting a carry and it's been ages since she had one.

Many people are very gracious. Others say the kindest things, and I just don't feel worthy of them. I'm just a dad, out with his kids. I'm not a doctor, not a fireman, not a policeman. I play rugby. That's all.

Anwen says I don't celebrate the good stuff enough. She's probably right. It's the Welsh thing again, being horrified at the idea anyone might think you fancy yourself. I won my 100th cap on tour in New Zealand, and with Mali only a year old, Anwen couldn't really fly out. So when I got home, Anwen organized a joint party – a second one for Mali, to make up for the one I'd missed, and a celebration of my landmark, which she hadn't been able to witness. Two cakes, one with a single candle, one a marble cake for me.

And I just felt embarrassed. I didn't want the fuss. I didn't want to be the centre of attention. Anwen had to put the cake back in the box, hide it in another room. And her friends were saying to her, didn't you say this was a joint party? Texting her afterwards – what happened to the cake? Her texting them back: don't ask. The cake's gone to waste . . .

I hope I'm better than I used to be. I love buying the girls presents. A sense of guilt when I'm going away again, back into camp, manifesting itself as a Fairy Princess Playmobil set. Maybe a selfish gift, something to make me feel better: ah, I've given them something, maybe now it'll be okay.

You give so much to rugby. Stuff that maybe isn't yours to give.

I make sacrifices to the game; those around are drawn in. Anwen was an athlete with a degree. She was racing and winning. That came to an end; she did a Masters, got a PhD. She became Dr Anwen Jones. A lecturer, an author, publishing papers.

And all of it put on pause, to give the girls a constant in their lives. She had been working in Cardiff. With the drive there and back from our home, that meant she wouldn't be able to take the girls to school and she wouldn't be able to pick them up. So she stopped it all. And we could afford to do it, with what I do, but that didn't make the decision any easier for her. It didn't ease the switch in self-identity from independent woman and earner to full-time mother. It's still hard when people describe her as a WAG, or assume she spends all her time getting her hair and nails done. She made the decision for our family, and I would have supported her whichever way she had chosen.

Sometimes I use the rugby shield. Ans, it's my job. There is an element of laziness on occasion. Sometimes Anwen protects me, and I don't even realize it. There were points early on when she would get her parents to pick Mali up from creche rather than me, in case I needed to stay later at training or add in some extra stuff. It was maybe only in the first national lockdown during Covid that I began to realize quite how brutal a regime I'd left her with. No camps for me to disappear on, training on my own, no one to blow the whistle to stop play. Coming back to the house and being forced to help out through sheer proximity. 'My god, this is full-on . . .'

But I need to catch up, and I need to sleep. I've stayed in Mumbles when I could perhaps have chased a career elsewhere. I've got better at chores, at clearing up when Ans has cooked, or cooking when she's been doing it all the time. I appreciate now that there is no domestic fairy who magically cleans the island in the kitchen. There's no fairy who magically fills the fridge when I've opened the door and been shocked to find there's no ham in there.

I'm institutionalized. That's the problem. You play international rugby and you spend half your time in hotels. Someone makes your bed. Someone else makes decisions about what you eat and when you eat it. You're actively encouraged to eat only things that others have made for you. There is a timetable someone else comes up with, and you're fined if you don't adhere to it.

You get home and find yourself absentmindedly asking where the toilet is. You finish a meal and take your plate to the kitchen surface by the dishwasher, but not inside it. You have a shower and leave your towel in the bath, because that's the universal signal in a hotel that you'd like a fresh one, please.

I don't wake up. When Anwen went away on a hen do I had to sleep with the baby monitor on the pillow next to my head, turned up to full volume. There's been nights when both the girls have had screaming nightmares, and Anwen is up comforting them, going downstairs to get them milk, and I haven't flinched.

I'm better at the big things than the smaller things. And I'm conscious I need to get better. My dad was a workaholic. We barely saw him, my mum, my sister and me. I can't let history repeat itself. It's not fair on my family and it's not fair on me.

I am better than I was. I'm not saying I'm great. I'm just trying to improve.

I can be around more than a lot of dads. I'm not pulling late nights in an office somewhere. I'm not taking calls at home at weekends and having to shut myself away in an office. And it will come to an end, at some point. I'm sure I'll try to train all the same. But I won't need to perform, and tweaking that part of the equation will change the final sum. I won't need to sleep as much, won't need to recover the same way. I'll be able to get up earlier, train hard and it will be done.

The rugby player and father and husband becomes a father and husband. The rugby will always be there, of course it will. But that love affair will be over. There'll be more room for the most important people.

17

PROFEDIGAETH | LOSS

I'd always found it hard, knowing what to say when we went into hospitals to do visits as rugby players. You're young, your world is full of sport. You spend your days running about outside, thinking of yourself, worrying about a little muscle tweak here or a touch of tiredness there. When you're younger, you don't have the life experience to cope with it. I'd meet people who were ill, confined to beds. I'd meet kids who had been stuck inside, who might not be getting out for a long time, and yet gave you a massive grin.

And I was awful at it. People thought it was just me being me, but I have been terribly conscious of saying the wrong thing at the wrong time. It doesn't get easier as you get older, but you realize that sometimes people are just happy to see you. They don't notice your awkwardness or shyness. They see a rugby player, and that's enough.

But I didn't have the emotional tools. I wasn't ready for it, when it happened to us.

I was at home. The family house, halfway up the steep road from Rotherslade beach.

That was the place. The two-storey house with big windows looking out from the ground floor, dark brown tiles on the roof, a sloping lawn in front.

It was in the kitchen out the back. The smell of my dad's cigarettes in the air. My mum and dad sitting there at the table.

They told me in simple terms. My dad had cancer.

It was shock, at first. For a long time. Not shock as in scared. As in, this doesn't happen. Even when I knew it did, when I'd done the hospital visits. The statistics with cancer are stark. Everyone at some point will know someone affected by it.

It was never talked about, how it made us all feel; not then at the start, not at the end. The focus was on the practicalities of getting Dad well. They were protecting me. Let's get the treatment. Look forward, carry on as if all this is normal – even as it was anything but.

There were bouts of it. Radiation therapy and chemotherapy, as soon as it could be done. A gap when we all thought it had regressed.

It hadn't gone. It came back.

Dad and I had never had that stereotypical affectionate relationship. Sometimes almost the best part of our time together was when we were going at each other. He loved to keep me on my toes – *what are you doing now, you shouldn't do this. The ball is faster than a man, why did you do that, why haven't you done this? I've sent you another letter, why haven't you replied?*

From me: *oh, leave me alone. Leave me alone.* Always.

It's odd the things you miss. And I couldn't deal with it, in the moment. I could speak to Anwen about it but I didn't want to bring it up with my parents. I didn't feel I could broach it. What this all meant, what might happen. How we felt about it. How we were going to cope. It felt that every time I tried to raise it, I was heaping pressure on my parents. As if my mum would think I was being selfish for asking those questions, or trying to confront those feelings.

The journey from home into training with Wales at the Vale seemed to get longer. On my own for long, unbroken periods of time. You know what it's like when you're driving the same stretch of road, five or six times a week: the drive becomes easy, you go onto autopilot, and then the cogs start turning. Thoughts come into your head that you can't escape. Staying there, going round and round; so many questions, so few answers.

Most of the players who had been there long enough knew what was going on. There were staff who had known me since I was 20, others who had known me for half my life. So I just tried to carry on, because there was nothing else I felt I could do.

And that's where the question of guilt comes from. Looking back and wondering, should I have carried on? Should I have been more self-aware? I think Mum and Dad were trying to do the parental thing. 'You don't have to come to this, you don't have to do that, you get on with your rugby.'

My sister was the one who held the fort with Dad's business. She was working there. It made sense. I couldn't do that; I couldn't do the work, and it's highly likely I would have struggled if I could. I was full-time with the rugby, I didn't work in the office, and I wasn't retired, like Mum.

The questions over whether I was selfish. On an island, all on my own. Mum essentially becoming a carer. Lowri in the office. Me running up and down a pitch, hitting rucks, catching lineouts.

I wanted to be more involved, but I wasn't forcing it, because they were still protecting me, and I wasn't forcing it, because I was scared, too. The stubbornness, the conflict. I felt like I'd been told not to come; I didn't want the conflict of going against that, of making such a difficult situation even worse. Maybe part of me was hiding behind my stubbornness, not helping more.

There were times when I knew I was coming into camp and I wouldn't get back in time to see Dad before he went to the hospital for treatment. I felt trapped. I was where I wanted to be, but nowhere near where I needed to be.

Suddenly the world seems twisted around your own peculiar grief. I drove early to the hospital one morning. There were no parking spaces, but I had to get to the ward. I left the car and ran in. And when I came back out, someone had written a note and left it on the windscreen: 'Just because you drive a BMW doesn't mean you can park like that.' As if I'd wanted to. As if I would have, if it had been an ordinary morning.

It catches up with you in the strangest small moments.

We went to the funeral of a friend. The treatment had taken its toll on Dad, beyond any doubt. His clothes no longer fitting as they once had. And as I was standing there, a little away from it all, I overheard someone saying – as if it was a joke, because they can't have known what was really going on – 'Someone's got the wrong suit on . . .'

Is it unfathomable that it takes these things to bring home the severity of a situation? I must have realized. But I didn't want to accept it. I didn't want to let it in. And so it didn't hit me until it was too late to change any of it, not that you could change what was happening to him. Was it the selfishness of sport, or the fear of a son not wanting to confront something so terrible?

Dad couldn't make the Lions tour in 2013. He couldn't travel to Australia in that shape. At my wedding he couldn't enjoy things as he traditionally would have done, in his own indomitable way. He was still the Tim Jones that Swansea knew, but not necessarily the force of nature that had shaped the family, as big a presence when he was away as when he was home. I leaned on Anwen and then we had the life-changing arrival of Mali too. A son, but a husband and a father as well.

So now I ask myself the questions I didn't want to ask myself then. Should I have gone on that Lions tour? Dad and his father, Ken, had always been so supportive of my rugby. He'd gone on the tour to South Africa in 2009; he'd been to every Wales game, to every Ospreys game he could. I'm certain he would have wanted me to go away with the Lions. He would have hated me to stay at home for him.

But as time went on, he couldn't come to as many games at the Liberty Stadium, just up the road from Mumbles, down there at the bottom of the climb up to Bonymaen.

That realization took it out of him. It took it out of us all. Took away some of the remaining simple little pleasures in life. Mum would drive him places in the car, and a lot of people hadn't seen him in a while. Some wouldn't recognize him.

Knowing he felt like that, and how he was, isn't how I want to remember him. The Dad I want to remember is the lessons in cleaning my boots. Dubbin and rolled-up newspapers stuffed inside to dry them out. Holding court at family functions.

A workaholic. Him sitting in his office, one fag in his mouth, another smouldering in the ashtray on his desk, talking on the phone whilst also dictating a letter into a tape recorder. 25 years ago, a frustrated son. Now a son with memories that raise a wry smile.

A positive energy. I probably only realize that looking back. You learn things, when you yourself become a father.

The house, halfway up the road from Rotherslade beach. That's where he said goodbye.

And that's where we all stayed, for a while. I stayed, lost between different worlds. Knowing I would have to go back to my own house, as a husband and a father. Wondering, what can I do now? Is this all too late?

All of it so strange. All of it the confusing mix of the intensely practical – organizing funerals, telling people – and the totally emotionally bewildering.

You understand you're not the first person to lose their father and you know you're definitely not going to be the last. You don't want to be selfish about it. You don't assume you should be the centre of everyone's attention. The world should not make space for you to pass.

But it's still happening. It's still all you can think of. There is no avoiding it, when it hits you.

It's a horrible feeling, when you first have to tell people. It's the first and last time you'll say something you know you never wanted to say. I had to phone Rob Howley to explain that I was going to be late coming into camp. Rob was in charge of Wales with Gats stepping back ahead of the Lions the next summer.

'Howlers, I'm going to be late . . .'

The Wales coaches had always talked about how family came first. It was one of Gats's central tenets. And they lived it for me that day.

I know any workplace would have done the same. I also felt

this strange serendipity that Dad had died just before the autumn internationals. Now he knows I can't forget him. Now he knows that every time the autumn comes round and I'm playing a game or watching a game, I'll remember the day he left us. Knowing his sense of humour, typical of his eloquent timing.

But all the coaches got it. All the players. Shaun Edwards understands grief. He's had it in his own life. And every time I see him now, he always asks the same question: *how's your mum?*

Those genuine emotions and efforts go a long way. We've all made our mistakes and we've all got our own demons, but however different a character, empathy is genuine. It isn't a skill, it isn't a characteristic. It's an emotion. The empathetic and sycophantic can seem very similar at times, but when you're in the darkest places, you know when it's authentic.

The funeral.

Of course Dad had organized the whole thing. Written out exactly what he wanted, who he wanted there, which songs he wanted playing. Print-outs of the service, photocopied so each family member had a copy to keep.

Meeting at the funeral parlour in town. Driving past his office, all the staff standing outside in the street. Driving on to the Mumbles Road, to All Saints Church, just back from the seafront, just along from the rugby clubhouse. The beach beyond, the sea and the gulls. The square grey church tower, the sloping roof, the green grass and the gravestones.

All my teammates were there. All in their suits, all soaked. Warm autumn showers coming through. Another stray thought: I'm driving past the Welsh squad, following my father's coffin. This is not supposed to happen like this.

We carried him in. Dunvant male voice choir there, singing the songs he had chosen. I spoke, as a son. We sang his songs and said his words, and then we went back to one of his favourite places, the rugby club. A room at St Helen's, the pitch out in front of us, the grass where he and the F Troop had played. Where he'd trained, where he'd watched me play. Too much black, at the home of the Whites.

The thoughts you have, the people you see. Swansea is a big enough city in Wales. And I looked at the faces there, the characters, and I realized: it's a small place too. Spotting Filo Tiatia, five years gone from the Ospreys but still loved for all his seasons tearing around in the back row, for the way he played, for his commitment. Asking him, in pleasure, what he was doing there. Finding out he was in the country but came to Mumbles just to support our family. Small gestures that mean a great deal.

The waves and the ripples reach out, from a day like that. And then the rugby began again, or rather, kept going, and I rejoined it.

Back for the game against Argentina at the Millennium Stadium. The boys were good. They knew what had happened, of course, but they were professional, too, and that's what we needed, what I needed right then. When the rugby stuff was happening there wasn't time for me to lose myself in the grief again. When it wasn't – when it fell silent in the changing rooms, or we were given the afternoon off training – I tried not to let it show through. You don't want to be a distraction; you don't want to affect anyone else.

Now Gats understood me enough, felt the link between rugby and family. Before we played Australia in the group stage of the 2019 World Cup, when I was setting a new caps record for Wales, he brought it up in our team meeting before we left the hotel.

Just one line. 'Alun, your dad would have been really proud . . .'

The Lions tour of 2017. We were in the Ibis in Hamilton. A team meeting had been called. I couldn't work out why. What's this for? Usually you arrive at a new hotel and settle in.

I was coming downstairs in the lift, and then realized it was Father's Day. Knowing that would mean we would be getting video messages from our families. It hit me afresh: my dad wasn't with us any more.

Other times it just catches you from nowhere. Little incidents and moments that are maybe strange to remember. And of course it changes you. You know what they say about how true the words are that are spoken during the pain of grief. You see the fall-out around you. In how your relationship with some people close to you is strengthened in those fires, and how others are weakened.

I probably speak to my dad more now he's not here than I did when he was around.

Grief is a complex feeling. It's a shared selfishness. You feel as if it's only you experiencing it, and you know at the same time that it's self-centred to even consider that no one else has felt this way too. And there's a selfishness too in how you grieve them. It's all about you and your closed world. The days I found hardest were the days when he missed out on what he would have loved. The things he would have taken most pride in.

When I got my 100th cap for Wales, he saw it on television. Too ill to come to the game. He was gone by the time of the 2019 Grand Slam; he wasn't there when I became record cap holder for Wales, when I went past the world record number of Test appearances. Sometimes I think: my dad missed all the good bits.

And the dark irony is, my stubbornness would have been true to form. I wouldn't have shared it with him enough anyway. So maybe it serves me right. All those years of me being an independent kid, and it's taken until I'm older and a parent myself to understand the reasons why he was the way he was.

Dad was always alternative. He was different as a man and not the usual father. But now I can feel the empathy of a boy become a father, rather than the resentment of a son. That's how I feel his gaze, his support.

I was a relatively young parent when he passed. Mali was a year old. Efa hadn't been born. So he never met her, and he barely knew Mali. It's not just the rugby stuff he couldn't experience.

Now Mali remembers her Pops. Both of them will. We're going to make sure they know more as they grow. They need to understand where they come from, feel the connections and the sense of belonging beyond their parents.

But I wish it had been different in those last few years. Because Dad was Dad, he continued to work pretty much until he couldn't. Those first two or three years of treatment he pushed it as hard as he could. Work was his obsession, his escape. Work first, family second.

And he was increasingly tired, when he did that. He'd get home and have nothing else to give. Mum would have to look after him more.

Would he have been your typical grandfather? Afternoons on the beach, taking the girls away, ice creams in summer and sleepovers in winter? I don't know. But I know he would have made them smile. He'd have revelled in their wit and energy and life. Mum would have had more time with them as babes in arms. The waves and the ripples.

Fathers butt heads with their sons. It happens. You get to your teenage years and you begin to define yourself in opposition to that figure rather than wanting to faithfully replicate them. If I'm destined to have girls, so be it. It's wonderful. I don't know if the love and affection you have as a father with a daughter is different to the affection you have for a son, but the only reason I'd want a boy is to try to improve the relationship I had with my own father.

That sounds harsh, when I say it like that. But through my own failings, I probably wasn't emotionally aware of anything. He always made sure we would be secure in the future. I was lucky, in lots of ways. But it can't just be about work all the time. And it wasn't, early on, yet as time passed, he worked more, and I became more aware. And maybe that's selfish of me too, because he was who he was. I'm expecting him to bend to who I was. You can't change someone's nature.

It's not being soft; it doesn't even have to be long chats when you're both pouring out exactly what you want to say. Nothing like that. It's just being there, essentially.

And maybe that's why it was easy for me to just carry on. They were doing the parental thing. And maybe I was hiding behind that. It was easier for me to deal with it that way, using their attitude as the excuse. Maybe I just wasn't joining up the dots emotionally.

Because no one trains you for any of this. They don't teach it in school. It just happens to you and then you have to react. And even if they did teach it, it wouldn't help. It's different for everyone. It catches you in your own personal way.

Something else you don't expect? You hear your dad talking in you. You feel yourself sometimes acting as he would, or finding some of the same personality traits embossed on your character.

I had a dad who literally worked until the end. And if I can replicate that commitment, I will. The older I get, the more determined I become. I don't want to take any of this for granted.

Why did I do a law degree? Was it because it would give me a solid career if anything happened to the rugby, or did I do it because Dad did it?

I'd like to say it was the first. But the reality is that I probably wanted to make him proud, too. I knew he was proud of whatever I did. And because I started my law degree, I made sure I finished it. Another trait so similar to him.

Not all of my law degree was enjoyable. I'm not saying I would definitely have become a solicitor. I'm certainly not saying I would have been anywhere near as good at it as he was, or my sister is. But I think I was trying to follow in his footsteps, whether I was doing it consciously or not. And the hardest part was probably not admitting it to him at the time, because you can't let them know.

Never say never, but it's highly likely that when the playing comes to an end, I won't go into coaching. It would be the time away from my family. And that has to be a positive lesson I learned from him. He's taught me the things I should cherish, both in work and with family, and the need to look after myself, in a strange way.

I'm trying to be more hands-on with my girls. I hope the older they get, the better I will be. It'll be easier. It's the rugby, the being away so much. When you're going into camps or on tour and then come back, it's their routines at home. It's like the lodger is back for a few days, and then he clears off again. I'd really like to think I can give them more of me when I don't have the devotion to rugby to maintain.

Sometimes with your dad you wait for this big cathartic moment when it all comes up. When you tell each other exactly what you want to say. What you both think. And for us it was through the worst means. When there's nowhere else to go. When it's almost too late.

I go up and see him, before big games, after big wins. Get in the Land Rover and drive over to Oystermouth cemetery. Over the road from Underhill Park, where Mumbles play, where I started my own first games of tag. Climbing up the narrow road through the trees, past the little grey chapel on the corner. Up into the open air, the views out over the sea, the wind coming in.

Dark polished stone, gold lettering inlaid.

> In loving memory of TIMOTHY GILBERT JONES
> And when the final whistle blows
> It is not who has won and lost
> But how the game was played

It probably makes it easier to process feelings for me, when I crouch down by that headstone. It's a good way to share moments with him, to bring him there with me. To talk him through what I hope he's still seeing.

I will never forget him, but I worry about losing him from my thoughts, or rather from my present consciousness. Days when you get halfway through a busy day and suddenly stop and realize, oh no, I haven't thought about him today. The double-edged sword of guilt – that I didn't spend more time with him when he was with us, that I'm not thinking about him all the time now.

My grandfather was everywhere with my rugby. I'd go to see him when he was still alive, and all we would talk about would be rugby. I'd want to say to him, let's talk about you, what have you done today? And he'd say, *ah, I've been in the garden. How was the game?* So I want to share things with Dad. I want to tell him how things are. Make up for lost time. For time I'll never find.

There's a certain image of my dad, when I think of him now.

He loved to be the life and soul, the mischievous wit, holding court. To be ordering drinks, to be at the centre of the conversation. To be talking and dishing out opinions. To be organizing. *You do this, you do that.*

But for me it's him behind his desk, in his office.

Me sitting there between a pile of files. Dad focused – *I've just got to do this* – and then he's sitting there looking at me, dictating letters.

Details and explanations as he carries on. *I've just got to do a couple of letters, then we'll go. Wait there. I've just got a phone call.*

And that's what I'd do. I'd wait. Look at my dad, and wait.

What I would give to still be waiting there, now.

18

DEWRDER | COURAGE

You think of a lot of things, when you look back on a Lions tour. When you look back on a life in rugby. What you did, what you wanted to do.

I think about courage, a lot of the time. Not mine, ours. The bravery of those around you, in ways that make sense if you haven't played the game, in ways that'll maybe surprise you.

Courage is a full-back going up for a high ball, knowing the opposition blind-side is going to smash into them when they land. It's a prop wanting to scrum again even knowing the forces coming through them. It's a back row going in to jackal knowing they've got a target on their backs. It's the 10 taking a long-range penalty into the wind; it's a second row calling the high-risk, high-reward lineout when it's bedlam all around and the game is there to be won or lost.

It's all those individual roles and decisions that make a team courageous. It takes time to build, within a group of players. And you don't have time on a Lions tour, not now. Not when you're touring against the double world champions, and your first game comes when you've just stepped off a plane after travelling a day and a night, and every midweek or weekend game they want to knock you backwards and show just what they've got that you haven't.

Courage is not the absence of fear. When you have no fear you're a danger to yourself and to the team. Courage is sometimes having the confidence to challenge a train of thought. The right thing can be easy. Sometimes you have to take a step back and get a broader perspective on something. An openness to change; sticking to what you know.

It all starts with discipline. You don't think about being brave on a daily basis as a rugby player. It's just your day job. We're not soldiers, we're not surgeons. We occasionally sit in ambulances; we don't drive them.

Discipline is the things you do at the worst of times. It's the stuff you do when no one is watching. When you could get away with something else. All the little invisible things that go into the pot and enable you to use your courage. Courage on its own is a fast car with no wheels.

There's courage when you're coming back from injury. When you go through the rehab and the hurdles that come with it.

You build up the ability to hurt yourself for rugby. It's not an intentional thing. It just comes when you get to a certain level. You know an injury is going to come eventually, even if you're one of the lucky ones. I've been fortunate with a few – the ones a grade away from an operation, the extra months out, the risk of infection or failure. I've done my ankles a few times, I've done the medial ligaments in both knees. I've had Achilles tendinopathies, I've dislocated my shoulder. You think, I am going to be a rugby player, I am going to get injured.

Below a certain age you think you are indestructible, or at least that it's not going to happen to you. Then you pick up one, and you pick up a few. You see guys coming off who've just come back on. We all get the one that's a wake-up call.

There's things you used to do and not get injured. You do it again and it gets you, and it doesn't seem to make sense. You go up the levels, and you're in with players who do it better, faster and harder. There's the flukes – the flailing elbow from your own teammate, like the one that got Stuart Hogg in Christchurch on this tour, or when Tom Shanklin and I tackled the same man in 2010 and I perched my elbow. It's the sport. So many parts of the game of rugby are so messy.

You don't feel scared. You couldn't play the game if you were genuinely frightened. And I've never felt like I wanted to escape the pressure of the biggest moments, the most anticipated matches. You're not scared of the expectation a Lions tour brings, and you're certainly not scared of another team of 15 men, no matter how well deserved their reputation. I walk out of the tunnel and onto the pitch thinking: this is what I've done a lifetime of work for. I feel lucky that the big occasion comes round so frequently in rugby compared to a sport like athletics. Six Nations every year, either a Lions tour or a World Cup every other year.

Bravery isn't being individual. It's not taking things into your own hands and trying to be a hero. Often bravery is sticking to the game plan and trusting those around you. Individuality has won games for Wales in the past, hands down, but first and foremost you've got to be brave by trusting in the group effort. It's a form of trust for the collective and it's probably a form of control for the individual.

And it's facing criticism, positive and negative, and being strong enough to ignore it and keep going. That's a form of courage too. I would find this Lions tour a very different beast to my first two. In 2009 I could go under the radar as a youngster. In 2013 the attention was elsewhere – on the coaches, on their decisions.

So here's what Warren Gatland did. He knew what we'd done with Wales. He knew how England had won the Grand Slam the previous year, how Ireland had won one a few months before. He looked at the domestic and European successes of Saracens and Leinster. He pointed out the big names the All Blacks had lost since winning their third World Cup in 2015, and then made it clear how good their replacements were. Letting us feel the comparison, the competition.

To be on my third Lions tour felt pretty special. I'd never thought I would do one. And this one felt big. The whitewash of 2005, New Zealand's World Cup wins in the intervening years. Our win in Australia in 2013 revitalizing us.

You land in New Zealand as a British and Irish Lion and you are among the obsessives. The cafe owners who can discuss the most subtle nuances of the game, the little villages built around the rugby pitch and the rugby clubhouse. Playing or watching the club games that you don't get on any other sort of tour. I could still remember seeing Simon Shaw take a restart against Manawatu in Palmerston North on the '05 tour and running the ball back 55 metres. I could see the effect on Gats, coming home again with a different side: how they saw him as a threat, how he relished all the stuff that was thrown at him. Gats is happy when he knows he's getting to you. He's not a man for a flap or a panic.

And of course he understood the culture we would be immersing ourselves in. That everywhere we'd go we would have a Māori welcome, and we would honour that welcome and challenge by responding. Giving our thanks for what they were giving us.

That's why our four squad songs worked. 'Calon Lân', 'The Fields of Athenry', 'Highland Cathedral', 'Jerusalem'. We all learned the words and we all practised – the good singers, the non-singers, the ones who thought they were in the first category but belonged in the second. We had done the same with Wales at the World Cup in 2011 and on tour in 2016: a small thing, but something that goes a long way. And for such a simple activity, it brings you together. A response to the hakas and traditional welcomes we would face during the tour; a connection, too, to Lions tours gone by.

It's the learning that sets the foundations on the early days of a tour like that. Steve Borthwick was our forwards coach, and he's a man who understands detail. Who craves perfection. He sat down with me early on and talked about previous experiences and expectations this time. He'd organize walk-throughs in the team rooms, taping a 15-metre line on the floor, rehearsing the calls. He'd put a clock on it too: we start now, we finish as soon as the alarm goes. 'Boys, that's our time now, we'll have to catch up again.'

The other coaches. Andy Farrell, an intense character but enjoyable all the same. Specific and concise with his set-piece drills, which is what you want as a player. A natural leader, a great man-motivator with his words.

You watched Faz Senior and saw a lot of Owen Farrell in him. The character, the attitude. You could imagine being a kid of Owen's age when his dad was playing, looking around that Wigan dressing room, at the men there, how they went about their lives. You could appreciate how special it was for the two of them.

Owen was vocal in training from the start. And I never mind having a bollocking from an outside half, particularly when they're right. I'd rather know than not know, when I can improve and it's in context.

It was the same with Johnny Sexton. Two 10s, both switched on all the time. I got both barrels from the two of them in one session early on, which I suppose makes it quadruple barrels. Johnny at 10, Faz at 12, me missing the jump on a play. And it was fine. They weren't wrong, and it didn't feel personal. It was just, this is what we're doing, this is what we expect. Do it.

I'm not an over-familiar person. You know that by now. I'm not phoning old teammates up and asking how they are. But you settle in with some people. Rooming with Rory Best, maybe us two put together because we were more mature than the rest. Enjoying the company of Jamie George and Elliot Daly. Dan Cole, a sense of humour dryer than the Sahara. Kyle Sinckler being good fun, a connection between us in Adam Jones, the tight-head ahead of me for Ospreys and Wales for so long, a coach for him at Quins in his formative years. I'd like to think we get on; I like his aggression and energy on the pitch. Those are assets that can be harnessed, not controlled.

All the time the tour accelerates around you. I didn't play against the Blues in the rain at Eden Park; I captained against the Crusaders in Christchurch three days later. Not involved against the Māori All Blacks, on the bench against the Chiefs in Hamilton, wondering if I was going to be involved in the Tests at all.

And then you're back in Auckland, in the rain, on a coach driving out from the city centre, Eden Park all lit up like a fairground in the middle of what seems like a perfectly ordinary, perfectly pleasant suburb. Different to a year ago, when we'd been there with Wales; great temporary stands, a huge Meccano colosseum. Black shirts and red shirts everywhere you looked.

The first five minutes of play so quick it felt like being on fast-forward. Not necessarily doing impossible things, but doing it all flat-out. One of the first passages of play was three minutes long or something close. At that level it feels like two days. You're just trying to breathe. To think. To hold on, to hit back.

A lot of the time the All Blacks play without the ball. They're happy to get into the kicking battle. They're direct. As a forward, you're focused on tackling and filling the line. The ball handling capability they have in the forwards is a huge facet of their approach to the game.

And you stay courageous. When Anthony Watson passed the ball back to Liam Williams deep in our own 22, he had two main options: kick to touch, or have a crack. This time, he saw space, and had a go.

Sanjay has pace. He's got a step. That's how that try began, from one end of the pitch to the other. Being brave, having done all the work on detail that got Jonathan Davies in support and Daly outside him, Foxy on his inside to take it on, Seán O'Brien cantering up to take his pass and dive over the line.

A defeat, but you don't fall apart. There were plenty of stats against us – the Lions only ever winning one series in New Zealand, and never having lost the opening Test; 23 years since the All Blacks had lost at Eden Park, where we'd be returning for the third Test; a 47-match home winning streak.

But there's always stats, and they're always about the past. With Wales, we had the mentality of always wanting to counter history. To make our own. And as we travelled down to Wellington for the second Test, we let the problems of the first slip away. Always look forward, never look back. Why obsess over something you can't change? Start working on what you can.

I liked Wellington. The coast and the weather, the hills and the little coffee shops. There was a hint of Swansea about it all, if you came from Swansea. There were memories of beating Ireland there in the 2011 World Cup, pushing the Springboks close a few weeks before. Even more fans around now than there had been in Auckland – around the hotel, in those cafes, around the waterfront.

I had to get out, the morning of the match. Escape the hotel for a little while, get away from the build-up. Now it's not easy when you're six foot six and decked out in Lions gear, so I tried to put on as few badges as possible. We were in the Ibis, on the front, only a five-minute walk from the stadium. Out the door, across the petrol station forecourt, towards Wagamama. Out of the bubble for a few minutes, the fans in the bars, getting ready their own way. Bumping into Sean Holley and Ryan Jones, an exchange of pre-match pleasantries. And then I was spotted by a few fans, and had to get back before I couldn't get back. One photo on a morning like that and you're done for. It's five photos, 10. It's appearing rude for pushing your way out of a different scrum.

Into the game. Into that same mad pace as Eden Park. Rain everywhere, wind. Penalty, kick, penalty, kick. Sonny Bill shoulder-charge, red card . . .

They played well with 14 men. Jerome Kaino taken off so it was seven forwards and eight backs, but they were never unbalanced. And it's hard to pull out specific moments, when you're working that hard. You're deep in it all. Nine points each at half-time, into the dressing rooms taking in air and liquids, out into the storm once again.

You never know in advance how long you've got in a game like that. You don't think about it. They've selected you, so you go flat-out for every second you're on the pitch. It's the same reason I've never asked for a day off. When I've been asked if I want to sit out a game, I always want to say no. I want to be involved in every game I can be.

The perfect scenario in a match like that? When the game comes to you. You're not thinking about being replaced, you're not thinking about trying to squeeze an 80 minutes into a 50 or 60 and giving three or four penalties away as a result because you're trying to do too much. You don't chase it and you don't get left behind. Then you know you're in the right space.

I got almost an hour before Gats sent Courtney Lawes on for me. An hour passed in the blink of an eye; 21 minutes on the bench as if time had slowed to a trudge.

I'm not a good watcher. You have no influence, when you've come off. No other way you can affect something which is incredibly important to you. The All Blacks ahead by nine points, Taulupe Faletau thundering over in the left-hand corner, me jumping up in delight, smacking my head on the roof of the dugout.

Another penalty from Beauden Barrett. Jamie George breaking through. Recycle, recycle. Conor Murray dummying a pass to his right, wriggling through and over the line.

21–21. Three minutes left on the clock. Kyle Sinckler taking a short ball and charging. Charlie Faumuina taking him out in the air. Sinks at his combative best, Jamie George on the harness.

Penalty.

And so we come back to courage. You're watching Owen Farrell kneeling on the soaking grass out in front of you, placing his kicking tee just so. You're looking round at this great bowl of a stadium, silver roof, bright lights, thousands on their feet all around.

And you trust him totally. You've seen what he does. You've seen the hours after training, the time out in the rain with a bag of balls and that tee and a set of posts in the distance. You know you couldn't do it, but you know he can.

The courage? It's not taking that kick now. He's not thinking about bravery. It's a job, a routine. The courage comes in the effort put in down the years. Pushing yourself when others would say, hey, that's probably enough. Stepping up as a youngster to a level that probably feels too hard, at the start. Giving yourself the chance to do what you're going to do now.

You know it's going over, when you're watching. When that trust is there. You celebrate afterwards, and you also hold a great deal back. You're in a three-Test series. You've done more than most people would have thought, but nothing has been won yet.

We gave away 13 penalties in that game. We only had 39 per cent possession. You're aware of that, afterwards. As you sit there in the dressing room, amid the grins and the cold beers. There's a lot of frustration and reflection, mixed in with the celebrations. Shouldn't have done this, shouldn't have done that.

You have to force yourself to move on as quickly as you did in defeat. It's too easy to dwell, too seductive. You get left behind in what was, not what is going to be.

Warren could see that. It was 2013 all over again, in some ways. A huge, decisive match coming up in a week's time, all manner of pressure there if you wanted it, an instinctive desire to do more to make sure it all came right – more training, more weights, more planning, more prep.

You dial it back, when you've been there before. You fight the temptation.

Long training sessions aren't going to help, not now. You're not going to build extra muscle in five days. You know the calls, the tactics. There's so much in there that to squeeze more into the mind is to stifle it, not set it free.

We went to Queenstown. Home of the adventure, the big night out, the buzz. Gats felt it. We'd all worked so hard for those first two games. Don't review straight away. Have some days off, clear your head, free your body. Only then do we start again.

It had worked for us in 2013, when we'd headed up to Noosa on the Sunshine Coast with the series at 1–1 and the decider in view. Surfing back then, a little SUP, a few scoops. Not everyone outside the camp was happy then, and not all the critics were happy this time, but maybe they'd forgotten the intensity of a Lions tour in the modern game. Your preparation time for each game is essentially cut in half. You come into your final game and you need a physical and mental release to get the slingshot effect working once again. Take a breath, wind it up, let it come out at maximum velocity when game time comes around on the weekend.

We all realized the red card had an influence in the second Test. We also knew how many penalties we'd given away, how the yellow card we conceded had hurt us. So you try to balance on that fine line, as player and coach. Reflect on the recent past but don't get lost in it. Look forward but don't forget what you need to get you there. It's going to be 80 minutes of hell. A week of purgatory beforehand is not going to help.

It was the jet boat for me. Up and down Lake Wakatipu and the Kawarau River, spinning round, fizzing about in cold spray and fresh air. Just what I needed.

Now, not everyone was convinced. Usually when you have a day off, you come back together and have a slightly sloppy training session. You shake it out of your system and rebound the next day. This time there was a slight edge among some of the training staff. Had we had too many days off? And it was a messy session, that first one back – no problem with the knowledge of the drills, of the set moves, but issues around their execution. Dropped balls, loose passes. But that happens. Courage tells you to trust that it will come good. Don't panic, not now. Get the plane back up to Auckland and Eden Park, be thankful that New Zealand is short hops rather than four-hour epics like Australia and South Africa.

You have to manage the excitement in a week like that. Balance the anticipation and the foreboding. Outside the camp, certainly from some of the media, there was a sense of, it's not going to happen for the Lions, it's too good to be true. Inside the camp, gently steered by Warren Gatland, it was different. We've got an opportunity here to do the impossible.

Gats is in his element in these moments. Switching it on after letting you all switch off. Doing his own prep without leaking any tension to you. Understanding that you get that far into a campaign and there's only so much you can change.

There wasn't much to tweak. Sometimes you can motivate

better by saying little and doing little than throwing the kitchen sink at it. The training session in Queenstown had been poor, but you trust in the slingshot to bring the pace and intensity back. Gats loves the siege mentality. He loves the idea of doing what others consider to be impossible. Backs against the wall, rubbished by the locals, given a shot by almost no one? Perfect.

Trust, in us players. Trust, coming from confidence in himself as a coach and what we were all doing. If you become uptight or overly controlling as a head coach in a situation already loaded with external pressures, it quickly spreads to the other coaches, to the players who are likely to be involved.

It's not a looseness. That's too much. It's giving you an independence. Trust coming from confidence, leading to confidence. Maybe that sounds too profound. An attempt to find wisdom when really it's common sense. It's hard to explain. But you know it when you feel it, as a player. And you can't fake it, not with that experience all around you.

He had the right men around him to balance it all out. Steve Borthwick, the architect of the set piece and its execution. Graham Rowntree on the scrum, the sort of authentic rugby man you want to work with. You can't buy that. Andy Farrell with the aggression, the switch to attack. It's never just the pure rugby that matters, when people talk about appointments and selections. It's personalities, characteristics. You're picking people as well as coaches and players.

It doesn't have to be shouting and snarling. Obscenities don't always need to be used. Sometimes words can be more powerful if they're eloquent and simple. They don't need to be Shakespearean. Poetry is seldom required. Just make it to the point. Clear. That's all we need.

And the messages that come through from above are seldom revolutionary. They're the things that make sense. The things you've heard many times before.

Keep our discipline. Stop giving away penalties. Keep the accuracy in the set piece. All messages from the general heap in the rugby locker. A lot of the same messages that a lot of teams will use at different stages of their progression.

*

13 mins: Lions 0–0 New Zealand
This is fast. Us nearly in on the right, them intercepting, brilliant chase and tackle by Foxy.

Take the short ball. Hit the ruck. Go again.

Coming at us in waves. Forwards in narrow, wingers holding their width.

Ruck, five metres from our line. Warby with his hands on ball . . . cleared off it.

Beauden Barrett. Time in the pocket. Spotting the space outside.

Tough D this, we're all marking our men, but Jordie Barrett's out there on the right.

Kick going his way. Up first, coming onto it.

Over Elliot Daly. Knocking it down. Laumape inside him, gathering, diving over.

Walking back under our own posts. Bobby on with water and comms.

34 mins: Lions 6–7 New Zealand
Smashing it up the middle, 30 metres out. Caught low, down badly. Hands all over me – Retallick, Read.

Fuck, done for holding on.

Barrett kicking the penalty to our 10-metre line.

Lineout. We're all cramming down to mark the option – they've messed this up, but Retallick's got lucky, it's fallen into his hands.

Through our line. Four-metre dent.

Fast ruck speed. Can't slow it down.

Aaron Smith to Barrett – shit, that pass has taken out five of us . . .

As soon as they made that dent, they were going wide. Lienert-Brown – us short of numbers, Jordie Barrett outside him . . .

From blip at the lineout to a marginal dent, then getting the ball to the edge. Almost like a trick play, when it goes wrong to then go right.

Barrett's missed the conversion. 6–12.

39 mins: Lions 6–12 New Zealand

Nice work, Foxy, cleaning up that short kick. Laumape's not rolled away there – pen for us, inside our half.

Daly fancies this. With his boot, why not? This is worth a shot – could be a three-point game at half-time, stick them on alert for the rest of the game.

Whoah, nailed it! Great time to score, back in the game now . . .

49 mins: Lions 9–12 New Zealand

Phase play inside our half. Te'o, having a bash.

Conor Murray to me. Got to check a little on the ball to get that – low carry now, not in full control of the ball.

Sam Cane on the inside, Kaino coming from the outside.

Nowhere to go. Impact on my jaw.

Get up.

Romain Poite speaking to me. 'You good? You good? You sure?'

You can get those 10 times and it won't affect you. This one? Not malicious. Just right on the spot . . .

Poite blowing his whistle, signalling to the bench. 'Red five!'

No choice. HIA. Can't kick off, or they definitely won't let me back on.

Courtney Lawes coming on . . .

76 mins: Lions 12–15 New Zealand

On the bench, soaked in sweat. With Sexton and Jamie George.

Farrell to Itoje. Cane trying to stop him. On the wrong side. Murray slapping him on the back – come on ref . . . pen! Yes . . .

Farrell crouching by the tee. Farrell striding back. Farrell glancing up at the posts.

Stepping in. The slap of boot on ball. The ball arcing, dropping, dying.

Over the posts.

Yes yes yes . . .

78 mins: Lions 15–15 New Zealand

Everything's there now. We win the series. They win the series. A draw? Maybe. Dunno what happens then.

Kick-off. We're going all in.

Sanjay goes for it. Ken Owens, running back.

Has he caught that?

Faz shouting, no! Penalty?

The boys getting ready for a quick tap.

Poite calling the skippers in. Read shaking his head in disbelief.

Knock-on!

Okay – he's made his decision. Scrum to them, hold on boys, hold on . . .

Final score: Lions 15–15 New Zealand

*

When that final whistle went, most of us genuinely weren't sure that we weren't going to extra time. On the pitch, the players looking around as if to say, do we swap sides here? All of us on the bench talking about it. Bobby Stridgeon shouting at us – 'I don't know! I don't know!' The fans behind us falling silent, as if waiting for something else. All the wind emptied from everyone's sails.

No one had even talked about the draw. Not a word, in all the detail of our preparations. It almost came to pass in 2009, had South Africa not won that late penalty in the second Test, had Morné Steyn not banged it over. But there was still another game to come, a game we would have to win to level the series. So we slowly walked on, from the bench, and you could hear Romain Poite trying his best to explain it all. 'No, no, that is the game . . .'

Their coach Steve Hanson used the analogy of it feeling like kissing your sister. I prefer the awkward looks on our faces when both teams attempt to stand on the same podium, when both captains raise the trophy. No one knowing what to feel. Smiling without being happy but without being gutted too. Caught in between. Is this it?

They weren't sore losers, the All Blacks. Partly because they weren't losers, but you know what I mean. They were professional about it; we were professional about it. We'd missed winning a series in New Zealand. They'd missed out on a series win over the Lions.

But afterwards? You don't obsess over isolated incidents like supporters do. Like the media. They fade away into the overall picture. Into the exhaustion, the desire to find your family in the crowd, to get back to the dressing room and open a beer and let it all slide away.

Only then do you begin to reflect. We didn't achieve the impossible. But we probably achieved more than anyone thought we would, so there was an element of celebration along with the disappointment.

You go out there to win. That's where your head is, as a professional rugby player: you want it all. In those minutes afterwards, soaked from the rain and sweat, pulling this precious shirt off over your head if you can, peeling the strapping off your shoulders, off your thighs. You don't move on, sitting in the dressing room, steam coming off all of you, the injured ones lying on the physio's tables, boots on the floor, mud and rolled-up socks. There will be others, watching from the stands, in pubs and on sofas back home, who would look back at the twists and turns and bite your hand off for a draw. A better overall result than many thought possible. As a player? You don't take consolation from not having lost, but you accept it.

There's always those stats again, in the aftermath. We had led, across those three matches, for a grand total of three minutes. Did we care? Of course not. The number that matters is the final score. No more, no less.

There's parallels with how South Africa would win the World Cup, two years further on. Two tries in the final, yet in the majority of their games, getting to that point, they had a strong kicking emphasis. A set-piece, a carry game that worked for them.

New Zealand? They kick maybe more than anyone else. They counter-attack brilliantly. Their start point is from opposition ball, not their own. Their kicking game gets the ball back to score the tries that win them games. We had held our own. We had got close. And that would have to do, for now.

I wasn't surprised when Jonathan Davies was given man of the series for us. He played some of his best rugby on that tour. He'd been playing some of his best rugby leading up to it.

I've played a lot of games with him, Foxy. He's one of those unassuming characters that some don't appreciate because there's never a song and dance about it. He just goes about his business, on and off the field. Not looking for the spotlight, not looking for fame.

But he has been the glue in the back line for Wales for a long time, and he was the glue for us that damp southern hemisphere winter. Some people questioned his rise in 2013. Why was he being picked ahead of men with more caps and a more public reputation? Then you watched him carefully – not just as part of a team, but in isolation – and you could see how quietly imperious he was.

He's a good man, too. He's a talkative one in the dressing room, but all of it productive. He's a calm voice, and that's critical in the number 13 shirt. Everyone goes on about his defence, because it's easy to spot from the outside. They don't always appreciate what he does in attack. We talk about the importance of the scrum-half and 10, and never enough about the support they have from their centres. Well, 12 and 13 are just as critical to the success of your fly-half as anything else. You hear nothing out there and you're all at sea. Foxy was constant and consistent in that.

And he's an athlete. Not a glider, with ball in hand, but he's got a hell of a stride when he gets going, and the power to match it too. One of those players where supporters underestimate their size. It's an optical illusion. He's fast, but he's built, too.

He's been an ever-present leader, someone who has supported me on and off the field in my time as captain of Wales. And something else. He's always smiling, which may be due to the fact that he barely seems to have aged since he came into the team, all those years ago.

19

ARWEINIAD | LEADERSHIP

I had solid thoughts about how I wanted to be, as captain of Wales. Or rather, I had solid ideas of how I didn't want it to be.

That was actually more important. I'd had my eight years at the Ospreys, and I'd gone in green and learned a little more with every season that went past. I always led the way I played, the way I trained. I never tried to force anything; it was me trying my hardest, it was me being authentic to who I am.

I looked at the senior players like Shane Williams, Adam Jones and Jerry Collins, and quickly realized that there wasn't much more I could say to them than to keep being myself. When it rolled on a few years and a younger generation came in, I think I probably expected too much of them early on. I probably rubbed people up the wrong way. *Why is he being so harsh all the time? Why does he never let up?*

But I don't regret it. I still don't believe you can go as slow as the slowest man. You've got to pull some along with you. And it's simpler at international level, in many ways. You're locked in for two or three months at a time, the distractions at a minimum. On average, you have better players around you – the majority of the senior players from each of the four regions. Even with the younger players, 90 per cent of them are more mature than the ones you've experienced at the next tier down. That's how selection works for the international game. It cherry-picks. It should pan for the nuggets of gold.

So I had all that preparation behind me. Still going to be true

17. Warren Gatland transformed Welsh rugby. He absolutely knew what makes me tick. And he had a way of carrying you with him, of making you believe exactly what he told you.

18. Lions 2013 series win against Australia. You can't quite see it here, but the Wales flag has Bonymaen written on it. From a special place in my rugby education, to a Lions series win on the other side of the world.

19. All aboard with the new Mr and Mrs Jones!

20. Celebrating our win over England in the 2015 World Cup.

21. Taking on the All Blacks with the Lions in 2017. Nowhere else obsesses over rugby union quite like New Zealand. Unless it's Wales.

22. 24 hours of travelling for Anwen to New Zealand for the third Lions Test . . . all worth it.

23. 2019 Six Nations. Efa, Mali and Anwen with the rain and a trophy or two. The whole family makes so many sacrifices for my rugby that it's wonderful to share the big moments with them.

24. With Anwen and the girls at the Liberty Stadium, Swansea, at the end of the 2018/19 season.

25. 2019 Six Nations. Winning a Grand Slam at home and having the trophy presented to you by the future monarch. Wipe the mud off your hands, Alun Wyn.

26. Covid lockdown with new coaches at Underhill Park, Mumbles.

27. Dadi doing sea recovery, Mali and Efa on towel duty.

28. Earning cap no. 149 v. Scotland in autumn 2020.

29. Family walk on Rotherslade beach, down the hill
from the house where I grew up.

30. Six Nations 2021. Although we won the championship,
we were 90 seconds away from the Grand Slam.

31. It was the most profound honour to be named British and Irish Lions captain in 2021. I understood all that it meant: the heritage, the privilege, the responsibility.

to myself, still wanting to be the one leading with energy and commitment, as I'd always wanted to be in the Welsh set-up. And in my eyes I am always a player first and a captain second. It sounds like the old lead-by-example stuff, but it's more subtle than that. It's not a conscious decision, thinking – right, I'm skipper now, I'm going to do this and that. It's me being me, and dealing with the other stuff afterwards – not always in the right way, but willing to learn.

You don't try to do it all. You don't start believing you have superpowers. Look after what you're good at. Trust those who know a great deal more than you. I'm not going to tell the front row how to scrummage. I'm not going to tell our 10s how to kick. I will ask questions – *why are we doing this now, what will this do, what do you think we should do?* – but I'm not going to make their decisions for them.

Asking those questions might not make you popular. Fine. Friction can be a good thing. It brings debate. It sharpens your thinking. It stops an issue building, because you have to confront it head on. You're not deviating from the end goal.

Elite sport can be like most other lines of work. It won't always be rosy. As captain you're a leader, but you can't be a dictator. You're not the only one making big decisions. There's the coach above you, the chief exec, the money men. You're way down the food chain, even though you can push for change. You're boots on the ground.

So don't hope for a world without confrontation. I'd always been in or on the fringes of senior groups within teams I'd played for, and you see too often how easy it is to say too much. Sometimes I've fallen into that trap myself. At times you have to give other people the opportunity to challenge you and ask questions of those you report to. It's the impossible balance that you'll always find yourself searching for: there will be those who don't think you're doing enough, and there'll be those annoyed that you're doing too much.

Trust. Trust those around you. The ones who can do what you

can't. The ones who can see what you can't. In that Wales squad that began the 2019 Six Nations, it was clear for me. We had the personnel in the right spaces to share the decision-making. Jon Davies in the backs, organizing the defence. Gareth Anscombe and Dan Biggar at 10, calling the plays, directing the attack. Ken Owens on the scrum, Justin Tipuric looking after the break-down. All of us helping police the gaps in between, because it's never that neat and compartmentalized in the mad hurly-burly of a Six Nations ding-dong.

It makes it straightforward, when you have a blend like that. Tips doesn't need to say much. You just watch the way he plays. Ken's Ken. You know what you're getting. Foxy sees it all happening and deals with it. No dramas. You have these men on your side? It's almost seamless. It's natural, not forced.

It works on the pitch and it works off it. You save so much time. You don't need the team manager calling a half-hour meeting after training every day. Issues resolve themselves. Problems sorted before they begin, others dealt with as they pop up. And half an hour saved every day is two hours more rest per Test week, or two hours more training, depending which way you want to play it. You're in camp for four weeks, six weeks? You might just have made the difference between coming close and winning the thing.

It did take me time to learn all this. Back in the day, I was the stickler. *We need to do this, we need to do it again. Let's sit down, let's go through everything together.* And that was maybe where I alienated people. I assumed what worked for me would work for everyone. I thought that if you were doing a team run the day before a big game, you should run through most plays. Some players have come to know me and what drives me. Why I do what I do. I've mellowed and realized my performance needs it. And there are still some who probably think I do too much, ask too much. And that's fine too. Sometimes you've got to be comfortable not making everyone happy. You win, there's always a few pissed off with how you did it or how their role panned out. You lose, there's just more of them.

I could feel a good blend, at the beginning of 2019. A solid year behind us; runners-up in the 2018 Six Nations, beating the Springboks in the autumn, beating the Wallabies. There was something else, too, that I'd learned about captaincy during my time with Wales: captaincy isn't as important as people on the outside think it is when you're winning, but it's more important than they think when you're losing. You win, and everyone's pulling in the same direction. There's a natural harmony created by the good times and optimism. Defeat? That's when the pressure comes on. That's when the cracks can appear.

I've never minded showing a little vulnerability. There are so many moving parts to a game that it's madness trying to look invincible. I've got loose on some nights out, like most of us; lads have seen what I've done, seen my remorse afterwards. I've shown that I fuck up and make mistakes like anyone else.

Which isn't always okay, but I'm not trying to hide anything or pretend to be someone I'm not. I would rather be thought of as being a pain in the backside for having lived on the edge at times than have players muttering, *what the hell do you know, you've never made any mistakes*. You try to be someone you're not, and experienced players will see through it pretty quickly.

From the outside, the only thing that matters is the 80 minutes at the weekend. As a professional player, what you do all week in training before a big game matters too, because it's the foundation for your performance. It's the intensity and consistency you bring. You can't get yellow- or red-carded in training, but you can get sacked. The more competitive you are from Monday to Friday, the better you will be on the Saturday. Not everyone in the team agrees. Okay. But I'd argue that my competitiveness is always for the betterment of the team. The purpose of training is to replicate the standard and speed of what you want to bring. If you're not bringing that, or doing things you won't get away with in a match, it absolutely kills me.

That's the practical stuff. The bedrock of it all. The emotional side? When you're younger, when you're starting to work out your aspirations, dreaming your dreams. I just wanted to play a game for Swansea RFC. I loved the idea of a single game at St Helen's. Then I played there in a school cup game, and I thought: right, done that now – do I reckon I could one day pull on the famous white shirt my dad wore, and my grandad wore before him?

You play for Swansea. You go to the Ospreys, and train with Welsh internationals. Men you've watched on television in massive Six Nations games. At World Cups, for the Lions. Now the dream shifts on again: could I win a cap for Wales, ever? A game in that red shirt, running out to represent my family, my nation.

It keeps building. With each fresh summit you climb, the next one comes into view. You're telling me I could go to a World Cup with Wales? You're telling me we could win a championship? We could win a Grand Slam?

Layer upon layer. And the peak to it all? Running out of the tunnel at the national stadium, packed out from front row to the rafters, red shirt on your back, thousands around you, millions behind you.

It's almost too much to describe. It's a priceless thing to be part of. You could be the richest man or woman in Wales and never have the chance to experience it. It only comes with a lot of help and sacrifice from those around you. It's still mind-blowing to me, knowing everything that goes into it, that it can't be bought. The international game is 140 years old and the number of men to be capped at Test level by Wales still hasn't broken 1,200.

And to be captain? Only 136 men had captained Wales by the start of the 2019 championship. Only 13 had done it on 10 or more occasions. You look at some of those men and what they achieved, and it's almost baffling that you could be part of its history in some small way.

I don't like to turn it into a numbers game or indicate any lack of respect to those who have captained less frequently or led the team in a more unofficial capacity. What matters to you is the detail in that bigger picture. It's the scale and importance of this cultural and emotional entity that you become part of. It's what you're a part of, rather than it being part of you: it's far greater than you, something almost impossible to envisage until you've experienced it as a Welshman. On one hand, a simple dream built on a work ethic; on the other, a passage to a sacred place.

You don't pretend you're the most important one there. You don't delude yourself for a moment. Half of Wales grows up wanting to wear the number 10 shirt – the legacy of the 1970s, of Barry John and Phil Bennett. Of Jonathan Davies. That magic still transcends a great deal else in this country. The weight of expectation, of how you should play the game. You travel to New Zealand and everyone there still wants to talk to you about John and Bennett. They want to talk about the great Welsh captains. You keep playing and you almost try not to think about it too much. You don't want to lose yourself in the beautiful history of it while there are still so many things you want to achieve.

Walking out of that tunnel first? It's the same noise that hits us all, but it's you it hits first. Now sometimes being halfway back can be decent as well, because you can see it all in front of you. It's like being on a rollercoaster – you see the impact on those ahead of you; you see the scene opening up; you get the context and the scale. A player on a white-knuckle ride.

But the symbolism is inescapable, when you lead the team out. It's Welsh rugby. Pound for pound, I'd like to think we're the most passionate nation about this sport in the world. Always the sense that we have so much to prove, because of our size relative to other nations. So much to back up, after the successes of the last 15 years, the four Grand Slams since 2005, the two championships.

Life can change around you. You know me by now. I'm a private man; I keep my cards close to my chest. There's more media, more press conferences. You're at the top table after every game, happy win or heart-tearing defeat. You'll get the nods out on the street, the supportive ones and the passive-aggressive ones.

'Have a good run this weekend, Alun Wyn . . .'

'Don't ruin my weekend now, will you?'

So much of it depends on how well you do as a team. Like anything, if you're winning, everyone wants a slice. If you're losing, then everyone wants to tell you how you cut the cake all wrong.

And when you start a Six Nations campaign and you're 16–0 down at half-time? You have to stay calm. There's no point ranting in the dressing room. You're all soaking wet, you're all cold. Steam coming off backs and heads where scrum caps have been pulled off.

We'd had something we called a crumb emphasis from Gats all week. Keep the pressure on. Force the mistakes, in the opposition handling, in their kick returns. When the little chances come, when the crumbs are there, hoover them up.

No great stirring oratory. Just patience, and precision, and effort. Chase down the kick when it looks like they have it covered. Hunt the crumbs.

Sounds rather prosaic, doesn't it? This was the game that Warren Gatland had said in the media would decide our entire Six Nations. Win this, and we could win the lot. But premonitions matter less than process in elite sport. Work out the game that the conditions have dictated. It's a February night, it's a deluge. We're not going to win by flinging it about and chasing miracle tries. You can slide faster on this ground than you can turn. This will be about the aerial battle; this will be about territory. The curious contradiction of rugby union: sometimes you're better off playing without the ball.

Okay. Boys, we will get an opportunity. Once we get that opportunity, we will probably get another one. Be a consistent team at critical moments, whether it's a kick-off, a restart or an unforced error. When we get on it we stay on it. Sometimes trying too hard is as bad as not trying hard enough in the first place.

*

0 mins: Wales 0–0 France

Kick-off. Here we go.

I'll be defending if they shift it. So. Fill the line, keep the width, try not to get too narrow.

Clearing kick. Race back, try to beat the chasers. Don't get overtaken.

Read the ruck.

Keep the options open. It's safe, we have it, we could shift it or kick it.

Rain coming down hard. We'll be kicking here.

Two men inside me. We're kicking – decent distance. Great chase, Bigs, good tackle.

Now they're coming at us, ball in hand.

Control our line speed, don't leave a hole. Stay connected.

Huget's off his wing, he's getting the pass here.

We're not in control, now. Danger. They're outside us . . .

My tackle.

Jackal attempt. Taking me off the ball.

In to it now.

First lineout. Them on our 22.

Picamoles standing in at nine.

Got to defend this, got to get up.

Picamoles breaking out. Inside to Fofana?

Spilled it.

Decent start for us.

23 mins: Wales 0–5 France

Foxy's up fast there, he's scragged his man behind the line.

Perfect. We need another positive now, back it up. No – where's Penaud come from there? He's making yards. Inside me, taking two more of us out.

They're going left.

One pair of hands. Two. We're short of numbers.

Three passes, four.

Offload. Huget's free . . .

Got to get him into touch. Scramble.

Try.

Get the boys under the posts. No need to panic, that won't help.

37 mins: Wales 0–13 France

Their lineout, 10 metres from our try line.

Don't compete for this one.

Maul.

Stay square. STAY SQUARE! If we get turned, we're in trouble.

Beardy on the ball. Get those long arms out. We got this . . .

There's the whistle. Come on, ref, easy one this – yep, scrum for us.

'LET'S GO!'

45 mins: Wales 0–16 France

Where we going here? Josh Adams taking it up.

Me keeping width on the left.

Josh off his wing. He's going to step here. Just like Penaud in the first half.

Through!

Great positive line from Tomos Williams, one pass here and we're in . . .

Good time to score . . .

51 mins: Wales 7–16 France

Scrum to us.

So tight in here, like your head's in a vice. The pressure coming in sideways on your ears, down through your shoulders.

We're going down here.

Face in the wet grass.

Up fast.

Going left, we're going wide. Sanjay will have this, he's calling for it.

Anscombe's kicked – too far . . .

Chase it, George – Parra's given it up. Huget's there, go George . . .

Yes George!

Look at Huget, he can't believe that's come out of his hands. Chase those crumbs and you get your chances . . .

Okay, Gareth, send this conversion over and there's only two points in it.

Happier.

54 mins: Wales 14–16 France

Foxy breaking down the left. I'll chase that grey scrum cap, get in support.

Bigs on the carry; 15 out.

Hit the ruck, hit the ruck.

We're through – try! Tomas Francis.

Hey, what's that? Penalty to them?

What? For what? Me at the ruck?

Okay – 50/50, they get given.

Move it on. Two-point game. We're going forward. Come on.

Run to next set piece. Recover there. Breathe.

Run it.

60 mins: Wales 14–16 France

Penalty to them. Kickable . . . Lopez has missed it!

Chase our kick. Chew up the ground, don't let them get back. Flat line, take territory, take their space.

Picamoles on the carry. Me and Navs, two-up tackle. Navs on the ball. Me holding him up.

Where's the ref?

'MAUL! MAUL! MAUL!'

He's given it. Our scrum.

Now then. Big shove. Penalty to us.

Bigs setting up for the kick.

Wave at the bench. Need the sticky spray for my hands, restart coming. Wet night, cold night. Think ahead.

Kick goes over. Could have been 14–19, 17–16 now.

66 minutes: Wales 17–16 France

Repeat sets. Exit. Go again.

It's a 14-minute game now. One point up. Might as well be 80. When you're up like this, time slows. When you're down, it races. 14 minutes goes like a click of the fingers.

67 gone now. We've got good shape here. Them kicking deep, searching for the space behind us.

Intercept – Ntamack. Shit.

Not in great shape now. Play's breaking up.

Come on. We train for this.

Drop goal coming. Lopez is back there waiting.

Go on, Tips, charge him.

Half a block. The ball spinning on. They're all onside now.

Scramble. Cory's done well on the tackle. I'll jackal.

Turnover, knock-on.

Applaud the decision. Let the ref know you've seen it.

But . . . we were in control, we've gone back.

Scrum, 25 metres out, in front of our posts.

Scrum under pressure, not getting away with this one.

Penalty France . . . Look up at the screen, watch the replay.

Lopez – too easy for him.

Still 10 minutes to go. Two-point game their way. They've got to take the restart. They won't want to go wide, not now, in this rain.

We'll get another chance.

71 mins: Wales 17–19 France

High kick from them. Come on Bigs . . . nah, Fickou's got it. Best outcome for them.

They're getting it wide. They got numbers?

Long pass from Vahaamahina.

George moving – high into the line.

Interception! He's away!
We're in . . .
This isn't over yet. Too long left. Too long . . .

Final score: Wales 24–19 France

*

There's a reason why, if you go to the launch of the Six Nations, five out of the six captains there will be talking about the importance of momentum. You win a game like that away from home in your opening fixture, and everything you have to do as a leader is suddenly given greater clarity. The sun shines a little brighter. The days become a little shorter – fewer meetings, fewer answers to be found. Training gets a little bit quicker; everyone around the place is a little bit happier. Momentum in a game brings momentum outside it.

Italy next. Not a pretty first half, but a charge from the bench in the second period and we pulled away. More momentum. England up next, after their impressive start, but us at home. Us happy to play without a rest week if need be. Keep the sun shining, keep the smiles coming.

That middle game is the one where your campaign can flip. England had come out on top in the previous five Six Nations matches between us; they had beaten Ireland in Dublin in their own opening game, running in four tries, and scored six more in hammering France at Twickenham in their second.

I felt we were still building. 16 points down in Paris, a narrow win in Rome. A long winning streak, but still searching for a better performance and a result that reflected where we felt we should really be.

Of course it was close. This is always the great myth when you glance back at Grand Slam seasons rather than study them. They're always close. They're never romps. The key games are frequently won by a single score, hang by a thread for what seems like most of the 80 minutes.

Beating Ireland at Croke Park in the 2008 Slam with Shane's late try. Beating England at Twickenham in 2012 with Scott Williams's steal. Games where there's horrible tension in the grandstands at 60 minutes, pints being thrown back at 70, that awful feeling for those at home that maybe they're better off going out into the garden, or for a long walk, or the shops – anywhere but sitting on that sofa, wanting so much for it to come good but being gripped by the realization that there appears to be almost nothing between these two teams.

But you don't win those close games by accident. There is a physical element to it and a mental one. We train constantly to be fit enough to be in the fight in those decisive minutes. You might not make all the right decisions. You might still make handling errors. But if your fitness is as good at 60 minutes as 10 minutes, if you can keep the pressure on at 70 minutes, if you can hit that ruck on 78 minutes and chase that cross-field kick on 79 – well, then you're bending the odds towards you.

We never cut loose against England. We clawed our way back into it after Tom Curry had squeezed through for their try. The game was deep when Cory Hill took that short ball in the right-hand corner to crash over. We had gone through so many phases to get there – patience, process, fitness. Keep it clean, make it work, keep it going. And there were only three points in it and a few minutes on the clock when Dan Biggar kicked long to Josh Adams on the right wing for him to out-jump Elliot Daly and seal it.

Romance can wait for the aftermath, in a game like that. You're exhausted at the end. You're hands on hips and sucking in the wet cold winter air. Trying to get the legs moving again to find your teammates for a slap or a hug and their players for a handshake.

You won. They lost. That's all that matters, in those shattered moments. In that Six Nations, England scored 32 points or more on four occasions. We never scored more than 26 in a game.

England scored 14 more tries than us across the championship. They scored 70 more points.

We won the Grand Slam. Another strange contradiction for you, from the top level? The better and more expansive and adventurous your attack is, the better your defence has to be. Why? Because there will be more errors. It's why the southern hemisphere blueprint is as it is: kick the ball, score your tries off counter-attack, through broken field. Keep the defence water-tight at all other times.

Three games, three wins. Scotland to come away from home.

And then a storm breaking that none of us could have seen coming. A weekend away with Anwen, and the Welsh rugby jungle drums suddenly beating. Phone calls flying about, head-lines and denials and accusations. The revelation: the Ospreys and the Scarlets had been in talks about merging. Two regions into one, two squads into one. Two sets of coaches, of support staff, of groundsmen, of canteen staff.

Project Reset. That was the official name. A very Welsh rugby way of doing things: a secret plan, coming out and then falling apart in the build-up to the penultimate game of what was shaping up to be a Grand Slam tilt.

A national squad meeting on the Monday. A meeting with the Ospreys on the Tuesday. Wednesday the usual rest day, a day this time to talk and stew and argue and shrug your shoulders at the whole madness of it all. Thursday travelling to Edinburgh. Friday the team run at Murrayfield, everything domestically in disarray as we ran our moves.

You could fear the match itself after a week like that. Find an excuse to underperform. A fair few of the players and teammates at the time back home hadn't been re-signed by their regions. Rugby's a sport, but it's business and employment too. It's how you pay the mortgage, feed the family and put petrol in your car.

Instead, we tried to relish the game. We'd been hearing about the merger all week. Worrying about it. We weren't being distracted from the game. The game was the distraction from the distraction.

Get on the pitch. Feel a ball under your arm. Get your shoulder and arms hitting and tackling. Play rugby.

And be realistic. If you play rugby in Wales and you can't perform until there is no stress, until the backdrop is perfect, until the domestic game is functional, when the players have the time they need to focus on it – well, you'll never get out on the field.

It was anything but simple, that second half. Scotland coming right back into it, narrowing our lead to four points, battering away at our line. Hamish Watson a dangerous combination of frustrated and fresh, almost forcing us to change our game plan.

You keep it simple again. Get numbers to our feet, don't overcommit at rucks. Wait for the opportunities, for the knock-ons and turnovers. The training and the trust in the system and each other.

You train for this. You train at speed. You make a lot of errors, but you don't make them at the weekend.

That's what experience gives you. What maturity brings. It doesn't all need to be perfect in the week before, because it won't be perfect on the Saturday. You've got 20-odd blokes who are going to try to make it very imperfect for you.

Intent is important. You need to know where you are and get set to do it. You do as much as you can on the shallow side of imperfections so that you are ready for when the pressure comes on.

If I'm running a line, I'm not going to look back to see if you're doing your job. I'm not going to wait until you say go. But when you're under intense heat like that, leadership is not trying to do it all. You don't need to control everything because you have Foxy, you have Biggs, you have Ken.

And so to Cardiff, and a Grand Slam day, and Ireland.

The week before, I was conscious of not trying to change too much. You've got a lot of rugby and running in your legs by the final weekend of a Six Nations. Do physically what you need to, when you need to do it. A captain doesn't need to create big emotive moments when you're going to be running out in front of 74,000 people for a Grand Slam.

Only a few easy points from me to the players, as the rain hammered down that afternoon. You do what you need to do in the warm-up. Get yourself ready for what is to come. Get ready to go at scrum time. This one is on us.

Sometimes when you speak to your teammates, context and tone is everything. Everyone can drop the f-bombs. You don't need to, because they don't impact. All you hear is a load of fucks and shits, sometimes, when you say something. Staying focused is staying with the men around you.

The last thing? It had been six years since we'd won a trophy. Enough of us in the dressing room to realize what it takes and what it means. So I just said, *Make sure you do it for the people who aren't here, as well as the people who are.*

That was all. Not just for me, thinking about my dad. Other players too who were missing parents, or grandparents. Staff who had been through the same thing.

Out onto the pitch, into the rain. Looking down and noticing that the little mascot with me was freezing cold, shaking.

Everyone in our squad would have done the same thing: give the lad your own jacket. If I had been his parent watching on, I would have hoped someone would do that for my child too. I just felt the reaction afterwards was over the top. I didn't do it for anyone except the mascot needing to be warm.

In a world where people are sometimes looking to act in a certain manner for praise or affirmation, this was a natural thing to do. I know some people in the public eye say they want a normal life. I'm not bothered if I look normal. I don't care if you thought I was an idiot and then found out I'm a nice guy, or thought I was a nice guy and then found out I'm an idiot. I'm just most comfortable being me.

The game. Scoring early: 16–0 up at half-time, a mirror image of Paris in similar conditions on that opening night of the tournament.

Inside a contest like that it never feels easy, never feels comfortable. You look at the scoreboard weeks later and it's easy to remember Hadleigh Parkes's try off Gareth Anscombe's kick right at the start, but harder to recall his try-saving tackle on Jacob Stockdale down the wing, or the classic Irish driving maul that got moving and grinding all the way to our five-metre line, only for us to keep them at bay. All the pressure we came under in the final 25 minutes, when Ireland had all the possession, when they kept attacking us wide. Supporters in the stands all around us launching their own Grand Slam celebrations even as we fought for every inch. It always feels different on the pitch.

Ireland scored their first points with the 80 minutes gone and us 25 points up. It shouldn't have mattered. I looked around at the faces around me and saw that it did, and I loved it. Still disappointed to concede a try, even when you've won the Grand Slam. It encapsulated our group and our attitude. Never feel that you've done enough.

It was attritional, for us out there in the middle. The early try and then forcing mistakes from them at the breakdown, at the set piece. Gareth kicking our penalties, taking us incrementally further away from Ireland, closer to the prize.

My own performance? I've been uncomfortable in the past looking at my numbers, my own display. The bloke next to me has worked just as hard as I have to be here. The vicarious liability of team sport, where it might not always happen but if you've done the best you can as an individual, you're one-fifteenth of the way there.

You're not conscious of playing well. I'd like to think I can perform in big games. I think that's what my career has been about. Sometimes the hardest part is getting to those games. Playing in them is what you do all the hard stuff for. It's what all the graft of the previous seven weeks hopefully takes you to, so you can perform instinctively when you get there.

You feel the collective release. The happiness in the faces of your mates, the noise coming from the stands. The knowledge of how it will be in the pubs outside, in the living rooms of houses, in the villages and towns across the land.

Those moments, when the red and gold ticker-tape is floating down, and the cannons are launching great feathers of flame up into the sky, and you're on the podium in the middle of the pitch, hands around the trophy . . . that's what you do it all for. For your place in it; for what it means to all those you care about. You play the game to feel these emotions. To create those memories and the memories you'll never be able to remember. The trophy lift? It lasts 10 seconds, and you can never recreate it. To have a moment with your children on the pitch. To think of the people you'd love to share it with but can't any more.

I love being with the boys on those afternoons and long nights. I love being with my girls. The collective experiences that make rugby what it is. You also need the silence on your own. Those deep breaths, the comedown after the intense release of energy. A feeling of elation that cushions you against the pain and fatigue and exhaustion that should be overwhelming you. A freshness that doesn't make sense, that wouldn't be there had the result been different.

We weren't thinking, as we hugged each other, slumped back on the benches, peeled off the white strapping gone brown, that this was Warren Gatland's final Six Nations game in charge. You don't, when there's a World Cup still to come, when the narrative of his departure had been around for months. And when you speak then, as a captain, it's never anything intentionally pro-found that comes out. You're aware some blokes aren't listening to a word you say. Others just staring into space, shattered from their physical efforts, from the emotion. It doesn't mean more or less; it just means something different to each one of you. Some lads a few games into a career, others long years. Easy years, years ruined by injury. Self-doubt, confidence, sacrifices. It never gets any easier to win. That's why team sport is difficult. It's also the beauty of it. Those moments mean different beautiful things to each of us.

Once it was all over – the parties, the drinking, the drinking the day after, the hangovers – there was something else I wanted to do.

When I was home, Six Nations trophy on the seat beside me. Back to Mumbles, the salty air and wheeling seagulls, the views across the bay. The pier and the lighthouse, the clouds racing by on the wind.

I'd envisaged a conversation with Dad on the Thursday before the Ireland game. A way of involving him when I probably didn't allow him in as much as I could have done before. He would have been bristling with pride, just like my grandfather. So I wanted to share the build-up with him. To find a few words, to ask for advice that I once wouldn't have taken.

So of course I talked to him afterwards too. To involve him as he had always been involved. I know, as a parent, how much you want to be part of everything your children enjoy, no matter where you are. Of what they achieve.

For all my frailties as a son, the selfishness and independence I displayed in my younger days, I wanted to share it all with him again, and more. Maybe it was selfish again – for me, to make me feel better. But it was the first Six Nations we had won since he passed. For all the times we argued, for all the times I didn't listen, you would have enjoyed this Grand Slam a few years ago, so there's no reason why you shouldn't now.

You never forget that they're gone. The hole they have left remains.

I saw an analogy of loss, after he passed. You draw a circle, and a black dot in the circle is your grief. The black dot never gets any smaller. The circle around it just expands – your life, your children, your commitments. Everything changes around it, but you never forget. The grief remains the same.

Getting caught in the contradictions, but embracing them too. Thinking, if I wasn't so fiercely independent and so stubborn at times, I probably wouldn't have got to where I am today. Some of those traits are among my best attributes as well as my most challenging. But thinking, a lot of those traits came from you, Dad.

Trying to continue what had and hadn't come before. Sharing the pleasure and pain of victory, once more. Because he was a father, and I am a father, and I understand more, now.

20

TYNGED | DESTINY

You do things in your career you'll never forget. Things that are special to you, that you don't want to shout about but will keep close to your heart on the long days and nights to follow. Dreams crystallized into solid memories; moments that seemed impossible to the kid looking forward all those years ago.

A fourth World Cup, another chance. A fresh adventure, beginning in the familiar surroundings of Fiesch in Switzerland. Pine forests on the hills, steep church spires, a yellow-and-red cable car whirring its way overhead and up the mountains.

Familiarity doesn't need to mean boredom or sterility. Warren Gatland was always comfortable in an environment that had been shown to bring results. You can graft when you're locked away. You can suffer together. You can go deeper and come back stronger.

The World Cup is always there in front of you, but it's not always on your mind. You cannot look too far ahead. There will be some players getting over issues, others trying to get things right. The squad is not entirely finalized, at this point. You're fighting the fatigue and you're working for the team, but you're working for yourself too.

I thought it might feel different as captain. Preparing to lead my country to the greatest competition in our sport. But it didn't, when it came to it. Playing for Wales couldn't mean any more, when it already meant so much. The captain's armband simply added me to the list of prestigious names to hold the honour previously, rather than overtaking or eclipsing the emotions I had carried with me before.

We had confidence, and we had levity. A 14-match unbeaten run, a time – albeit briefly – at the top of the world rankings. The surprise of seeing Bobby Stridgeon, strength and conditioning coach and pocket dynamo, arriving direct through the alpine air.

Bobby is a self-identified energizer. An intelligent man who can read people, and make those people understand he cares for them – and that's a rare thing in elite sport, and explains why players will go to the well for him again and again. Never quiet, never still, always keeping us on our toes. Maybe that should have warned us that something was up when the theme tune to Mission Impossible played on the speaker by the training pitch, and then again, and again. But you don't expect to see your strength and conditioning coach paragliding into the middle of a session, and you don't expect to see Huw Bennett – 16-and-a-half stone of former Wales and Ospreys hooker, now the assistant S&C coach for Wales – paragliding in to land alongside him.

You all need an escape, sometimes. A time to let go, when you've felt something building up inside. And that's the way it was one afternoon, for a few of us, when our training camp moved to Turkey.

It wasn't a big night out. It was more a big afternoon out. Given some time off from training, pushing on too far. Taking in too many, thinking that going back early to see some of the lads coming off the pitch and show them our support was a good idea. Timing has never been my strong point.

It was a decompression, more than anything else. That's how it felt. The second camp of a long preseason, the second residential camp away. You come to feel it more, as you mature. You realize there's enough people telling you what you shouldn't, can't and won't do. A part of you pushes against it all. Sometimes it manifests in the great escape. In too many beers in too many bars.

Not a binge, but a way of releasing all that pressure. Going big so that you don't feel the need to keep doing it. Enjoying the freedom to be a different version of you, for a few short hours. And Warren Gatland and the coaches were phlegmatic about it, when the six of us rolled home. A look that said, you're old enough to know better, but boys will be boys.

I didn't drink often, in my younger days. I was intent on being the perfect professional. I thought it was what I should do, not what I wanted to do. You don't realize, in those intense days, that finding a balance is more important. It shows control and maturity. You try not to do it at all and you end up chasing it.

This impromptu session changed nothing about the World Cup and our preparations. Way too far out to have any physical effect, as much about the anticipation for what was going to come in Japan that autumn. A welcome for us in Kitakyushu in keeping with the atmosphere around the entire tournament: energy, animation, warmth, passion. 15,000 locals piling into an open training session, all of them singing a spectacular version of 'Hen Wlad Fy Nhadau'.

We were blown away. I'd learned a few Japanese words and phrases, read a few books. And you're still not ready for the reality of the country, when you get there – the food, the onsens (hot springs), the traditions. Oysters as big as steaks, onsens where everyone is starkers and you just crack on. Our team manager taking us all to a restaurant he had recommended which turned out to be an all-you-can-eat place, the boys smashing their way through plates of chips and Fanta refills while he just had to sit there, dying inside, and let us fill our boots. A liaison officer who seemed unassuming until he took us to a kendo hall and turned out to be a master, the local academy treating him like the star he was, carrying his *shinai*, his sword, for him, lacing him into his protective gear. 'Hey, that's Alex!'

Japan's players backed it all up. A style that was fantastic to watch, results that should have been shocks but weren't, not really, if you watched the way they played, particularly after beating South Africa in the 2015 World Cup.

And us? This time we got the group stages right. Past Georgia, treating their forwards with the respect they'd earned. Uruguay tougher than it should have been, us pulling away at the end. Fiji, because there'll always be Wales and Fiji in World Cup groups, and us going 10 points down early on, because that's what Fiji always do to Wales at World Cups. A short turnaround for us and a physical experience: Josua Tuisova running as hard as a bullet train, Josh Adams with two tries in the first half to haul us back in front and third going into the final quarter to help steer us home.

Australia? That felt like the game against the Springboks in the 2011 World Cup. It felt like the game against Australia in 2015, not least because so many of their starters then were starters again.

You don't dwell on the performance, in those games. It's purely about the points, about the way the draw for the knock-out stages should open up for you a little more if you get it right. But you start well, and the confidence flows. Dan Biggar's drop goal in the first minute, his cross-field kick over Marika Koroibete for Hadleigh Parkes to jump and score in the right-hand corner. The Wallabies hitting back through Adam Ashley-Cooper; Gareth Davies picking off Will Genia's looping pass to outsprint Bernard Foley and Ashley-Cooper to put us 23–8 up at half-time.

You just obsess about stopping them. When they work a try early in the second half, when they drive over from close range and Michael Hooper burrows over you. When Matt Toomua brings it back to a one-point game, when you see Liam Williams limping about with all your replacement backs already on the field.

Just stop them. Tackle, get up, tackle. Hit a ruck, protect a ruck. Look for the ball, run hard, make yards.

And you never think you're lucky, when you come through. You don't listen to those who say you were fortunate, or that you were hanging on. They weren't making those tackles, hitting those rucks, making those carries. They weren't there when you were training in 40-degree heat in Kitakyushu, or doing double days at altitude in Switzerland. They weren't in the weights room in the training barn at the Vale, and they weren't doing repeated sessions at minus 140 degrees Celsius in the cryo-chamber afterwards.

You get through it, and you use the momentum it brings. You could see what it was doing for Japan, beating Ireland, keeping that going to do the same to Scotland and top their group. You could see how South Africa were trying to get it back, having been beaten by the All Blacks. Us heading back to Oita for the quarter-finals, staying up the coast in Beppu, watching the number of Welsh supporters and red shirts growing by the day.

A glance at the Webb-Ellis trophy as we walked out that grey Sunday afternoon, all shining gold and close enough you could have picked it up. The taiko drummers, all dressed in black kimonos, hammering away. The gong, ringing out, signalling it was about to begin.

They came on to us at a thousand miles, France. A strange stadium an hour out of town, a first 10 minutes when the game feels like it's blowing through you and past you.

Sébastien Vahaamahina, in his black scrum cap, smashing over from a few yards. Virimi Vakatawa, crashing through one tackle, watching him slip in Romain Ntamack on his inside, then Antoine Dupont on the supporting line, then Charles Ollivon inside him. Tracking back desperately but chasing heels, chasing space. George North trying to come across, all of us too late.

Eight minutes gone, 12 points down.

Up in the stands, on the sofas back home, there might have been the doomsday thought: France are having a France day. On the pitch, you don't worry about that. Not much you can do about what has come before. Individual errors, missed tackles – they happen. Unless someone is a repeat offender, there's no point tearing into them. You've done it yourself; how do you know you're not going to do it in this game, too? As a captain, you must tread that line between maintaining standards and motivation.

12-point leads today are not what they were. The game is faster; there are more points to be taken. Two tries, but one missed conversion. You're not dead and buried. You're just not going forward.

Get back to it. Think: we were 16 points down against the same opposition on their home patch eight months ago, and we won that one.

Move on. Start again, for it is what it is. And gain perspective from the time on the clock, rather than fear. You'd rather they score those tries early, when there's more time for you to respond, rather than late on.

It comes back to you. A loose ball, bobbling out the side of a ruck, after a hit from Jake Ball on their captain Guilhem Guirado; Aaron Wainwright seizing it and galloping half the pitch to score. Conversion, 12–7. A different game, in a handful of seconds.

Now the fight begins. Penalty to us for 12–10, game open.

A high one on Gaël Fickou. You do things under extreme pressure that reflect the speed and the scramble, and when you've just come on as a replacement, it's that much harder. But try defending with 14 men for 10 minutes, and there will be gaps. Vakatawa taking advantage of the space created by his forwards.

Conversion knocked over, 19–10. Half an hour gone, and it felt much longer.

Into the second half. France with a lineout on our five-metre line. Forming the maul, driving for the line.

I didn't see the Vahaamahina elbow on Aaron at first. I heard his shout. I saw Jaco Peyper's arm go out for the penalty, although at that point he was talking about an arm around the neck. And then I watched it back on the big screen, and I knew the referee had a decision to make.

You understand the laws of the game, and the fact that most players will try to stretch them when they can. You know, too, when you're coming into a World Cup, what they're going to be tight on. You know what offences they're looking for, and that you can't make contact with the head.

There's nothing you need to say, as the opposition captain. No need to remonstrate with the opposition. You expect the referee to have a look. The offence is obvious, the action that follows it likewise. You have no choice but to trust the officials and the system backing them up to get it right. You might ask them to have a look, depending on how the game has gone. And the attitude you have to that point in the game makes a difference. You and your teammates.

You play the game. Getting a carry in, the support coming in to drive you on. France not rolling away, another penalty that Dan Biggar could kick.

They often slow down, the contests that begin that fast. And this one began to fall into the sort of patterns we had experienced before under Warren and Shaun Edwards. In high-pressure games, we've often gone on to play some of our best rugby. Not always our most beautiful, but our most effective. When we needed to, we knew we could turn it on.

Six minutes to go, France scrum eight metres or so from their line. France a forward light, a big shove from us. A rip from Tomos Williams, the ball going straight up in the air. Justin Tipuric grabbing it, going head down for the line. Me sprinting in to clear their men off the ball. Ross Moriarty behind, picking and going across the line.

I clenched my fist when I saw we'd scored. A point down, a point up if Biggs knocked over the conversion. But you never think of the game as won. You never think of one instance as the decisive play.

We waited for the TMO to have a look, to decide if the ball had gone forward or just straight up in the air. Me still gesturing with my palms down. You don't over-celebrate if it's given and you don't fall apart if it isn't. You don't know how it all ends, in that moment. Just play the game in front of you.

You go back again to the critical moments. How many times do you see a team concede straight after a score? The role of the front five has changed; the demands of the game are greater now. You've got to fill far more roles. I ran back to our half acutely aware of the significance of securing that restart.

And we secured it. A big jump, boosted from below, reaching

back high over my head, almost landing flat on my back. Tomos kicking long, Maxime Medard kicking too long. A scrum back from where he had kicked it.

Five minutes left of a World Cup quarter-final. Leading by a single point.

Wheel. Reset. Get your binds right. Front row collapse. Reset. Another messy one. Remind the referee whose put-in it is.

Three minutes, we burned through like that. A penalty to follow, a nod of affirmation to the referee. Biggs kicking to their 10-metre line. A throw to Adam Beard at the front.

Maul. Burning away the seconds. Short carries, rapid clear-outs. The clock going red, Biggs booting the ball deep into the stands. The only time France touched the ball in that final six minutes was Medard's catch and over-done kick. You're not lost in the quarter-final disappointment of four years before, not wondering about the semi-final ahead. Messy thoughts in your head instead. Why do we make this so hard for ourselves? Maybe we've dodged a bullet there. Maybe instead we've created our own destiny again. We've waited until we've needed to. Not a good habit to have.

You reflect on yourself, in those moments. Wet grass on your face, dirt in your eyes. Shirt turned dark red with sweat. How did I do?

Character matters, in games like those. You either have that inside you or you don't. You can't grow it, from the environment you build around a team.

Remember – trust matters, too. A trust in the leadership group that took us to the Grand Slam in the spring, a trust in those around us now. It's not the same as getting on with people. There can be players you get on with and others you seldom agree with. There can be friction, plenty of it. If you trust each other to per-form each of your roles – if you trust that each will do everything they can – then you have the foundation for everything else.

Those players didn't need me talking all the time before and after games. They didn't need my physical presence when we were away from training. But they knew I would do my job, and I knew they would do theirs. That's the reality of life in or outside of sport. It's not about friendship. It's not about letting personal feelings get in the way. It's about success through collaboration. The delegation of shared responsibility that doesn't need to be talked about. Believing in yourself. Believing in each other.

And so it moves on. A World Cup speeds up, as you progress. You get through one epic, and that just gives you passage to another.

A flight north from Beppu to Tokyo, a hotel in the middle of the city. Bright lights and more fans and bigger buildings.

Your senses are heightened at this point in a World Cup. Training sessions are shorter and sharper. The anticipation of Test week is all around you. The girls and Anwen on their way out to Japan, thousands of others back home trying to get plane tickets to do the same.

Rugby being rugby, it never goes smoothly. On a simple lineout drill early that week, I tweaked my groin. Not so badly I feared missing the semi-final, but bad enough to limit my time training. To require diclofenac, the strongest anti-inflammatory pills we can have. A pill to protect your stomach, another to get you through. No reason for the injury, no sudden trauma. Every now and then, you just get an injury you've never had before.

The game is in your mind all the way through that week. As the days burn away, as kick-off gets closer. I found, as always, that it helped me to think about the magnitude of it. You can try telling yourself it's just another game, but you won't fool yourself for long. It's special. You don't want to get away from it. You're where you want to be. Embrace it.

It had been a theme with Warren Gatland, all the way through. The bigger the performance required, the bigger the performance will be. We had confidence in what we were doing – in our preparation, our plans.

We felt ready, as we did our captain's run, our final trot around the Yokohama pitch before the game. I left going out for my warm-up for as long as possible, so there could be no stories swirling around about a potential injury. And when we walked out of the tunnel and towards the pitch that Sunday night, I felt that tropical dampness when night falls and the temperature drops and there's almost a dew in the air.

Always thoughts of what could be, always pushing them away for what the next few hours would bring. Bright floodlights, shining from the roof of the grandstand opposite. From the roof of the stand behind us. Flames shooting skywards from the launchers behind the posts.

It started as you expect it to start against South Africa. A towering kick-off, them slowing our ball down. The clearing kick from Gareth Davies, Handré Pollard hoisting a high cross-field kick of his own. Leigh Halfpenny taking it, but their forwards piling in to hold him up and win the scrum.

First penalty kick to them, ruck infringement. Us levelling it up through Biggs after Willie le Roux went offside. Scrum penalty to them, 6–3.

Driving maul, Ken pinged, 9–3. Ken opened up on his head for his pains. Aaron Wainwright taken out off the ball, Biggs for 9–6. Five minutes into the second half, levelling it up through Biggs after Etzebeth jumped across a lineout.

Attritional. But where we needed to be, in a game like this.

*

55 mins: Wales 9–9 South Africa
George North off. Tomas Francis off.

South Africa just outside our 22. A couple of carries centre-field.

Faf de Klerk behind his forwards to Pollard. He's spotted a gap here, cutting right, curving back in.

Attacking the weak edge of the ruck. Through a tackle. Leigh bringing him down.

Scan left, scan right. Them recycling the ball. Coming to our right, towards the left-hand touchline.

Me centre-field. Pollard to Damian de Allende.

Defensive system looks okay here. Three of ours for three of theirs.

De Allende, stopping, accelerating.

Pushing off Biggs.

Fighting past Tomos Williams.

Through Owen Watkin.

Try . . .

Okay.

It's done. Move on.

Not ideal, in a game this tight. 20 to go. We'll get one opportunity. We'll have to take it.

61 mins: Wales 9–16 South Africa

Done well off the kick-off here. Going hard at them, eight phases, nine.

Into their 22. Phase 11.

Carry carry carry. Hard for the line.

Stopped, shoved backwards.

Five metres out.

Options to attack both sides, if they shorten up.

Collisions have to be decent now.

Phase 16. Fighting for every inch.

Phase 18.

Me on the carry. Decent defence this . . .

Pen coming!

Their forwards off their feet. Quick kick left, nothing doing.

Okay. Hauled off the deck by Ross Moriarty.

Decision time.

We kicking the three points? Kicking for the corner? Taking the scrum?

So. We go for the corner, they're strong on lineout D. On maul D.

We kick the points . . . we're still four points down. In a game being won by three points at a time.

The scrum? I've gone that way before, and it's gone wrong. But now . . .

Ask the front row. Yes?

Scrum.

'LET'S GO!'

Quick strike, channel one.

Nine's gone in. De Klerk's out the picture. Three on two.

Muz's done well there at 8, had to dig for that . . .

Tomos going left.

Good hands from Fox.

Josh on the left . . . TRY!

73 mins: Wales 16–16 South Africa

Got to get close enough for a drop goal. Got to clear them out.

Carrying.

Rhys Patchell waiting, still too far out . . .

Not making dents. Not sucking them in.

We go through too many phases here, the ref will see something. Make a decision.

Short ball to me. Carry hard. Green shirts.

Done for holding on.

Fuck.

Now they'll kick to touch. Now they'll have field position for a driving maul.

Tough at the best of times.

Lineout throw to the front.

Them getting a roll on.

Maul collapsing.

Penalty South Africa . . .

I want Pollard to miss. He won't. He hasn't.

Three points down, four minutes to go.

Have to get the ball back.

79 mins: Wales 16–19 South Africa

Still their possession.

Scrum South Africa, our half, right-hand side.
Big shove. Scrum wheeling. Whistle going.
Clock going red.
Pollard kicking it out.
It's gone.
Done . . .

Final score: Wales 16–19 South Africa

*

I was dark afterwards. Everything stops. It stops, but you've got to carry on, on lots of levels.

I was called for dope testing. Straight from the pitch into a small room with two South Africans, François Steyn and François Louw. I'd been in there with Louw after the quarter-final in 2015. You don't say much, in those circumstances. You shrug. Breathe. Try to find a piss.

I was lucky my girls were there. It helped. I wouldn't see them until later, back at the adjoining hotel to ours, but they were a great distraction. Mali just wanted to know where we were going next. Probably more likely to remember the giant candy floss she had rather than the game she'd just watched.

Staying away from the boys was better for me, that night. Everyone's feeling the same. There's nothing you can say, because you end up having these hypothetical conversations – *what if we'd done this, what if that hadn't happened, how did they get away with that?* And they mean nothing, because you can't change any of it.

And you're drained of emotion. Thinking about Gats's last campaign, how it had started with a Grand Slam and ended with a Grand Slam. Gats making sure it was never about him.

I thought about the journey there. The past and the future. Four World Cups now.

All these thoughts go through your mind. And then you

remember you've got another game to come, a game no one ever thinks about or plans for. A third-place game that feels, at best, a touch perverse, but helps, a little, because you have to think about it.

The girls joined me on the pitch after that one. Both in red Wales jerseys, JONES in white lettering across the shoulders, a big number 5 on their backs. Me showing them my office.

And the following night, when the World Cup final was taking place, the squad went out in Tokyo. We didn't watch it, although it was on in most places you went into. You worked out the result when the Springboks fans piled out into the streets and began celebrating.

And you still felt the blackness of loss, in that bright neon city. The closer you are to something, the further from your grasp it can be.

21

HANES | HISTORY

A final Six Nations game against Scotland in Cardiff. Straight-forward. Familiar.

Until Covid came. We had played England at Twickenham as the pandemic was beginning to sweep across Europe, but no one saw it coming at that stage. Within the camp, most of us thought it was going to be another Sars or bird flu: we'll move on, and we'll keep playing rugby.

As late as the Friday morning, the Scotland game was still officially going ahead. Thousands of supporters with trains and flights and hotels booked, many already in town or travelling down. But we'd felt it by then – the waves of pressure, through the media, the ripples from meetings far higher up the food chain. And when lockdown came, at first we fell into limbo. Trying to stay match fit, ready for the Six Nations to resume at short notice. Preparing for a summer tour to Japan that seemed so far away, it surely had to go ahead.

We all learned fast, in those springtime weeks. That we wouldn't be playing again for far longer than we'd imagined. That we would be training by ourselves, with what we had.

It's strange how your body reacts after years of elite rugby. A freakish opportunity to recuperate, to let a troublesome Achilles tendinopathy finally heal. A chance to see if the home gym I'd ordered by chance just before could do what I'd hoped. Anwen looking down at my feet in bed one morning and saying, *I think that's the first time since we got married that I've seen you with a full set of toenails.*

I tried to keep a routine. A morning session, an afternoon session. To refill the tank while also trying to build it around the family, in my usual slightly selfish way. I know myself now; if I'm not training, I'm grumpy. At one stage I even seriously contemplated training in my full Ospreys kit, just to feel slightly more normal. I took Anwen out with a bag of balls to work on the skill-based stuff. Another grand romantic gesture.

Here's how my head works. I kept a log of every session I did. Written on the white board in the gym at home, photographed afterwards. Following a programme but doing extras afterwards as well. I recalled the great track athlete Michael Johnson talking about doing the same, and it all made sense to me. Being able to check what you had done and when, finding a calm in replicating the feel of the gyms at Llandarcy with the Ospreys and the Vale with Wales: session on a white board, walk up, take it in, go do it.

I missed playing. A sense of incompleteness around the Six Nations, a strange sort of intent to blocks of training. You train to compete, for a goal. I surprised myself: I missed the people. I play rugby to win games. The communal side of it is more special than you realize, until it's taken away.

The simplification of it all, of daily life? That suited me. Not being able to make plans, not being able to be spontaneous. Anwen spotted it straight away. *You quite like this, don't you? Not going out, not having to make social engagements.* I don't dislike people, but I naturally keep myself to myself.

And as restrictions gradually began to ease, you appreciated it all afresh. Ospreys training moving to St Helen's in Swansea, with Llandarcy requisitioned as a field hospital; another new link to my past, a career coming full circle. The clubhouse, the black wooden cricket scoreboard, the grey concrete terraces with the white metal barriers. Feeling privileged because we were getting to do our jobs when millions of others weren't. Pubs shut, restaurants shut, theatres and music venues closed. We could work; we could spend time in closer physical proximity than other people.

A chance, too, to reflect. A trial for life with no rugby, in some ways. The first prolonged pause since the very start, all those years ago at St Helen's. No job is difficult when it's going well, when you're getting promotions or winning things. It's when it gets tough that you get a true sense of how much you care.

I still did. That's what Covid confirmed to me. I saw beyond the sport to a time when I wouldn't have it any more. I saw it, and thought: I want it back. I'm ready to do some more.

The autumn of 2020, the Six Nations finally ready to resume. Isolation at our camp in Wales, temperature checks every day. Medical masks on the plane to Paris, individual letters signed by President Macron in case we were stopped by the police for being outside after the 9 p.m. curfew. As the game didn't kick off at the Stade de France until 9.15 p.m., this was perhaps a decent precaution.

Maybe that's why so little felt real around the idea I would equal Richie McCaw's international caps record. Why so little felt real as we flew home and began preparing for the Scotland game, where the record would be broken. Isolation in camp. Temperature checks. No seeing the family, no seeing any fans. And then a coach the other way along the M4 from usual, west to Parc y Scarlets rather than east to Cardiff, with the Principality being turned into an emergency NHS Nightingale Hospital. Fewer cars on the roads, no flags being waved. No fans in either stadium. We might as well have been playing in the car park.

My overriding emotion on both occasions? Immense disappointment that we lost. Antoine Dupont outstanding against us in Paris, Ali Price killing us with two fine kicks to the corner a week later. And those results dictated how I reacted in the aftermath. I didn't want to do a presentation on the pitch in Llanelli, smiling and waving a bottle around having been beaten at home by Scotland for the first time in 18 years. Anwen had a bottle of champagne waiting in the fridge when I got home. And I looked at her as I walked in the door and said, *yep, shall we leave it until tomorrow?* A tense evening, that one.

I know what you're thinking. Stubborn. And you'd be right, in many ways. But I was intensely proud, deep down, and I was genuinely grateful for the effort that so many went to: a commemorative watch from the Welsh Rugby Union, with the number 149 engraved on the back; a bottle of single malt Penderyn. The boys in the squad chipping in for a case of 2006 Patagonian red, a nod to where my international adventure had begun. The messages that came in from players who I had the utmost admiration for, some of the ones who had been my heroes coming through: Shane Williams, Victor Matfield, Jason Robinson, Paul O'Connell. So many of the Ospreys boys; contemporaries from the international game like Stuart Hogg, Maro Itoje, Julien Bonnaire. A lovely chat with Adam Jones the night before. Richie McCaw himself.

I'm not great at taking compliments. If someone says I played well, I assume they're also thinking that I could have played better. If I know I have played better, it still feels uncomfortable, because I'm still only one bad game away from being dropped.

When I was younger, I was blunt about it. Never believe your own hype. If someone tried saying something nice about me, I shut them down straight away. Now, I appreciate it a little more, or at least the effort they have made. For all those men to take the time to bother meant a great deal to me. A personal one from Ian Foster, now head coach of New Zealand, who had once done a brief stint of consultancy for the Ospreys. It had been one of theirs who held the record before. The Kiwis I've met always do things the right way.

I didn't crack anything open in the changing room – not the wine, not the whisky. I drove home. And leaving the family celebrations until the Sunday worked better, anyway; we could let the dust settle on the Saturday, bring the cake out, let the girls share in it, when Covid restrictions had meant they weren't allowed to watch from the stands the afternoon before.

I felt fortunate the matches were going ahead, after the long wait, in the context of what was happening around the country. Beyond that? If I'm honest, a big part of me couldn't understand the hype about the record. Now, I don't know if I'm missing something, or I'm insufficiently emotional; although I am emotional about lots of things. The pangs for me were around my family. Around the fact my dad couldn't be there to see it. Being a parent myself, knowing the emotions I'd feel if it were my son or daughter. That's what I thought about, as we ran out onto the pitch in that swirling autumnal wind, as I sat in the dressing room afterwards, mud on my face and hands and knees.

The actual numbers of caps? I almost had to have it explained to me by Anwen. With her athletics background, she understands stats and world records and special numbers. I just kept thinking: but I'm just doing my job. I'm just chasing an egg. In my eyes, the records belong to the game, not to the players. I'm just holding onto one for now.

I wasn't comfortable with any of the comparisons with Richie McCaw. He has two World Cups. I don't. I've got those holes in my CV, and then I'd lost the Scotland game, too.

So now, with the distance of a little time, I think: because we lost at home to them for the first time since 2002, I can never forget the game, can I? My skin crawls at the idea of me elevating myself above the team. I felt a greater satisfaction in the combination of my Welsh caps and going past 240 appearances for the Ospreys. There's a saying in rugby that if you work harder, you get your rewards. Well, I know when I've played with nerve damage and infections and a back spasm. I know how hard I've gone to get there.

You strip it back, and rugby is a job. For you, for your family, for the nation. You embrace all the privilege and emotion that comes with it, but you can never take it for granted or you'll be spat out fast. No one counts how many kitchens a carpenter has fitted, or tells a plumber he should pack it in when he's done a certain number of bathrooms. Keep working, keep trying to improve. Some like the old saying that you're only as good as your last game. I think you're only as good as your next one. Me? I just drove to work.

You know me now, more than you did before. I hope you can see this is authentic, not fabricated. I look forward all the time; I don't like looking back. I fear the complacency that might follow, the possibility that satisfaction might lead to boredom, to monotony, to failure.

You can tart anything up with numbers. Someone told me I've played in almost 20 per cent of Wales's total international matches. But I've never beaten the All Blacks, never won the World Cup, so it doesn't matter, and I'd far rather have won a World Cup than be the record caps holder. It's an achievement from the collective, for the nation.

Maybe that's how you keep going. How these records appear on the horizon and move closer. You strive to be consistent, even though no supporter ever made a song up about the virtues of consistency. We had a guest speaker once, with Wales, who had been in the special forces. He told us that whenever he went out as part of a unit, he felt better about being the worst performer in a great team than the best performer in a poor team. That makes sense to me, even if I'm not. I'm comfortable with a mentality like that, because there's somewhere to go. Somewhere to improve.

It's not that difficult to be consistent every Saturday. It's much harder to be consistent throughout the week that leads to a Test match, too. I've lived the equivalent of three years in Test weeks. When you know what those weeks are like, all that goes into them – well, that's a mind-blowing thing, for me.

You, on the outside, see only the performance. You don't see what produces the performance. When consistency becomes almost an art form. You walk from the kitchen to the front door and you could ask yourself 10 questions about what you have and haven't done, about how ready you are for the day ahead or just gone: can I eat this today, have I had enough protein, do I need to do my stretching, do I need to do my 20 minutes on the bike tonight?

There are days when it's all emotion that carries you through and onwards. Those are the easy ones. Consistency gets you through the rest, when it's monotonous, when you're bored. It's a cliché, but it's the stuff you do when no one is looking, not the bits you do when everyone is looking.

There is a balance. A sweet spot, where you're on it but not allowing the OCD part of your personality to win out. Hence why if you live it, it's not a chore. I wouldn't have half the things that were put in front of me. Now there's the family to think about, emphasizing the need for balance.

So I'll have the slice of cake now, when it's a birthday, a celebration. As a young man, I was an absolutist. I remember Christmas parties and buffets where I'd walk to the table and think, oh, can't have a sausage roll, there's pastry on it. And I wasn't shredded, I wasn't going to get shredded. Now? I might not necessarily be on it all the time, but I'm aware of it. I think you're in control as long as you're asking the questions. When your conscience stops poking you, you could be in trouble. You need to learn to work with it.

I was the same on the training pitch. If I dropped a pass, I would be beside myself. If someone else dropped one, I'd be all over them. But you can exhaust yourself before the weekend if you try to tie up every loose end. You end up carrying too much baggage into the game. I'm more in control of it now. If I drop a ball, it might only be a press-up as a reinforcement. To remind myself.

It's addictive, this life, this mentality. Yet I like to think I would be the same if it hadn't been rugby. If I'd fallen into something else. Whatever I did, I would want to be as good as I could be at it. I wouldn't necessarily be the best in the world, but I'd be the best I could be. Doing things the right way takes a lot longer sometimes, and a lot of people don't enjoy the honesty of that process. But that's where the satisfaction comes from.

And it all has to come from you. In my career I've seen some people who do things to satisfy others. Not everyone sees through them, but most of our peers will know. You've got to work on remembering and maintaining your core attributes too. Don't spread yourself too thin. If you're good at something, keep being good at it.

So. The caps record. Maybe there'll be a point in the future where I'll look back on it with a slightly different perspective. If the game lets me go.

Not many people fancied us, when we began the 2021 Six Nations. Those defeats to France and Scotland leaving us fifth in the table for the previous edition, defeats following in the Autumn Nations Cup to England and Ireland.

But we had played sporadically, in November and December. Very good defensively against England, in patches against Scotland. A poor start, but a sense of something building. Our discipline letting us down, probably trying too hard at times. Just needing to be smarter and a little more accurate.

That's all it often is, in international rugby. Your memories of successful campaigns are full of free-flowing rugby and bursts of unforgettable tries, always more romantic than they should be. You seldom romp a Grand Slam. You chisel one out. There will always be that one game you win by a single score, or come from behind, or win late.

And so much, always, hinges on that first game. We were 13–6 down at half-time against Ireland. We came through, and the world was a different place for us. George North looking a natural, playing out of position at outside centre, competition for places across the side. Competition creates pressure; pressure, in a game, creates opportunities, and opportunities lead to points.

It was close, at the death. Us missing touch after deciding to try a grubber with 10 seconds on the clock, Ireland's fly-half Billy Burns putting his penalty kick dead rather than finding the corner as Ireland marched back at us. But close games set you up for other close games. We were 17–3 down to Scotland six days later, and I still felt calm, even when Stuart Hogg scored a try we should have prevented. There is no point in screaming at people, or showing off when something goes right, when you win a scrum penalty. Wear stress as a leader and those around you feel it too, which I may have been guilty of at times. We know where we went wrong, so why are we still worrying and shouting about it? Just don't do it again. And if you ask a question to a referee about a decision of his, and he says no, you have to think – okay, that one's on you. I don't feel the need to remonstrate or shout at them or chase them around.

You spend enough time on the field, and what seem to be the decisive moments from the outside appear to you instead as one part of a chain. The Owen Watkin tap-tackle on Duhan van der Merwe right at the end looks like it was decisive; Liam Williams slipping and out of the picture, Owen just reaching Van der Merwe's heel with his outstretched fingertips. But how do you know it wasn't a breakdown penalty a few phases back, a defensive mistake that allowed Finn Russell to get out of the initial tackle to put away his offload to then set his winger away?

Small margins, big shifts in momentum. Had Van der Merwe got away at the end, our overall performance wouldn't have changed, but the result would have done. Instead, we were two from two, with England to come at home and Italy away. Relief, at the final whistle, but also frustration that it had come so close to going the other way.

The red card, to Zander Fagerson, to match the red card given to Ireland's Peter O'Mahony? Everyone was made aware pre-tournament of the referees' focus areas. I've played in enough games where similar decisions have gone against us, and we've lost them. And when, two weeks later against England, Dan Biggar took a quick tap penalty and kicked to Josh Adams in the corner? You play to the whistle. We won that game with a 16-point margin, scoring the most points Wales ever had against

England. It wasn't all about that moment; it just appeared that way to some watching from the outside.

It was tight. Only two points in it with 13 minutes to go. The time when the attitude and attributes of your replacements can make all the difference. You have two choices, coming off the bench: either come on to make a difference, to lift it without standing out too much, or come on to be seamless. It's harder to do than it sounds – add to the flow, when you're winning; change the direction, if you're losing.

Ours did their job. A few of the opposition's replacements were guilty of trying too hard, on a couple of occasions, and we cashed in from the subsequent penalties. In a strange way, it may have helped them had the referee given a yellow card. In all our previous games, the teams had been galvanized by exactly that.

We closed it out. Leaning on our kicking game. Three wins from three, and a performance against Italy in the penultimate week that gave us even more confidence. We were expected to win. We did. We also felt something else – a cohesion, a pace to our play. You can feel form coming, and you can feel it kicking in.

You can feel a team binding together sometimes. That's how it felt, travelling out to Paris. Still in lockdown, still the temperature checks and the masks on the plane and the curfews, but the strange now the familiar. So much experience in players who still have so many games ahead of them – George North, past 100 caps, Ken Owens and Taulupe Faletau past 80. Dan Biggar past 90, Jon Davies not far off 100.

You add in youth, and you use everything the younger ones have. Not just what they can do for the team, but what they can do for you. Questions for you to answer: what's he doing differently, what's he trying to do, what can he add to me? These talents make a difference to everybody. Josh Adams had done it when he first came in; Johnny Williams raised a few eyebrows in the autumn. Raising the competition, pushing the team towards perpetual motion.

No one was doing that more than Louis Rees-Zammit. One of the quickest players I've ever seen, a kid built to go fast and with loads of growing still to do. A brilliant finish in the corner against Scotland, maybe a better one yet to get us in front against Ireland. Another against Italy, having only made his debut off the bench against France in October. Everything simple. A time in your life when the game opens up in front of you, when everything seems possible.

The game. The one to win the Slam.

Flat-out rapid, at the start. Romain Taofifénua scoring early for France, us hitting back through Biggs. Antoine Dupont with their second try, two minutes later; Josh Navidi with our second, four minutes further on.

17–17 at half-time.

Josh Adams going over. Daylight. A driving maul from us, brought down illegally. A yellow card, but not a penalty try, when a penalty try felt like the only option. Zammo going so close in the corner.

Paul Willemse with a finger in the eye of Wyn Jones. Red card. And so into the final 11 minutes, not thinking about the prize, not thinking about anything except the game. No idea at all what was about to unfold. Where it would take us, what it would do.

*

69 mins: Wales 30–20 France
Bigs and Foxy off, Callum Sheedy and Halaholo on.

   10 points up, 13 to play. France down to 14 men, but they look like they're liberated by it.

   Our ball, pass back to Callum, Callum kicking.

   Penalty, France. Offside from the kick.

   Not ideal, but hey. We're a man up, they're chasing.

Kick to corner from Ntamack.
Lineout coming. Reading shapes.
Overthrown! Let-off, that is. Now let's get our exit right . . .

72 mins: Wales 30–20 France

France lineout on our 22. Watch them round the corner. They're not going to be spreading too wide, not a man down.
   Tackle Toby!
   Penalty. It can't be for interference, he's trying to get back.
   Offside? There's the yellow card. Is the ref trying to even this up?
   14 on 14 now. We had the warning. Can't do anything about it. He's not going to change his mind. Move on.
   Ntamack kicks to the corner. Lineout.
   Decent line D from us – nah, they're moving, this maul isn't stopping, Chat charging for the line . . .
   No time for a tackle – get under the ball, stop him getting it down.
   One, two, three of us here.
   They'll try to hit Vakatawa and send him over.
   Callum's got it. He's kicking clear . . . not into touch.
   Not ideal. Ebb and flow.
   Chase.
   France coming back at us from halfway. Got to force them to the edge.
   They're going right. Sanj is there.
   Penalty advantage?
   Penalty France.
   Hands on knees. Take a breath. Right call that, probably . . .
   Yellow card?
   Right – 13 plays 14.

76 minutes: Wales 30–20 France

Deep in our 22. Another penalty to France.
   Ref wants a word with me.

What's he saying? 'You need to change your discipline. You're making life really hard for me . . .'

I'm listening. But what really am I going to say to my players? They already know.

No more pens. It's simple.

Scrum.

Can't hold them.

They're over. Ollivon.

77 mins: Wales 30–27 France

Three minutes to go. They've still got to take the restart. They'll be deep.

Hold it.

Here they come. Tackle! Get back onside . . .

Knock-on! We got it. Advantage . . . advantage over . . .

Minute and a half left. Could have had the scrum there, that'd be it.

Short ball, take this, into contact. Present it back. Tomos there to pick up and pass.

Another carry. Not made any ground here, could be back for the scrum.

Advantage over? Okay . . .

Nicky Smith carry. Stay up.

Cory following through.

Alldritt jackalling, feet back.

Penalty.

Sealing off.

Fuck.

50 seconds.

'NEXT JOB!'

Kick to corner from Ntamack.

Maul coming. Pinned it all right.

Chat in front of me. Clock in red.

Need to get them going backwards.

These numbers aren't good. We send one man into the tackle, plus the jackaller. That only leaves us 11 in defence. We need 14, 13 of them on their feet . . .

81 mins: Wales 30–27 France
France 10 metres out. Blue shirts everywhere.
  Nine metres out. Eight.
  Short ball. Good carry.
  Quick recycle from them.
  They're going wide.
  So much space.
  Overlap . . .
  Fickou holding George.
  Louis going in. Man outside.
  Dulin . . .
  Get there get there get there!
  They can't score, not now.
  They're scoring.
  It's gone . . .

Final score: Wales 30–32 France

*

There's hindsight when you win, and there's hindsight when you lose. Should I have said more earlier? Was I asking the right things?

You can't say much, afterwards. You do the media stuff. You don't hear what the coaches say.

You think about the mistakes in the last 10 minutes. You think, were these mistakes from trying too hard? Not panicking ones?

You think about the clearance kick that led to offside, the decision to yellow card Liam Williams.

Another night staying at the hotel. Wishing you could just press a button and be home.

A long, long week to follow. A game to come where we were

involved but not involved. Scotland to stop France to give us a chance to win the championship.

You have to process it.

You have family. One day, you'll be someone different. The processing takes a long time, but you have to attempt it. You don't want to be haunted by games gone by. By what could have been.

22

BALCHDER | PRIDE

I didn't know my shoulder was dislocated, when it first happened.

One of my Lions teammates making a tackle, me spotting the chance to compete for the ball. Hands on it, head down. A Japanese forward coming in to clear me off it. A good hard hit, with textbook technique. No malice in it.

Bang.

Right on the sweet spot. The angle he hit me, the position of my body.

You feel it straight away. The pins and needles. And you hope – this is a stinger. It's pinged a nerve. I'll get up and it'll all fade. You get the feeling back, with a stinger.

And I stayed down, and nothing eased.

This isn't a stinger.

Staying on my haunches. My knees. Supporting my weight on my right arm. Left arm resting on my thigh.

The physio and the doctor with me, yellow bibs, face masks. Cradling the arm. Looking at me. Me not wanting to look back.

I've dislocated this, haven't I?

Your brain starts doing the sums you don't want it to do. We're seven minutes into the 2021 Lions' final warm-up match before the tour proper begins. A flight leaving Edinburgh for South Africa tomorrow afternoon. The next match against the Sigma

Lions at Ellis Park, Johannesburg, on Saturday. The first Test just three weeks further on.

Shoulder dislocations usually mean a lot of time out. They can mean pins. They're often six months. If you work hard.

Onto my feet. The physio holding my left arm gently at the wrist. Walking me off the field. Away from my teammates, away from the action. From everything I'd worked for.

They give you gas and air first, to mask the pain. The embarrassment of the Entonox not being enough. I've dislocated shoulders before. Watching them try once to put a shot of morphine in, then again, finally getting it in on the third attempt. Like it's happening to you but you're watching on at the same time.

They put the shoulder back in. A soft dropping-in, masked by the morphine.

You sit there in the dressing room, listening to the roars outside, the peaks and falls of the crowd noise. Quiet in there. Just you, your breathing and the calm voices of the medical staff.

I had my protein shaker. You're always looking to the future, until suddenly you're not. So no protein in there now. Two cans of beer emptied in instead.

You don't want to be a distraction. You clean yourself up, shower as best you can. Pull back on your red Lions tracksuit top, your red Lions face mask.

I walked back out and watched the game. I tried to put a brave face on it. Positive body language, a smile. The first outing for a new team, the official start of a grand adventure. You don't want to bring everyone down.

But you know. What this means. What you're going to miss out on.

It had felt like a full international, that game against Japan at Murrayfield. The first time I'd played in front of spectators for 16 months. 16,000 in there, sounding like 60,000. Seeing fans in the streets as the team coach made its way from hotel to stadium, seeing the red shirts and the banners. Hearing the songs and the cheers. A happy wildness about it all, everything to remind you of what you'd missed.

And all we had done as a team in preparation for the tour had felt like everything the British and Irish Lions is supposed to be. I loved those two weeks we had on our training camp in Jersey. A mixture of playing and getting to know people.

In Jersey, I'd like to think the players and coaches saw a slightly different side of me. A more mature man, a little less blinkered with the game and life. A captain who would lead and trust in those around him too.

In meetings I tried to keep it short and sharp, to keep the energy levels high, to delegate to others. There was no point in me trying to give it the *War and Peace* treatment about our attack; I could leave that to Dan Biggar and Owen Farrell. I can chase all day. Tackle. Ruck. Tell me where to be, and I'll be there.

I was the most mature player in camp by a few years. Almost as if it were coming full circle for me – not just players who had been teammates or opposition, but coaches I had played with or against too. I had played with defence coach Steve Tandy when he was an open-side in my early days at the Ospreys, and I'd then been captain when he was promoted to head coach; I had played in Gregor Townsend's last game, Border Reivers against the Ospreys at Netherdale, Galashiels, in 2007.

You've always kept an eye on the younger ones, but you realize as you mature that you have to make an effort with some of the ones in between too. I got on well with most I spoke to. The usual suspects – Louis Rees-Zammit was his usual cheeky self, entertaining us all. I took pleasure in seeing him flourishing. When I needed to let off steam, Ken Owens was there by the coffee machine.

We worked hard. A couple of really tough days early on, when the weather was scorching. The new facilities at Strive, the sports complex up by the airport; the staff bending over backwards to help us. An element of errors from us in training and combinations coming together, which is always how it is in the early days of a Lions tour.

The simpler you can get it at this level, the more productive you can be. A good night on the beers, on our first Saturday on the island. Paddle-boarding in St Brelade's Bay, taking fast inflatable boats round the lighthouse at La Corbière. Burgers and buckets of chicken wings waiting for us when we got back. The Saracens and Bristol boys arriving after their club seasons came to an end with Championship finals and Premiership semi-finals, the fresh faces and their energy and enthusiasm almost making it feel like the first week all over again.

There was nothing in those final few days before we flew to Scotland that gave any hint of what was to come. A proper training session on the Tuesday. A day off on Wednesday. A training session Thursday morning; the flight north in the afternoon. A short, sharp warm-up on the Friday, the team run a mere five plays. You don't need to repeatedly drill new plays at this level. Some get it straight away, others merely need to walk through it once. Feeling in the best shape I'd been in for a long time.

All of it flooding back on that Saturday afternoon.

The crowd, the noise, the occasion. The team around me, the feeling of running out of the tunnel. What I said to the team, in the dressing room beforehand. *There is nowhere else I want to be.* Having no idea of the irony of my words.

Out of the darkness, into the Edinburgh sunshine. Throwing Bil down, him landing belly-down and good to go. The whistle going; getting a few solid tackles in, one wipe, a lineout.

The hit.

The shoulder went straight back in, when they manipulated it. No break. The call was made. I was going home.

I had found Anwen and the girls in the stands. There could be no hugs, no physical assurances or commiserations; we were still under Covid protocols, still in our Lions bubble. I went back in to get my jersey to give to Anwen to take home, just in case I was somehow good enough to go again.

That's when they told me. You don't need to. You're withdrawn from the tour. You're going home tomorrow.

I addressed the team, at the end of the game. Handed out the caps. Spoke to them from the heart. *This is special. Keep it special. Show South Africa what it means.*

Scans booked in at the Spire hospital later that evening, one for me, one for Tips. He shouldn't even have been there – only in the starting XV because Hamish Watson had suffered a head knock in training.

Seeing the girls again, as we were pulling into the hospital. Them walking along the pavement, tired from a big day out. Anwen telling me she'd come by the team hotel later to pick up my bags. To give me the keys for our house, since I would now be getting home before them.

The MRI scan. A report done with reference to labral damage and some stuff going on in the back around the HAGL – the humeral avulsion glenohumeral ligament. Damage to the capsule of the shoulder joint.

They explained my options to me. I could have something called a Latarjet procedure, where they take a bone graft from your hip and put it into your shoulder. You lose some range in your movements, but it can repair it. Or option two, the best case scenario: keyhole surgery, going in through my back just to repair the rear of my glenohumeral capsule. Option one: six months. Option two: closer to three. A bitter pill to swallow, whichever you chose. Whichever was chosen for you.

Everything speeds up, after that. Bobby Stridgeon packing my bags for me, Anwen picking them up from him. Tips and I told to be ready to leave the hotel on Sunday morning at 10.30 a.m. for a flight down to Cardiff.

I stayed up late that night. To try to make the most of it. To squeeze every last drop out of my Lions experience.

Doors close, and doors open. Conor Murray announced as the new touring captain in my absence. A brief chat with him, wishing him all the best. Hearing that Adam Beard had been called up to replace me in the squad, that Josh Navidi was coming in for Tips. You don't get to speak to everyone. Bobby, in his typical Bobby way, coming to give me a hug goodbye.

You just want to get home, that morning. You don't speak much in the car on the way to the airport. You see a private jet land and the Exeter boys step out first, after their Premiership final defeat – Stuart Hogg, Luke Cowan-Dickie, Jonny Hill and Sam Simmonds. Then Beard and Navidi. Ready to fill the dead men's shoes. That's how rugby works, sometimes. There's no time for sympathy or condolences. You nod, raise your eyebrows, wish them luck. They move on, you travel back.

I was glad Tips was there. Someone who could empathize, even as he spent most of the flight on his iPad with his head-phones on. I was grateful I would have the girls, by the evening time. The familiar sloping streets and salty air. Much sooner than I had expected, than I had hoped.

We had a lift home from Cardiff airport. Dropping Tips at the turning for Jersey Marine, where he was being picked up to go home, as I went on my way back to Mumbles.

I didn't do a lot, just sat there on the sofa. I probably had the TV on in the background, but I don't know whether I watched anything. Staring into space. Waiting for the day to pass.

The girls back late that evening. Anwen worried; Mali all obvious confusion. 'What are you doing here?'

Waking up in my own bed on the Monday. The kids going back to school. Our wedding anniversary, and nothing organized to celebrate it, except a CT scan.

I tried to make plans as I waited, staring down the barrel of six months without rugby. What I might do with a car or a motor-bike. How I might fill the empty days, the quiet Saturdays.

Anwen was as positive as ever. 'Alun, we don't know until we know . . .'. Refusing to let me go to the scan on my own, insisting on driving us up and along the M4 to the Spire hospital in Pont-prennau, Cardiff. Getting there and spotting Dr Kath Lyons, the radiologist who had done the scan on my injured MCL before

Christmas, who had done the two injections I'd had of PRP —
platelet-rich plasma. It was so good to find a familiar face, in
some ways. 'Kath, I'm sick of seeing you, but it's lovely to see you
too, okay?'

And that was when it really hit me. Not because I was in an
enclosed cylinder for 10 minutes, with nothing to look at but the
white plastic, but the realization that while the rest of the squad
were in Johannesburg, acclimatizing at the team hotel near Sand-
ton, I was back in south Wales, having a scan.

That was Monday 28 June. An appointment with the consultant,
Dr Richard Evans, booked for 7.15 p.m. on the Tuesday. Another
long day of waiting, wondering, coming up with increasingly
improbable alternative plans.

This was not my first issue with my shoulder. The time in 2017,
playing France in our last game of that year's Six Nations, when I'd
been wiped at another ruck as I tried to win the ball and felt my
shoulder pop into my armpit. Lovely.

Dr Evans had those scans from four years before. Yet as he sat
down in front of us – me, Ans and Matt Bowen, one of the
Ospreys' physios – his disposition was not that of a man about
to impart bad news. He then took me through the physical tests.
*What range do you have in the shoulder? Can you raise your arm
above your head?*

I could raise my arm. My range was about 70 per cent of what
it should be. And because I was focusing on not showing any
discomfort, for obvious reasons, I didn't initially notice the
expression on his face.

Surprise. Pleasure. Eyebrows going up.

The first revelation: *this is nothing to do with the previous
injuries. Doesn't matter that it happened when you were on the
ball jackalling again. It was just another freak one.*

The second revelation: *as far as I can see, you don't need an
operation. You can rehab this.*

The third: *you can take that sling off now.*

It didn't quite hit me, straight away. I could see it in Anwen's face, before I felt the impact of his words myself. I was still stuck earlier in the process, thinking: I was there when the medics were cradling my arm. I was there when the Entonox wasn't touching me, and they made the third attempt at getting the morphine in.

The caveats: *there's damage there. I can see the old damage from 2017. But I have seen people with potentially worse dislocations being able to rehab this.*

Anwen realizing first. There might be a chance here. There might be a chance.

So much to suddenly digest in a very small amount of time. I must have asked Dr Evans the same question, four or five times: so this is not related to the previous shoulder issues? The same answer every time: no, it's gone a different way.

It was almost like it was happening to someone else. I couldn't process it. It was bizarre, like it was too much for me. And so Anwen asked the critical question. 'Are you telling us he could rehab this?'

'Yes. If the shoulder is stable in seven days' time.'

Me now. 'Do I have to come back and see you?'

'No. Just send me a video, showing me what you can do.'

The long drive back. Now, rehabbing something is not the same as playing Test rugby on it. But there was a beautiful little green shoot of hope, where before there had been nothing. Starting to spread its roots, starting to stretch towards the sunlight.

Two thoughts forming in my mind. I will give this everything. And if anyone can, I can.

On that drive home, I spoke to a company about getting altitude equipment in my house. I started working on getting a hyperbaric chamber, as I'd used one for my MCL injury before the Six Nations. One for fitness, one for recovery. I spoke to those in the Lions organization who could help with such things. I spoke to the Lions medical team, who couldn't quite believe I hadn't sustained more damage. We began to formulate The Plan.

*

These were the numbers. The dislocation had happened on Saturday 26 June. Tomorrow was Wednesday 30 June. The shoulder had to be stable and capable of passing its tests with the consultant on Monday 5 July. The final warm-up game on the tour was scheduled to be against the Stormers in Cape Town on Saturday 17 July. The first Test was a week later.

Which gave me roughly two weeks. Two weeks to get a dislocated shoulder moving. Pushing weights. Rotating. Taking contact, hits. Back playing.

I'm good when it comes to projects. I was transformed, having a target. A man who smiled rather than stayed silent. A man who talked to Ans rather than wanting to be left alone. A player who thought about playing again.

I was on the Wattbike in my garage first thing Wednesday morning. Interval sessions, heart rate high, legs spent. By Thursday morning I was back at St Helen's in Swansea, just like the 17-year-old me, just like my dad, just like my grandfather. Running, with a rugby ball under my arm. Under the shoulder.

The Ospreys were fantastic. They took me straight back in. I did put the fear of God into the physios there, but I'm used to doing that, and I knew I had to anyway. And we all found the black humour in it: me going from being with the elite players of Britain and Ireland to running past a dead rat a seagull had left behind. The other players there stunned to see me – *What are you fucking doing here?* My reply a phrase that I would come to find comfort in: *You can't kill a dead man, boys . . .*

Treatment from the Ospreys physios every day I was in. Arranging a physio session at home every day I wasn't in training at St Helen's – so the Saturday, Sunday and Wednesday. The hyperbaric chamber for recovery delivered and set up in a spare room, doing two hours a day in there, either one two-hour block or two one-hour blocks. The altitude equipment to keep the cardiovascular fitness up, a mask on with restricted oxygen. The danger, knowing me, that I would do too much.

I wanted to do cryotherapy. I wanted to do ice-baths.

Vasodilation to help everything heal in the muscles after the trauma in the soft tissue. But that would have to wait. I could get in the hot tub at home every day for the heat. I could hammer it on the bike. I could run. I could do leg weights and upper body weights on my right side.

I took no painkillers. Not because they weren't required, or that I didn't want them, but because I couldn't afford to mask the reality of where I was. I needed the feedback.

But I had Anwen. As soon as we had that hope, she did everything. You need to get in the hyperbaric chamber rather than helping clear up? Fine. You need full nights of sleep? I'll look after the girls. We can't take the girls out of school, but we'll take them out of anything they don't need to do, because we can't risk one of them being exposed to Covid and you having to isolate, and that fragile little green shoot of hope getting stamped on.

I had moments of doubt. If she did, she never let them show. From the start she was telling me, *no you're going to be all right, you're going to be back out there, you're going to be fine.* You think you know someone, and then you truly realize what they actually do for you.

Saturday. Trying 45-degree press-ups. Working on point loading, trying to improve mobility with resistance bands. Anything more I could do, I did. Double days. Triple days. Quadruple days.

The second consultation, on Monday 5 July. I managed everything I was supposed to do. I did a bit more, to be on the safe side.

The shoulder was stable, as the consultant had expected post-scans. I could move to the next stage.

Three and a half kilometres of running a day. Keep loading the legs, keep working the lungs. Getting some speed in there. On the bike every day. Rehab weights on the shoulder, progressing towards proper weights. Hyperbaric chamber early in the morning and late at night.

Squeezing in as much as I could, getting help anywhere from anyone. Ready for the sweet relief of cold therapy, Swansea City FC making the cryo-chamber at their training base in Fairwood available to me. Everyone who I asked rallying around. A lot of people I hadn't asked too. The numbers who messaged me, wishing me well.

Working at home, working at St Helen's. As I improved, a couple of key days at the Wales team base at the Vale. Where all my great rugby journeys begin. In the barn there, in the gym, on the artificial turf. First thought in the morning, last thought at night.

The full Wales squad was there, preparing for the game against Argentina on the Saturday. I trained with the non-23s, the players not in the final match-day squad. By the second Thursday, 8 July, I was ready for some collision-based stuff. On the Friday morning, we tried it – 10 days on from sitting in the consultant's office, talking scans. It was controlled, but sometimes it's worse when you try to control it than when you let it happen naturally. You try not to run straight head-on at people; I know I do it badly sometimes. It's what happens.

Extra rehab work in the gym afterwards. Staying at the Vale that night, rather than travelling home to be with my family. More power endurance on Saturday morning, as the Lions were preparing to take on the Cell C Sharks in Pretoria. A reminder of where they were, a reminder of where I wanted to be. A further contact session afterwards, some wrestling, some prowl and push. Realistic functional rugby stuff, maybe one of my toughest days. A triple session on my third consecutive big day, a cumulative loading, a relentless fatigue.

A call from South Africa from a member of the medical team and Gats. Updates and assistance, encouraging words and cold logistics. They were worried about the insurance situation. The condition might be termed pre-existing. Another aspect you don't consider, when you're head down in it all. Finding out I had been cleared. Another hurdle passed.

Still the shock from other people, when they saw me charging about. On the Welsh boys' faces out on the pitches at the Vale when I arrived. From one of our bus drivers, Andy, who had also been our driver out in Jersey, an actual full double-take. Spotting me, looking away, looking back in astonishment.

I got through Saturday 10 July. More treatment that evening. Rehab on Sunday back at the house, more physio. I was like the spare part at home, or rather a part designed for a very different purpose. Not quite sure what to do, my mind somewhere else.

Monday 12 July, two weeks on from the CT scan. More working on down-ups, getting off the deck. Hand-release press-ups. A Turkish get-up, when you hold a kettle-bell above your head with a straight arm, push up and then tuck your legs under. Everything working the shoulder's stability, its strength.

I packed my bags that day. Packed for the possible. Got Anwen to take me back east along the M4 and drop me off at the Vale with everything I would need for South Africa, if I was getting there. Another rehab weights session that evening.

Tuesday was the big day. A flight was held for the Wednesday, London to Doha to Cape Town, at three in the afternoon. A car booked to pick me up from the Vale at 10 a.m. Get through Tuesday and they could pull the trigger for it all.

It was a full training session. Nothing held back, no holds barred. I was sore, but no more sore than I was used to being. I did more contact top-up at the end, and then more. And then I thought, do I need to keep going now, because I've done everything I can without actually playing a match.

Wednesday 14 July. Departure day. And also, quite by chance, Anwen's birthday. I left her a few cards. I cherished all the simple sacrifices she had made. A present? She said to me, *the best thing you can do for me is get back out there . . .*

Terminal 5, Heathrow. There all on my own, the strangest start to a rugby tour I'd ever experienced. In civvies, piles of Lions luggage with me. Paying excess baggage, because I wasn't yet with the team. No man has ever been happier to pay excess baggage.

A quiet business-class flight from London to Doha; no direct flights to South Africa in these Covid times. A far busier one on to Cape Town. A familiar face in Ireland hooker Rónan Kelleher at the gate in Doha. He had trained with us for two weeks in Jersey while Jamie George and Luke Cowan-Dickie were still busy with club commitments, and had now been called up to add cover to the squad. For the whole journey, me being incredibly conscious of the Covid risks. I stayed in my seat for most of it. I barely lifted my mask. I sanitized my hands like a surgeon going into theatre.

And I slept and slept. All that physical exertion, all that emotional exhaustion. Some of the best sleep I'd had in the entire two weeks. Waking up as we began to descend, and not feeling any soreness at all in the shoulder.

Landing on Thursday 15 July. The final tour match in two days' time, the first Test in nine. A call from Gats on the drive to the team hotel: did I want to be involved off the bench in Saturday's game against the DHL Stormers?

I knew I had to. Not just to give myself a shot at the miracle, at playing a part in the first Test, but to demonstrate to everyone – the players out there, the staff, those watching on at home – that it was the right thing to get me out to South Africa.

Two other reasons too. Firstly, because playing was what I'd done everything for over the past two weeks. The quadruple sessions, the pushing it every single day, the dawn starts, the late nights in the hyperbaric chamber in the spare room. And secondly, because I know how it feels, from the other side. Any hesitation and there would have been a question mark over me. Over my fitness to be there. I was never going to say no.

There was still trepidation, just not around my physical condition. At Murrayfield, I had thought I wasn't coming back. I had thought there was no hope. That's how I had addressed the team in the changing room after the Japan match. When the full-contact training session on the Tuesday had confirmed that I was ready, I had one doubt: *what are they going to think now?*

I shouldn't have worried. They were all great, as soon as I arrived. Some monstrous piss-taking, of course, and a decent fine for being two weeks late. Since Rónan and I also had to socially distance for the first five days, eating away from the others and travelling anywhere on our own in a Land Rover, I referred to us as travelling in the Toxic Taxi.

Walking through some moves on the Friday, the captain's run at the stadium. And finally the Saturday and the game came – and you're a rugby player, so you want to play rugby. Picked on the bench, Gats saying to us beforehand, *boys, you're going to get time.* The first half going by, half-time. The second half beginning, and a few boys coming off, and a few other boys going on. The clock counting down. Thinking, I need more than this. I've had seven minutes on this tour, and all of them in Edinburgh.

48 minutes, and the signal to get my warm-up top off. Here we go. Getting on and doing okay, and probably better than I thought I would, to be honest. Not relieved to have got through it, but glad to be back out and playing. Yes, because it was the Lions, but also not just because it was the Lions. Because it was rugby, and rugby is my profession, and a large part of my world. You almost do it for you, yet it isn't about you, equally. No midweek game before the first Test or once the series had begun, so the only chance I had to get back to the group, as much as getting in the picture for the Test. I'd like to think that if anyone else in the squad had been given the same opportunity in the same situation, they would have done the same.

Nothing had been said about the possibility of resuming my leadership role. Not before I flew out, not on arrival, not before the Stormers game. Only on the Sunday did Gats ask me again. *Do you want the tour captaincy back?*

I'd mulled it over. Inside, thinking: *to be honest, I do. I could bite your hand off.* But saying out loud instead: *you need to put this to the leadership group. I can't muscle my way back in and say I have to have it because I had it at the start.* I had too much respect for the leadership group and too much respect for the team.

I said the same thing to the group. *Look, it's not about me and it's not about the role, it's about the respect for you. I don't want to make an issue of it.* And they were all in agreement. It's yours.

Monday: the recovery day. Tuesday: the tasty one, a hard double-day. Doing everything in my power to make it difficult for Gats not to consider picking me for the Test team, even when he had told me at the start that there were no guarantees I was going to play. I didn't know whether that was just him leaving himself options, but I wanted to give him good problems as well.

He gave me a heads-up, in the end. Just before the official announcement on a big screen in the team meeting. He told me the other second rows had been doing well. He complimented Adam Beard, my replacement. He told me there were a couple of specific things he was looking for me to do. That was it. Pressure from him that I was used to, that I expected and respected.

There was disappointment for others. There always is. You can feel it for a good 24 hours afterwards. But sometimes that's what preps a team best. An edge in training, an energy and commitment.

The pride and pleasure I felt was as much for Anwen, and everyone else who helped, as it was for me. Those two weeks between the injury and the confirmation that I could fly out were among the hardest of my career. I could see that now. The two days from the Saturday night in Edinburgh to the Tuesday evening in the consultant's room in Cardiff were maybe the most surreal 48 hours of all. Not knowing; knowing. Finding out you should maybe be somewhere else.

You play for your country and you love it. You play well for your country and, once every four years, it can get you here. I knew what an incredibly special position I was in. I could have been thousands of miles away. Instead, I was heading to Cape Town Stadium.

Everything I had given had been worth it. Now I had to make it count.

*

The day flies by when you have a game like this ahead.

A 6 p.m. kick-off in Cape Town, a switch the night before from the Arabella Hotel in Hermanus, 100 km from the stadium, to our holding hotel 20 minutes from the stadium. I went to bed slightly later, did a last round of hot-cold treatment to prep my body. And it accelerates, once you're awake on game day – breakfast, brunch, watching something random on Netflix. A primer walk-through of lineout calls. Jersey presentations the night before done in a novel, Covid-era way: a video message from our families, expressing their pride, wishing us well.

To the stadium with a police escort. We knew the game plan we wanted. A big emphasis on not getting bored, on keeping our discipline. On looking for crumbs. And that's what I said to the team beforehand, as we huddled. I looked around and saw all that experience – the domestic finals, the Six Nations deciders, the World Cup semi-finals and finals. I could keep it simple. Nothing overly profound.

Do not give up on anything.

Maybe selfish, thinking of what I'd done to get here. But enough.

A fast start from them. A slower one from us. Too many early penalties, giving them the momentum. Them putting the pressure on to force the mistakes, us struggling to fight the temptation to give them away.

Our scrum taking time to get going. A couple of communication errors at the lineout. Nine penalties against us in all, in that first half. Sometimes trying too hard, sometimes having to remember that we could manage this game better. We can move the ball more. We can play further up the field. Chances will come, if we do. The pressure will fall onto them.

3–12 to them at half-time. It could have been worse. It could have been better. Not worrying about precedent, that the last time the Lions had won a Test from behind at the break was in Australia 32 years before. The game moves on. 2009 felt like ancient history. The comparisons work for the occasion, not the performance.

The messaging simple from me in the dressing room. *One chance is going to turn this game. Let's make it ours. Let's take it.*

Early in that second half, a penalty to us. On the outer edge of the kickable range. A decision to make: go for the posts, or kick to the corner?

It came naturally. A few of us all thinking the same thing at the same time. Elliot Daly had tried a shot from distance in the first half and fallen just short. I was comfortable making that call because we still had a half to come. But this time, 12–6 would still leave us a converted score away. I looked around. You could feel we were all on the same page. *Let's kick for the corner.*

You can feel the charge in the air when you go positive like that. Another penalty much closer in, and you have to go again, because you've backed it once, so you must back it again. A driving maul, gaining pace, rumbling on. Luke Cowan-Dickie at the back, ball under arm, burrowing over for the try.

Back in the game.

Now we started to go through a few more phases. Penalties coming fast from South Africa now. A try for Faf de Klerk, when we maybe felt Pieter-Steph du Toit had knocked on just before. Dan Biggar knocking over his second, his third, his fourth.

Replacements on both sides, our scrum getting better and better. But you can't get drunk on having a dominant scrum. It's a really dangerous thing. You end up putting pressure on yourself. The experienced voices in our team had the rugby intellect to feel that stuff. Conversations firing round about securing territory, about not rushing things. Sticking to the strategy. Taking back control, rather than worrying why we had to get out of jail in the first place.

Two points ahead with 17 minutes to go. Knowing we couldn't rely on them blowing up. Focusing only on ourselves.

The defence strong. Faz stroking over a penalty for 22–17. Makazole Mapimpi claiming the restart down the middle, them coming forwards, us knowing they were looking for a penalty so they could kick to the corner. Our discipline standing strong. A solid defensive set, decent line integrity. Maro Itoje doing what he had done all game and getting his hands on the ball to rip it away. Hoggy kicking it into the empty stands.

I think I may have tried to have a clock check. There was no chance. And when the whistle went, no relief, no over-exuberance. Gathering the boys together to say, they'll be a different team next week. Let's enjoy this – the moment, the night. But then we go again, because this is not done. They're going to come at us harder, and we have to go through that.

And I reflected, after a few beers, when a quiet moment came. Thinking, technically I shouldn't be here, not because of selection or rugby, but because I had been told I was done. Working in the four years before this point, blocking any thought of the Lions. Having just done two weeks when I had been pushed as hard mentally as I ever have been. If somebody had told me all this would have happened – how hard it would be mentally – I would never have believed them.

The next logical step, in my mind: if we don't win the series now, it won't have been worth it. I'd had to work too hard to get back out. I had to make it count.

Had I not suffered the injury and come back, I probably would have been happier. I knew in that moment, a few cold beers in, that it would be worse now if we didn't do what we set out for.

And I felt, too, a little bit more of the old Alun Wyn, rather than the more open, accommodating man I'd become. A return to being more resolute. A harder edge.

You can get swept up in the mystique of a Lions tour. The hoo-ha around it all. Quite accidentally, I'd had to strip it all back. Running around at St Helen's with a dead rat for company. The next day, a loose terrier careering about, cocking its leg on the posts. A dead rat and a dog don't care who it is, when you're running past them.

Sunday resting, Monday training, Tuesday training harder. On what we wanted to do better, on where we wanted to go next.

A sideshow, far from us. An hour-long video released critiquing the officiating in the first Test. We didn't talk about it at all in the team. I was asked questions about it in my press conference, but I hadn't watched it.

The Friday evening before the second Test, the same journey for us from the Arabella Hotel into Cape Town. The same speeding up of the hours after waking on the Saturday. Another jersey presentation the night before: a player from the second Test against the Springboks in 2009 recording a video message for a player in today's squad. Me – the playing link between the two eras – doing the one for Sinks. Keeping it short, since enough of the boys in the room had heard from me already. 'Alun Wyn Jones, jersey 761, to Kyle Sinckler, jersey 814.'

The messaging straightforward again in the dressing room. *Don't get bored. Stay in the game. Be prepared to use today. We have an opportunity to achieve something special.*

We knew the first five minutes were going to be different. We saw the niggle from the off. At one of the first rucks, Conor Murray had his head pushed into the ground. I pulled the player up off Conor. One of their players came onto me, which to be fair is probably exactly what I would have done in his position.

No one's dumb enough to swing. You'll get a red card. But if the whistle has gone and one of your teammates is having his head shoved into the ground, you have to do something. And it's posturing, because everyone knows you can't do anything. You can't allow yourself to be walked backwards. You stand your ground.

There was no pretty rugby. Both teams trying to counter the way the other team wished to play. Us not getting enough possession to string phases together, or possession in the right area. The Springboks controlling the tempo.

A clumsy trip from Duhan van der Merwe, a yellow card. Conor tackled in the air; it could easily have been a red card. The referee told me Conor had landed on his back, which wasn't what we had seen. In the aftermath, Dan Biggar taking a charge in the back.

Us with a scrum deep in their 22. Conor taking another shot. A few phases on, Robbie Henshaw jumping high to gather Conor's chip, landing over the try line and twisting to make sure of the grounding.

I thought Robbie got the ball down. His reaction indicated he had. There was no sense he was trying to blag it, and there were parallels with South Africa's first try in the second half.

I asked about the second shot on Conor. I was told they had looked at it, decided it was nothing.

We were still ahead: 9–6 at half-time. We hadn't had enough possession to get into the game, hadn't got past five phases. So the messaging was brisk. *Don't get bored. Stay disciplined, as we have for much of that first half. Try to get the tempo up.*

We could have played better in the second half. Much better. We began with a bad period, giving away three penalties in succession, get-out-of-jail-free cards.

We got caught isolated with some breakdowns. Having given them four lineouts the week before, we kept giving them away this time – 13 of them, by the end. We conceded eight penalties to their 14 in the first Test; this time we gave away 15 to their 10.

An hour gone, and only 9–11 down. Biggs with a penalty that bounced off the left-hand upright.

You don't stop. But it's the crescendo that gets you. The preceding action – the previous penalty given away – puts you under pressure in another area. We give away a penalty, they kick to touch on our 22. They set up a driving maul, it leads to the kick over the top from de Klerk for Lukhanyo Am's try. Our maul D had been pretty good. But if you give them 13 lineouts and 13 shots at it, sooner or later they'll get one going.

We just couldn't get tempo in the game. And it's the clock, rather than the game, that kills you. You can see the time ebbing away. The frustration comes from the fact that it wasn't even that quick a game. The more set-pieces they had, the slower the tempo of the game, the more time burns up. It didn't need to be ball-in-play control; it was management of that side of things. And we didn't have enough territory then, let alone possession in the right area, to put them under pressure.

We were gone, well before the final whistle. Lions 9–27 South Africa.

I addressed the boys on the pitch afterwards. I told them that with Gats notorious for making changes, we had to stick together. The pressure will come on now. We have been beaten, but we didn't play well. We didn't help ourselves.

It's always funny how many opinions are generated by a loss. It's just the same as in a domestic game or an international to a Lions Test. We hadn't been too far away; still in it at 60 minutes, the Biggs penalty an inch or two from going over. You lead, you make them chase, the pressure goes the other way. But we needed more shape.

We were all deeply disappointed. But there's a fine line between moving on without showing that too much, and moving on without showing it at all. You have to strike the balance. A few drinks on the Saturday, needed for the boys who haven't played and the staff as well as those weary from the contest. A trip to a vineyard 20 minutes away from the hotel on Sunday to recover, to begin to move on; an extra day off on the Monday, ready to return to a double day of training on Tuesday – a new team to be picked, a new day ahead. A greater challenge still.

A long tour, the final few days of an epic season. The last block of time off for anyone was way back after the 2019 World Cup.

You have conversations with the coaches, you do more detail on your prep. Day off Wednesday, light day Thursday, to the stadium for the captain's run on Friday.

It's tough, because you know there's no other chance after the Saturday ahead. You have a backstop after winning the first Test, but you never want to have to use it. I knew it would be my last ever game for the Lions, and I wanted to finish on the right note – for the squad, and for all I had done to get back from the shoulder dislocation.

You don't think about injuries. You don't think about defeat.

Do that, and you're beaten before you set foot on the pitch. The sideshow and the last show, both to be pushed away. A re-versioned team, Wyn Jones and Ken Owens starting in the front row. Ali Price back at nine, Bundee Aki in at inside-centre. Josh Adams on the wing, Liam Williams at full-back.

A winter Saturday on the tip of southern Africa, a day when the fog rolled in and covered the ocean and lapped at the land. The same stadium, a different challenge. The hours racing by, the comfort of a familiar routine.

The strapping of shoulders and legs, the stretching, the warm-up. Pulling on soft boots, checking studs, the tension of the laces. The feel of the kit, the sight of the badge.

Coaches keeping it simple, keeping it calm. Thinking not of the end result but how we would get there. A trust in the plan; a trust in each other.

We talked beforehand about three aspects of our game: phys-icality, discipline and tempo. In the tight huddle of the dressing room, I tried to keep it simple. *A lot has been said about the history of the Lions, about those who have gone before. It's all true. But let's do it today for our families – the ones who helped us get here. We put our bodies on the line today.*

Out into the eerily silent stadium. Empty white seats all around. A ring of bright lights around the edge of the stadium roof.

And we played well, in that first half. We kept the tempo, the discipline, the physicality. We showed an awareness of where the Springbok weaknesses might be; we had said we wanted to put them under pressure, and we did. I was happy with Finn Russell kicking penalties to the corner rather than the posts.

The first came off. Another strong driving maul, Ken Owens going over and Finn stroking over the conversion for a 10–3 lead. Almost another try from exactly the same source, until we were penalized by referee Mathieu Raynal. Another lineout on the South African five-metre line, the ball slapped out of my hands. A five-metre scrum where we were penalized again.

We had other chances in that first half. Josh Adams nearly put clear down the right. We had well over 60 per cent possession. We didn't have the points we deserved, but we had the momentum.

But we started the second half slowly. Better than the second Test, but still not great. They scored a try through Cheslin Kolbe that may have come from a knock-on, a 50/50 call that could have gone either way. One of a few calls that maybe went against us. That's the game.

I had sort of guessed I might be replaced at some point in the second half. The selection of Adam Beard on the bench pointed that way. I was still disappointed when the call came, at 61 minutes, even if I understood the reasons. I wanted to finish the game. And I shouted to the boys, as I ran off the field. *Keep the tempo up, and win it.*

13–10 down. Then 13–13.

Once you start trading penalties with the Springboks, you're in a different sort of contest. Mako Vunipola being driven over, the referee deciding he had been held up. No try. A scrum five metres out, and another penalty conceded. These are the margins, at this level.

16–13 down. Finn from way over 40 metres, 16–16.

In the game. So much behind us in the series, in the build-up, in even being on the far edge of that distant continent.

A penalty given to South Africa for us not rolling away in the tackle. Their scrum-half tapping and going, us bringing him down, winning the ball back. The referee deciding he had taken it from the wrong place, and calling it back.

You know Morné Steyn isn't going to miss a penalty from that distance at that straight angle. You watch the ball arcing and spinning over the posts, and you look around at your teammates, and try to stay strong for them and strong for you.

South Africa 19–16 Lions.

South Africa 2–1 Lions.

I said my words to the team on the pitch. I thanked the

players, I thanked the staff. For all they had done, for how close we had got.

If you go on the next one, good luck. And win it.

I didn't expect all my emotions would come flooding out. I thought I'd gone through it all in the struggle to make it back out on tour after my shoulder dislocation. Then I was asked in the television interview on the pitch about it being my last Lions match, and I realized the finality of it all.

I thought, too, in those quiet moments afterwards, of how much I had given to get back on the tour. The reintegration, the relentless efforts in training and those three Tests. I thought: I did all that to win this series, not to take part.

It was late when I spoke to Anwen. Too late for the girls. She was worried about me. A tough one to deal with, because she went through it all with me. She gave everything to it too.

I couldn't wait to see my family again. I'd had that two and a half weeks at home, but I wasn't with them. Not properly. I was focused on coming back. Doing everything I had to do.

As a spectacle, going ahead in this year, in these Covid times, the tour felt pretty special. To win the first Test; a second that was almost a tale of two halves, with us in it with an hour gone; a third Test where we played some of the best rugby we had produced all tour. You always sense the level go up, when you hit a Lions tour. A congratulations to the Springboks for their series win.

You ask yourself all those questions that have no answers. Should I have done this, should I have done that. Being injured and then coming back – was it a driver in my motivation, or did it take me out of my stride in the overall campaign?

Should I have stood up to this, could I have said something else here. A decision that came off, another gamble that did not. Defeat never gets any easier, no matter how many games you play. But those two weeks of doing everything I did added a new and different sheen to it all. A longer way to fall.

Playing in 12 straight Lions Tests, 13 if the game against

Japan in Edinburgh is upgraded. A little like my international caps record, it wasn't something I had planned to do. In the immediacy of the aftermath, you don't think about it. It's hard to accept it. You can't deal with much when you lose. Had we won, maybe I could have enjoyed those numbers more. As it was, I would have given some of them away just to have won the series.

A rollercoaster of a 12 months. Covid lockdowns. Playing the Six Nations in the autumn. The Nations Cup in deserted stadiums. The appearances record. A knee injury, eight weeks out. A fresh Six Nations campaign that came within a few minutes of stoppage time from a Grand Slam. Being picked for the Lions, being made captain. Thinking my tour was over before it had begun, fighting back harder than I had ever done before. Making it back out, winning the first Test. Losing the next two, and the series.

And I was ready for a rest. The first proper break, if you take out injuries, since the World Cup in Japan in 2019, almost two years before.

A rest, not to do nothing, but to tick over. Ready to get going again.

EPILOGUE:
PERTHYN | BELONGING

And so it comes full circle.

The long flight north from southern Africa, quarantine in Jersey, a drive from Bristol airport back out west. Over the bridge, past Newport and Cardiff. Past the steelworks at Port Talbot, Bonymaen up the hill to your right, turning south around Swansea Bay, all the way along the coastal road and promenade to the village of a man coming home.

Mumbles. The sea views and rocky headlands, the rugby pitch at Underhill Park, the old clubhouse on the sea front. The ruins of Oystermouth Castle up on the hill, the lifeboat station and the pier sticking out into the sea. The cemetery tucked up the winding path from Newton Road, the tide coming and going out in the bay. The smell of salt and seaweed.

I don't want to fall into clichés. The old ones, the ones that you tap and find hollow inside: 'If you work your dream, you will never work a day in your life.' It's never as simple as that, because there is bullshit around you, and you get hurt, and you carry regrets along with the triumphs. You don't have tendinopathies when you're seven years old, when you're 13 and charging about with your mates after school.

But the fire still burns inside. How could I ever fall for anything again as I fell for rugby? I was so selfish as a young man because I loved rugby so much. I couldn't see how much my parents did, all the driving to training, all the kit they bought.

You carry that on to today, and I'm probably still doing it in a different guise with Anwen and Mali and Efa. They still support me. I still don't see as much of them as I could, because of rugby.

When I play, when I stand there with arms round my team-mates, singing 'Hen Wlad Fy Nhadau', I'm representing my family, my girls. They mean everything to me. The game is a relation I will lose. The family will be there forever.

There's fear as well. I think I'm at the point now where I am always going to be Alun Wyn Jones the rugby player. When I finish, I'll always only be Alun Wyn Jones the former rugby player. I won't be Alun Wyn Jones, man, husband, dad – not to the world. And the hard thing will be that relationship I have with the game, and the knowledge, once it breaks, that I won't have another relationship like it ever again.

In many ways, the easiest way to finish would be if the decision were made for me. To walk away from something that's been with me for so long, that's carried us through so much.

But this is where we are, by the sea and the streets on the little hills. Remembering all the stuff now I'm back: the smell of my dad's cigarettes, my mum sitting by the kitchen table. The beach in summer, the rain splattering against the windows in winter or during a spring storm.

I like to hope, regardless of anything I've done outside the white lines of a rugby pitch, that I will have given everything. I know it's going to come to an end eventually. But part of me will die when I stop playing rugby, definitely.

I don't want it to be about me, when it comes to a close. I want it to be about my family.

I want to play for as long as possible. I don't care how shit some people might say I was in the final few years. But when that's gone, Alun Wyn Jones the rugby player will be gone, in my eyes. It won't be about me any more; it's about the girls. I won't be telling tales from my past. It'll be, *do you want to go the beach or do you want to go to Joe's for ice cream?*

I know it sounds contradictory. To take such pride and

pleasure in belonging to something far larger than you, and then leave it all behind. But you can't carry your past around with you. I can't live the rest of my life beginning sentences with, 'Well, I was . . .'

When I play my last game, part of me will die. And I'll accept it. I like to think I'll have it all planned; I'm going to try to write a letter to myself, to be opened in 15 or 20 years' time, or whenever I need it. A backstop, in case I need it. 'Alun Wyn, you haven't got any better . . .'

When you talk about love, you think about so much. If I didn't love the game, I couldn't have come this far. When Warren Gatland asked me if I would like to be Lions captain? I thought about sitting on the floor of the school assembly hall, aged 11, watching the Lions in South Africa – Scott Gibbs, Neil Jenkins, Martin Johnson. I thought about playing there in that same shirt, 12 years later. Adam Jones, Gethin Jenkins, Paul O'Connell.

To be asked to go out there again, with the best players from Wales, from England, from Scotland and Ireland? It's a profound thing, for me. Indescribable in words, but not in deeds.

So I come home, to the girls, to a house you probably couldn't tell a rugby player lives in. I'll talk to my dad soon. Have another chat with him.

I'm still the shy kid. I'll still have a grumble. I'll be quiet at first, when you meet me.

Not your cup of tea? Fine. But at least you know me now, more than you did before. You've seen where I come from, who shaped me. You know where I belong.

ACKNOWLEDGEMENTS

I'd like to thank all the management and players I've worked with. Thank you to all those who helped me along my rugby journey in my younger days, getting me this far in the first place. I appreciate everything you taught me.

Thank you to my family, who continue to support me within rugby and beyond it. None of it would have happened without you.

Thank you to everyone who has watched, suffered and celebrated in the big games along the way, whether in the stands, in the pubs or on your sofas.

To my ghost-writer Tom Fordyce – thanks for guiding me through the process. I've probably been a help and a hindrance over the last 18 months, but we got there in the end. Thank you to David Luxton for all his hard work and patience, and to all the team at Pan Macmillan for their efforts.

PICTURE ACKNOWLEDGEMENTS

All photographs are courtesy of Alun Wyn Jones except:

10–14. Huw Evans Agency
15. Stu Forster/Getty Images Sport
16. Mike Hewitt/Getty Images Sport
17. Huw Evans Agency
18. David Rogers/Getty Images Sport
20. Getty Images
21. David Rogers/Getty Images Sport
23. Huw Evans Agency
25. Huw Evans Agency
28. Huw Evans Agency
30–31. Huw Evans Agency